The Art and Science of
MINDFULNESS

The Art and Science of

MINDFULNESS

Integrating Mindfulness
Into Psychology and the
Helping Professions

Shauna L. Shapiro and Linda E. Carlson

With a Foreword by Jon Kabat-Zinn

American Psychological Association • *Washington, DC*

Third Printing, September 2010
Published by
American Psychological Association
750 First Street, NE
Washington, DC 20002
www.apa.org

To order
APA Order Department
P.O. Box 92984
Washington, DC 20090-2984
Tel: (800) 374-2721; Direct: (202) 336-5510
Fax: (202) 336-5502; TDD/TTY: (202) 336-6123
Online: www.apa.org/books/
E-mail: order@apa.org

In the U.K., Europe, Africa, and the Middle East, copies may be ordered from
American Psychological Association
3 Henrietta Street
Covent Garden, London
WC2E 8LU England

Typeset in Goudy by Circle Graphics, Inc., Columbia, MD

Printer: Maple-Vail
Cover Designer: Naylor Design, Washington, DC
Technical/Production Editor: Emily Welsh

The opinions and statements published are the responsibility of the authors, and such opinions and statements do not necessarily represent the policies of the American Psychological Association.

Library of Congress Cataloging-in-Publication Data

Library of Congress Cataloging-in-Publication Data

Shapiro, Shauna L.
  The art and science of mindfulness : integrating mindfulness into psychology and the helping professions / Shauna L. Shapiro and Linda E. Carlson.
      p. cm.
  Includes bibliographical references and index.
  ISBN-13: 978-1-4338-0465-6
  ISBN-10: 1-4338-0465-4
1. Acceptance and commitment therapy. I. Carlson, Linda E. II. Title.

  RC489.A32S53 2009
  616.89'1425—dc22

                                          2009006749

British Library Cataloguing-in-Publication Data
A CIP record is available from the British Library.

Printed in the United States of America
First Edition

For my grandparents, Benedict and Nancy Freedman
—Shauna L. Shapiro

To my parents, Lorne and Shirley Carlson
—Linda E. Carlson

Contents

Foreword

Shauna Shapiro and Linda Carlson are to be congratulated for an extremely clear and nuanced exposition of this rapidly expanding field and its various roots, growing edges, areas of promise, and potential concerns. Both authors are major contributors to the developing body of research in this area as well as to the actual clinical delivery of mindfulness-based approaches and other emerging applications of mindfulness. Thus, they speak from a place of ongoing experience and engagement regarding both the art and the science of mindfulness and its exploration as a framework for healing. They further examine its value in elaborating an ever-deepening understanding of what it means to be human and of the degrees of freedom available to us in the present moment.

In terms of the art of mindfulness, I would like to underscore a few points that may merit being kept in mind as one enters this field. One is that the teaching of mindfulness, especially in a clinical setting, really is an art form. Among other things, it requires that each individual client, patient, or participant be seen as a whole human being and be accorded the dignity and sovereignty that are intrinsic to being human—the counterpart of what Buddhists might call one's "true nature" or "Buddha nature." This, of course, is also the foundation of the core vow adopted by medical practitioners, the Hippocratic Oath. It is axiomatic that this vow and the view it is based on need to be inquired into continually and lived wholeheartedly by all who hope to skillfully introduce mindfulness into their work with others. It bears remembering that our patients and clients know far more than we do about what is going on with them, even if they are not always aware of it consciously, nor confident about or even cognizant of their internal resources. It is they who are being asked to shoulder some degree of responsibility for their own health and well-being. It is they who are being called upon, challenged, and encouraged, hard as it is, to cultivate attention, intention, and self-compassion as they engage in the interior work of "non-doing" for themselves, whatever the setting and context of the intervention. And it is they who will be the source of energy and healing within the practice of any mindfulness-based intervention, even in the case of mindfulness-informed therapy or in a therapeutic relationship in which only the therapist may be grounded in mindfulness. Every person's innate genius, uniqueness, and nature as a "miraculous being" requires authentic recognition and acceptance inside the framework of the therapeutic relationship. Nothing need be said along these lines. We are addressing something far more profound than speech: the unspoken awareness of the other's fullness of being. Carl Rogers's unconditional positive regard frames very well what is required from us as teachers or therapists to protect and deepen the intentional holding and honoring that lie at the core of all good therapy—and, in fact, relationality of any kind. What is required is its enactment, its embodiment, beyond all artifice or contrivance. That means that a reliance on mere *modeling* is inappropriate in such clinical relationships. The art is in the authentic *embodiment* of presencing, of mindfulness, of kindness and compassion. As the authors point out, these qualities are continually developed, refined, and understood through *practice*. That, in the end, makes us all somewhat humble students of our own experience, if we are willing to attend with resolve and openness and a sense of humor, especially when we catch ourselves observing how strongly we may be attached to the personal pronouns *I, me,* and *mine* in certain moments.

The art of mindfulness—especially in clinical situations in which the client or participant has no particular interest in meditation or Buddhism but is very much there because of his or her suffering—also requires sensitivity to languaging the meditation practices appropriately and situating them, at least for oneself, in a credible universal dharma context supported by science and clinical medicine. It also requires an ability to effectively ignite passion in clients and participants for their own possibilities for learning, growing, healing, and transformation, starting from wherever they find themselves. Related to this is skill in encouraging an interior motivation in clients and participants to practice with sincerity and consistency and to bring greater mindfulness to the challenges of relationships with others and with the world.

And all this is to say nothing of the considerable artistry required to effectively integrate and teach the essential elements of mindful yoga and mindful movement in mindfulness-based interventions; to make room with unalloyed acceptance for the expression of unbidden and often unwelcome emotions; and to skillfully make use of sensitive and respectful listening, inquiry, and dialogue for exploring together aspects of a patient's inner experience. Further artistry is required for understanding the various meditative practices and how they interface with the unfolding actuality and with the interior stories and tacit assumptions that frequently hinder insight and growth.

Then there is the domain of the nonverbal, of the reading of body language, spatial relationships, facial expressions of emotion and other fleeting perceptions, and one's own inner commentary as the therapist or instructor, as well as the challenge to midwife all of the above without resorting to romanticism or to idealizing either the practices themselves or their potential benefits. All these areas, and many more, will need to be developed and deepened by professional training opportunities and curricula, and investigated in future empirical studies as we refine our understanding of the essential elements conducive to effective teaching and cultivation of mindfulness in clinical and therapeutic settings. That would include exploring systematically the intimate relationship between mindfulness and heartfulness, or put otherwise, the seamless role of compassion and self-compassion in promoting well-being and integration within the framework of mindfulness. Here we have the art and the science converg at complex yet potentially fruitful interfaces.

Regarding the science of mindfulness, perhaps the most important issue at this point in time is to ask the hard questions about mindfulness-based interventions, and explore empirically what the most important elements are for obtaining and optimizing clinically meaningful outcomes, whether they be supported by neuroscientific data or by more clinically oriented measures, depending, of course, on the population of interest and or specific diagnoses or conditions, and the questions that are being addressed. As the authors point out, among the most compelling of these is the question of elucidating specific biological mechanisms and pathways via which observed clinical outcomes may be attained, and our basic understanding of the mind and its relationship to the body and to health deepened. Certainly the use of active and imaginatively designed control interventions balanced for all the elements of a mindfulness-based intervention or curriculum should allow the next generation of translational studies to clarify whatever roles specific mindfulness practices may or may not be playing in specific outcomes for specific populations—and elucidate the degree to which a positive outcome may be due to nonspecific factors having to do with set and setting, plausibility of the intervention, attention, teacher or therapist enthusiasm, tacit beliefs, and so on, rather than with the cultivation of mindfulness itself. This is, of course, a vast and problematic challenge, yet one worthy of attention. Another fruitful direction is the exploration of possible synergies between the first person experience of highly practiced contemplatives in the various meditative traditions and the development or refining of a next generation of mindfulness-based interventions that need to remain true, as always, to the nondual wisdom nature of such practices and understandings, yet also need to be accessible and commonsensical to those who, like most of our patients and clients, may have no background or even interest in meditation but who may benefit enormously from engaging in them. The authors have been diligent in pointing out these and other challenges, and in demonstrating how such synergies might be used for developing various theoretical models of the nature of self, and of perception and learning, that may help us to understand how mindfulness might be catalyzing its demonstrated effects.

I am sure that this volume will become an important and inspiring resource for those already practicing in this area, and for those who are increasingly drawn to mindfulness without having much of a grasp of what it actually involves or where its roots lie. It will no doubt contribute significantly to the development of the field and help many professionals drawn to integrate mindfulness into their work in psychology and psychotherapy to understand what mindfulness is and how it might be used and investigated further, to potentially great advantage, in various psychotherapeutic settings, as well as in hospitals, clinics, schools, and beyond.

Jon Kabat-Zinn
December 31, 2008
University of Massachusetts
Medical School
Worcester, MA

Preface

Intention is fundamental to any project, endeavor, or journey. We begin this volume with a deep intention that it may benefit both those who read it and those whom they are dedicated to helping. Our aim is to explore the art and science of mindfulness, drawing on Eastern teachings and wisdom as well as Western psychological theory and science. We believe that mindfulness is fundamental to effective therapy and to all the healing professions. We also believe that sound empirical investigation of mindfulness is necessary and valuable in order to advance the field. We hope this volume will speak to a general audience of psychotherapists, health care providers, caregivers, educators, students, and researchers interested in weaving mindfulness into the fabric of their work.

The purpose of the volume is to demystify mindfulness, drawing on the concepts of this 2,600-year-old Buddhist practice,[1] and exploring its potential within the current Western psychological and biomedical framework. Incorporating the perennial insights of mindfulness into the Western tradition offers something unique and profoundly healing to the field of health care. There is a growing need for new ways of seeing and new ways of being in the health care professions. Mindfulness invites such a new way of envisioning one's self and one's self in relation to others and the world. It helps us expand our vision of self, other, health, and healing, and invites us to inhabit our own bodies, hearts, and minds with greater presence, aliveness, and awe.

---

[1] Although we draw from and are inspired by the Buddhist teachings and practices of mindfulness (drawing particularly from the Theravadin tradition), we introduce mindfulness as a universal concept and attempt to place it within a Western medical and psychological context.

In our work with therapists in training, as well as through experiences leading continuing education workshops for thousands of health care professionals, we have seen the yearning to reconnect with the deeper calling that initially drew these students and professionals into the field of healing. Often, practitioners express feelings of frustration, disillusionment, and burnout. They report that the intentions that initially drew them to the healing profession are buried under seemingly impenetrable stress, pressure, and overwhelm. They are seeking refuge, honesty, and authenticity, a new way of relating to the chaos and suffering around and within them. They are seeking a wholeness of being and presence out of which they can facilitate their own and others' healing. Mindfulness offers such a path.

Our intention is to clearly define mindfulness and its role in psychotherapy and health care, exploring it as an empirically supported clinical intervention across a wide range of populations, a means of fostering self-care for helping professionals, and a catalyst for going beyond the profession's focus on pathology to include positive growth and development.

This volume is divided into three parts. Part I, "What Is Mindfulness? And How Is It Applicable to Clinical Work?" is composed of four chapters. Chapter 1 defines mindfulness, attempting to elucidate its multifaceted nature as both a meditation practice and a fundamental way of perceiving and being. Chapters 2 through 4 explore applications of mindfulness in psychotherapy from the perspective of the mindful therapist (chap. 2), mindfulness-informed therapy (chap. 3), and mindfulness-based therapy (chap. 4).

Part II, "Does It Help? And How Does It Help?" focuses on a summary of the research on mindfulness-based interventions for psychological (chap. 5) and medical (chap. 6) populations. This section also discusses potential mechanisms of action for the salutary and transformational effects of mindfulness (chap. 7). Part III, "Expanding the Paradigm," offers new ways of envisioning health care and mental health, expanding the field to include the well-being of the clinician as an essential part of the system (chap. 8) as well as expanding our definitions of health and human potential (chap. 9). Finally, chapter 10 offers directions for future research and applications of mindfulness.

Because the field of mindfulness is still young, we have attempted to provide a basic foundation that can be continually augmented with current publications that highlight the most recent research, theory, and clinical applications. Our intention is simply to offer those in the helping profession a foundation to explore the potential of integrating mindfulness into their work and their lives. Although this is an academic text, it is offered as part of a much larger dialogue within psychology and the helping professions as a vehicle to explore and expand our visions of health and healing. We invite you to read this volume as a form of mindful contemplation, and we hope that it challenges you to discover new ways of being with yourself and the people whose lives you touch. Throughout the volume we include mindful reminders as a way to infuse the reading with an experiential element of mindfulness. We invite the reader to spend time with these and to allow them to create a space of consciousness that will facilitate a deeper, fuller understanding of the reading.

Most important, we offer this volume as a journey into the richness and beauty of mindfulness. We invite you to discover for yourself what is true. In the words of the Buddha:

> Do not believe in anything simply because you have heard it
> Do not believe in anything simply because it is spoken and rumored by many
> Do not believe in anything simply because it is found written in your religious books
> Do not believe in anything merely on the authority of your teachers and elders
> Do not believe in traditions because they have been handed down for many generations
> But after observation and analysis, when you find that anything agrees with reason and is conducive to the good and benefit of one and all, accept it and live up to it. (Kalama Sutta, pp. 188–193)

Acknowledgments

I t is a pleasure to acknowledge the many people who have contributed directly and indirectly to the development of this volume. We are deeply grateful to our colleagues and teachers who continue to offer guidance to us in our many roles as therapists, researchers, teachers, meditators, mothers, and human beings. In particular, we would like to thank meditation teachers Sylvia Boorstein, Eugene Cash, Jack Kornfield, Alan Wallace, Sharon Salzberg, Joan Halifax Roshi, Robert Beatty, and Shinzen Young. We are also deeply grateful to the teachers at the Center for Mindfulness, Health Care and Society who introduced us to mindfulness-based stress reduction (MBSR) with such love, integrity, and grace, and most especially we would like to thank Jon Kabat-Zinn, Saki Santorelli, Ferris Urbanowski, and Elana Rosenbaum. We also thank our academic mentors Gary E. Schwartz, Richard Bootzin, Alfred Kaszniak, Barbara Sherwin, Barry Bultz, and David Spiegel, whose wisdom, guidance, and care supported us through graduate school and postdoctoral training, and continue to guide us. We offer our deep gratitude for the generosity, compassion, and wisdom of Frances Vaughn and Roger Walsh, whose teachings and guidance have been invaluable. We are also grateful for the support and encouragement of our respective colleagues at Santa Clara University—Mike Axleman, Susan Babbel, Diane Dreher, Dale Larson, Jerry Shapiro, Teri Quatman, Lucy Ramos-Sanchez, David Feldman, Jeffrey Baerwald, Patricia Moretti, Diane Jonte-Pace, and Tom Plante; and at the University of Calgary and Tom Baker Cancer Centre—Michael Speca, Helen MacRae, John Robinson, Guy Pelletier, Lisa Lamont, and Tavis Campbell. We acknowledge the venerable Anil Sakya for his help in understanding and defining mindfulness from a Thai monastic perspective as well as for his profound humility, kindness, and generosity, and John Dunne for sharing his wisdom regarding Buddhist scholarship. We also offer gratitude to the Center for Contemplative Mind in Society, whose contemplative practice fellowship (awarded to Dr. Shapiro) supported the development of the course "Mindfulness and Psychotherapy: Theory, Research, and Practice," which was an impetus for the current volume. We acknowledge the Enbridge Endowed Research Chair in Psychosocial Oncology at the University of Calgary, cofunded by the Canadian Cancer Society Alberta/NWT Division and the Alberta Cancer Foundation and held by Dr. Carlson, the Canadian Institutes of Health Research, the Canadian Breast Cancer Research Alliance, and the National Cancer Institute of Canada, all of which have funded aspects of mindfulness-based research described in this volume. We are grateful to the Mind and Life Institute for providing fellowship and support for our mindfulness practice and research, and for exposing us to broad perspectives of philosophy and research methods, in particular, Adam Engle, Richard Davidson, Matthieu Ricard, and Jon Kabat-Zinn. We also are grateful to the sangha of clinicians and researchers who are committed to decreasing suffering and increasing freedom, and we specifically want to thank John Astin, Robin Bitner, Willoughby Britton, Paul Choi, Cassandra Ann Curtis, Shamini Jain, Buffy Lundine, Johanna Murphy, Michael Speca, Sarah Trost, Maureen Angen, Shirley MacMillian, Eileen Goodey, Holly Minor, Lanice Jones, and Paula Fayerman. We thank research assistants Hooria Bittlingmyer and Joshua Lounsberry for their extraordinary attention to detail in referencing and collecting literature, and the energy and enthusiasm they brought to this project. We would also like to acknowledge our acquisitions editor, Susan Reynolds, for initiating this project and giving us the opportunity to share this volume; development editor, Emily Leonard, for her enthusiasm and care; and production editor, Emily Welsh, for her attention to detail. We are deeply grateful to grandparents Benedict and Nancy Freedman and parents Deane and Johanna Shapiro, all of whose insightful edits and tremendous faith made this book possible. Thanks also to parents Lorne and Shirley Carlson, who have quietly but unfailingly supported all academic efforts over the years. We also want to express deep gratitude and love for Jackson Ki and Nova Violet for being our most transformative mindfulness teachers moment by moment and to Joal Borggard for providing unfailing support and love. Finally, we are grateful to all of the students and patients we have had the privilege to work with and learn from, as we all journey together toward greater health, peace, and freedom.

WHAT IS MINDFULNESS? AND HOW IS IT APPLICABLE TO CLINICAL WORK?

What Is Mindfulness? 1

Yesterday is a memory
Tomorrow is the unknown
And now, is the knowing

—*The Buddha*

The widespread clinical applications of mindfulness are based on a few general principles whose simplicity and power have sparked a literature examining the effects of mindfulness as a clinical intervention, a theoretical orientation, and a means for training therapists in essential clinical skills. Our intention is to explore mindfulness, elucidating its multidimensional nature and its implications for psychology and health care.

Attempting to write about mindfulness in an academic and conceptual way is in some ways antithetical to the very nature of mindfulness, which is essentially an experiential process. However, if mindfulness is to be integrated into Western medicine and psychology, we must find ways of translating its nonconceptual, nondual, and paradoxical nature into a language that clinicians, patients, scientists, scholars— all of us—can understand and agree on. This volume is offered as one attempt to articulate the potential of integrating mindfulness into psychology and the healing professions.

Although the concept of mindfulness is most often associated with Buddhism, its phenomenological nature is embedded

This chapter incorporates material from "Mechanisms of Mindfulness," by S. L. Shapiro, L. Carlson, J. Astin, and B. Freedman, 2006, *Journal of Clinical Psychology, 62,* pp. 373–386. Copyright 2006 by John Wiley & Sons, Inc. Reprinted with permission.

in most religious and spiritual traditions as well as Western philosophical and psychological schools of thought (Brown & Cordon, 2008; Walsh, 2000). In this work, we draw from the richness and wisdom of Buddhist teachings; however, our intention is to present mindfulness as a universal human capacity. Although our understanding of mindfulness is inspired by the 2,600-year tradition of Buddhism, we define it within a Western psychological and medical context with the intention that it can thereby be accessible to anyone in the health professions.

What Is Mindfulness?

Mindfulness is the English equivalent of the Pali words *sati* and *sampajaña*, which as a whole can be translated as awareness, circumspection, discernment, and retention. Bhikkhu Bodhi, Theravadin scholar and monk, integrated these multiple definitions of mindfulness as meaning to remember to pay attention to what is occurring in one's immediate experience with care and discernment (Wallace & Bodhi, 2006).

What can be confusing is that mindfulness is both a process (mindful practice) and an outcome (mindful awareness). In *The Heart of Buddhist Meditation*, the Buddhist scholar and monk Nyanaponika Thera wrote,

> Mindfulness then, is the unfailing master key for *knowing* the mind, and is thus the starting point: the perfect tool for *shaping* the mind, and is thus the focal point; and the lofty manifestation of the achieved *freedom* of the mind; and is thus the culminating point. (as cited in J. Kabat-Zinn, 2005, p. 108)

Guided by this teaching, we attempt to bring this clarity and nuance to the way we speak about mindfulness, referring to it as both (a) *mindful awareness:* an abiding presence or awareness, a deep knowing that manifests as freedom of mind (e.g., freedom from reflexive conditioning and delusion) and (b) *mindful practice:* the systematic practice of intentionally attending in an open, caring, and discerning way, which involves both knowing and shaping the mind. To capture both aspects we define the construct of mindfulness as the awareness that arises through intentionally attending in an open, caring, and nonjudgmental way.

MINDFULNESS AWARENESS: BIG *M* MINDFULNESS

In exploring a definition of mindfulness it is helpful to begin simply and then add complexity. So let us begin with bare awareness, such as awareness of simple breathing. Are you breathing right now? Do you *know* you are breathing? This knowing can be an intellectual and conceptual knowing, but it can also be a felt sense, a knowing with your whole being. This deep knowing is mindfulness. As you breathe in, knowing with your whole being "breathing in." As you breathe out, knowing with your whole being "breathing out."

Notice the quality of your mind right now. Is it clear and interested? Is it dull and fatigued? Is it concentrated? Knowing the state of your mind in this moment, without judging it, evaluating it, thinking about it, or trying to change it, *is* mindfulness. Knowing your emotional state in the moment—joy, sadness, fear—is mindfulness. This practice of knowing what you are experiencing as you are experiencing it will continue with the prompting of mindful reminders interspersed throughout the book.

As the Buddha taught,

> Feelings are understood as they arise, understood as they remain present, understood as they pass away. Thoughts are understood as they arise, understood as they remain present, understood as they pass away. Perceptions are understood as they arise, understood as they remain present, understood as they pass away. (Samyutta Nikaya 47:35, as cited in Bodhi, 2002)

Mindful awareness is fundamentally a way of being—a way of inhabiting one's body, one's mind, one's moment-by-moment experience. It is a natural human capacity. It is a deep awareness; a knowing and experiencing of life as it arises and passes away each moment. Mindful awareness is a way of relating to all experience—positive, negative, and neutral—in an open, receptive way. This awareness involves freedom from grasping and from wanting anything to be different. It simply knows and accepts what is here, now. Mindfulness is about seeing clearly without one's conditioned patterns of perceiving clouding awareness, and without trying to frame things in a particular way. It is important to learn to see in this way because how a person perceives and frames the moment generates one's reality.

Theravadin scholar and monk Bhikkhu Bodhi referred to mindfulness in its simplest form as *bare attention* (Wallace & Bodhi, 2006). However, he went on to note that "bare attention is never completely bare" (Wallace & Bodhi, personal communication, October 2006). The context and intention one brings to practice and how one practices are very important (Wallace & Bodhi, 2006). What bare attention refers to is attention without one's conditioned "emotional reactions, evaluations, judgments, and conceptual overlays" (Wallace & Bodhi, personal communication, October 2006). Thus, mindfulness involves simply knowing what is arising as it is arising without adding anything to it—without trying to get more of what one wants (pleasure, security), or pushing away what one doesn't want (e.g., fear, anger, shame).

From a mindful perspective, suffering arises out of one's reactions to and judgments about what is present as opposed to what is actually present. A story exemplifies this:

> A teacher walking with his students points to a very large boulder and says, "Students, do you see that boulder?" The

students respond, "Yes, teacher, we see the boulder." The teacher asks, "And is the boulder heavy?" The students respond, "Oh yes, very heavy." And the teacher replies, "Not if you don't pick it up."

People are constantly pushing and pulling and trying to move the "boulders" of their lives into the places they think they should be. This constant reactivity and resistance to what is creates a great deal of suffering. Mindfulness offers a different way of relating, a different way of being. It involves becoming aware of tendencies to resist how things are and a letting go of trying to rearrange the boulders. It is simply knowing there is a boulder here in this moment and I don't like it—and that's okay. What does it feel like to be in this state? There is tension in the body. There is shallow breath in this moment. There is a thought, an emotion, a mind state in this moment. With mindfulness, there is no need to change one's experience; one simply apprehends it, knowing it deeply and intimately.

And yet, apprehending the present moment with acceptance does not mean that one allows unnecessary suffering or injustice. Whatever is arising in the present moment is greeted because it is already here. Then, from a place of clarity, a person can consciously discern what is needed and respond in an appropriate and skillful way.

Buddhist psychology teaches that suffering comes from wanting things to be different than they actually are. People crave certain experiences and reject and push away other experiences. They try to push or pull and force reality into the way they want it to be. And even if for a moment they get it just right, just the way they want it, in the next moment things change. And so, they continue to resist and hence to suffer.

Mindfulness is an antidote to this suffering. It is a way of being with *all* of one's experience. It allows whatever arises to be here, which makes sense because it already *is* here. As noted earlier, this allowing is not a passive resignation but a clear seeing acceptance that simply says, "This is what is true, here, now."

Mindful awareness involves an open receptive attention, but it is also a discerning attention, which invites insight. It allows one to see clearly which experiences lead to greater suffering for oneself and others, and which do not. In this way people can determine which aspects of mind are wholesome (those leading to the well-being of self and others) and which are unwholesome (those leading to the suffering of self and others). So, when we say that mindfulness allows and accepts whatever is present, this is true; however, it also discerns between wholesome and unwholesome.

In this way mindfulness offers a universally applicable system of ethics based on inquiry and the ability to discern the wholesome from the unwholesome. This *ethics as inquiry* (Wallace & Shapiro, 2009) simply inquires, "What is most conducive to my own and others' well-being?" As the meditation teacher Milindapanha stated, "Sati (mindfulness) . . . calls to mind wholesome and unwholesome tendencies . . . beneficial and unbeneficial tendencies: these tendencies are beneficial, these unbeneficial; these tendencies are helpful, these unhelpful. Thus one who practices . . . rejects unbeneficial tendencies and cultivates beneficial tendencies" (as cited in Wallace & Bodhi, 2006, pp. 37–38).

Mindfulness is the nondual awareness that holds all of experience in an open, accepting way. It is the abiding awareness that is always present within. As J. Kabat-Zinn (2005) put it, "Your awareness is a very big space within which to reside. It is never not an ally, a friend, a sanctuary, a refuge. It is never not here, only sometimes veiled" (p. 298). Through holding and being with experience in this way, without trying to force anything to come from it, deep insight into the nature of things can arise. One may realize that (a) everything is impermanent; (b) suffering arises out of greed, hatred, and delusion; and (c) everything is connected, nothing is separate. These insights begin to inform one's life, and mindful awareness becomes more and more a way of being.

Although, according to Buddhist teachings, this natural way of being or awareness is inherent in everyone, it is often masked by deep and endemic conditioning—parents, teachers, relationships, and society have influenced people in ways known and unknown. One's patterns have become so ingrained that often one does not realize one is engaging in them. People often live on automatic pilot, being pushed and pulled by these unconscious tendencies, not fully awake to the reality of the present moment. To counteract this conditioning, one can train one's mind in the innate capacity to be with and *know* one's experience as it arises and passes away. This requires sustained practice, the intentional training of the mind to pay attention in a caring, discerning way. This training is the formal practice of mindfulness meditation, which we discuss later.

At the deepest level, mindfulness is about freedom: freedom from reflexive patterns, freedom from reactivity, and, ultimately, freedom from suffering. Mindfulness can transform our relationship to what is. As a result, the strength of our unexamined and highly conditioned patterns can begin to diminish. Greater degrees of freedom from reflexive habits of perceiving and reacting can arise spontaneously. We can make more deliberate choices guided by a clarity of seeing, and a deep knowing what is true within ourselves. And so we begin to train our minds, to cultivate the ability to observe the mind with the mind. And we start in the present moment, because that is the only place we can start.

MINDFUL PRACTICE: LITTLE *m* MINDFULNESS

Mindful practice is one way individuals can intentionally pursue the big *M* of mindful awareness. Mindful practice refers to the conscious development of skills such as a greater ability to direct and sustain one's attention, less reactivity, greater discernment and compassion, and enhanced capacity to recognize and disidentify from one's concept of self (discussed in greater detail in chap. 7, this volume). Mindfulness can be a richly complex yet simple practice. In its most basic form, mindful practice involves paying attention on purpose and with acceptance (J. Kabat-Zinn, 1990).

A Model of Mindful Practice

In an attempt to elucidate both the simplicity and complexity of mindful practice, we developed a model of mindfulness composed of three core elements: intention, attention, and attitude (S. L. Shapiro, Carlson, Astin, & Freedman, 2006). Intention, attention, and attitude are not separate processes or stages—they are interwoven aspects of a single cyclic process and occur simultaneously, the three elements informing and feeding back into each other. Mindful practice *is* this moment-to-moment process.

INTENTION

Intention is fundamental to mindfulness practice, which for Buddhism was freedom from suffering for oneself and all beings. Intention (i.e., why one is practicing) is highlighted in Buddhist teachings as a central component of mindfulness and thus considered crucial to understanding the process as a whole.

Mindful Reminder: What is your intention right now? Why are you reading this book?

To understand mindful practice accurately and deeply, it is essential to explicitly incorporate the aspect of intention (S. L. Shapiro & Schwartz, 2000b). As J. Kabat-Zinn wrote, "Your intentions set the stage for what is possible. They remind you from moment to moment of why you are practicing in the first place" (p. 32). He continued, "I used to think that meditation practice was so powerful . . . that as long as you did it at all, you would see growth and change. But time has taught me that some kind of personal vision is also necessary" (J. Kabat-Zinn, 1990, p. 46). This personal vision, or intention, is often dynamic and evolving (Freedman, 2009). For example, a therapist may begin a mindful practice to decrease her own stress. As her mindful practice continues, she may develop an additional intention of relating to patients in a more empathic, present way.

The role of intention in meditation practice is exemplified by D. H. Shapiro's (1992) study, which explored the intentions of meditation practitioners and found that as meditators continued to practice, their intentions shifted along a continuum from self-regulation to self-exploration, and finally to self-liberation and selfless service.[1] Further, the study found that outcomes correlated with intentions. Those whose goal was self-regulation and stress management attained self-regulation, those whose goal was self-exploration attained self-exploration, and those whose goal was self-liberation moved toward self-liberation and compassionate service. Similar results were found by Mackenzie, Carlson, Munoz, and Speca (2007) when they interviewed patients with cancer who had been practicing meditation for several years. At first the practice was used to control specific symptoms such as tension and stress, but later on the focus became spirituality and personal growth. These findings correspond with our definition of intentions as dynamic and evolving, which allows them to change and develop with deepening practice, awareness, and insight.

Not only is it important to be clear about one's intentions, it is also necessary to reflect on whether they are wholesome or unwholesome, for the benefit or harm of self and others. Value issues are often seen as problematic in Western scientific traditions because modernist theory viewed science as objectively neutral. However, postmodernism, science, and technology studies challenge that assumption—there are always values driving behavior. So it is not a question of whether values are operating—in the individual, in the client–therapist interaction, in society—but how and to what extent these values can be brought to consciousness (Freedman, 2009).

> **Mindful Reminder:** Try pausing and reflecting to reconnect with your deeper intention for entering the field of healing.

Mindful practice helps people (a) bring unconscious/nonconscious values to awareness; (b) decide whether they are really the values they want to pursue, that is, are they wholesome, or merely biologically reflexive or culturally conditioned; and (c) develop wholesome and skillful values and decrease unwholesome ones. We suggest that discriminating between wholesome and unwholesome intentions can be based on universal values and does not necessarily have to be specifically steeped in Buddhist or other religious traditions. In fact, the concept of "wholesome" or "right" intention is not so much moralistic (i.e., "You should live like this") as descriptive (i.e., "This is a way of living that leads to freedom from suffering and enhancement of compassion, empathy, and interconnection"). It is not difficult to take this Buddhist concept of "right" or "wholesome" or "wise" intentions and interpret it within the ethical and moral framework of Western psychology and philosophy. For example, the commitments to "relieve suffering," "do no harm," and "cultivate compassion" fit comfortably into both Buddhist and Western

---

[1] *Self-liberation* refers to the experience of transcending (i.e., becoming free of or disidentifying from) the sense of being a separate self.

contexts. We believe explicit teachings of these guidelines are critically important to mindful practice.

Intentions should also be differentiated from the concept of "striving" or "grasping" for certain outcomes from meditation practice. Intentions are held lightly as the basis for undertaking practice in the first place, but intentions are not seen as goals or outcomes one actively strives toward during each meditation practice. As meditation teacher and psychotherapist Jack Kornfield put it: "Intention is a direction not a destination" (personal communication, 2007).

ATTENTION

A second fundamental component of mindfulness is attention. In the context of mindful practice, paying attention involves observing the operations of one's moment-to-moment internal and external experience. This is what Husserl referred to as a return to things themselves, that is, suspending (or noting) all the ways of interpreting experience and attending to experience itself, as it presents in the here and now. In this way, one learns to attend not only to the surrounding world but to the contents of one's consciousness, moment by moment.

It has been suggested in the field of psychology that attention is critical to the healing process. Mindfulness involves a deep and penetrating attention, not simply grazing the surface. As Bhikkhu Bodhi noted, "whereas a mind without mindfulness 'floats' on the surface of its object the way a gourd floats on water, mindfulness sinks into its object the way a stone placed on the surface of water sinks to the bottom" (from the Dhammasangani Malatika; as cited in Wallace & Bodhi, 2006, p. 7). Instead of this sustained and penetrating attention, our typical mode of attending is reflexive and superficial. As Brown and Cordin (in press) describe it:

> What comes into awareness is often held in focal attention only briefly, if at all, before some cognitive and emotional reaction to it occurs. . . . The psychological consequence of such processing is that concepts, labels, ideas, and judgments are often imposed, often automatically, on everything that is encountered (e.g., Bargh & Chartarand, 1999). . . . [W]e do not experience reality impartially, as it truly is, but rather through cognitive filters that are frequently of a habitual, conditioned nature, and that can furnish superficial, incomplete, or distorted views of reality.

Mindful practice involves a dynamic process of learning how to cultivate attention that is discerning and nonreactive, sustained and concentrated, so that we can see clearly what is arising in the present moment (including one's emotional reactions, if that is what comes up). As Germer, Siegel, and Fulton (2005) noted, "An unstable mind is like an unstable camera; we get a fuzzy picture" (p. 16).

ATTITUDE

How one attends is also essential. According to J. Kabat-Zinn, mindfulness is understood "not just as a bare attention but as an *affectionate attention*" (Cullen, 2006, p. 5, italics in original). The qualities one brings to attention have been referred to as the attitudinal foundations of mindfulness (J. Kabat-Zinn, 1990; S. L. Shapiro & Schwartz, 2000a, 2000b; see Exhibit 1.1). Siegel (2007a) used the acronym COAL to refer to a similar list of qualities: curiosity, openness, acceptance, and love.

Often, the quality of mindful awareness is not explicitly addressed. However, the qualities, or attitude, one brings to the act of paying attention are crucial. For example, attention can have a cold, critical quality, or it can include an openhearted compassionate quality. It is helpful to note that the Chinese character for mindfulness is composed of two idiograms: One is presence, and the other, heart (Santorelli, 1999). Further, heart and mind are the same word in Asian languages. Therefore, perhaps a more accurate translation of *mindfulness* from the Asian languages is heartfulness, which underlines the importance of including "heart" qualities in the attentional practice of mindfulness.

Mindful Reminder: Can you tap into the deep and abiding awareness inside of you that is always present?

EXHIBIT 1.1

Attitude

Nonjudging: Impartial witnessing, observing the present moment without evaluation and categorization

Nonstriving: Non-goal-oriented, remaining unattached to outcome or achievement

Nonattachment: Letting go of grasping and clinging to outcome, and allowing the process to simply unfold

Acceptance: Seeing and acknowledging things as they are in the present moment

Patience: Allowing things to unfold in their time

Trust: Developing a basic trust in your experience

Openness (Beginner's Mind): Seeing things freshly, as if for the first time

Curiosity: A spirit of interest, investigation, and exploration

Letting go: Nonattachment, not holding on to thoughts, feelings, experience

Gentleness: A soft, considerate and tender quality; however, not passive, undisciplined, or indulgent

Nonreactivity: Ability to respond with consciousness and clarity instead of automatically reacting in a habitual, conditioned way

Loving-kindness: A quality embodying friendliness, benevolence, and love

---

Note   These categories are offered heuristically, reflecting the general idea that there are specific attitudes that modulate attention during the practice of mindfulness

We posit that, with practice and right effort, people can learn to attend to their own internal and external experiences, without evaluation or interpretation, and practice acceptance, kindness, and openness even when what is occurring in the field of experience is contrary to deeply held wishes or expectations. However, it is essential to have the intention to make the attitudinal qualities of attention explicit.

Attending without bringing the attitudinal qualities into the practice may result in practice that is condemning or judgmental of inner (or outer) experience. Such an approach may well have consequences contrary to the intentions of the practice, cultivating, for example, patterns of judgment and striving instead of equanimity and acceptance.

The attitudinal qualities do not add anything to the experience itself but rather infuse the lens of attention with acceptance, openness, caring, and curiosity. For example, if while practicing mindfulness impatience arises, the impatience is noted with acceptance and kindness; however, these qualities are not meant to be substituted for the impatience or to make the impatience disappear—they are simply the container. These attitudes are an essential element of mindful practice. As J. Kabat-Zinn (1990) stated, "The attitude with which you undertake the practice of paying attention . . . is crucial" (p. 31); "Keeping particular attitudes in mind is actually part of the training itself" (p. 32). The attitudes are not an attempt to make things be a certain way. They are an attempt to relate to whatever *is* in a certain way.

With intentional training, one becomes increasingly able to take interest in each experience as it arises and also to allow what is being experienced to pass away (i.e., not be held onto). By intentionally bringing attitudes such as patience, compassion, and nonstriving to the attentional practice, one relinquishes the habitual tendency of continually striving for pleasant experiences, or of pushing aversive experiences away. Instead, bare awareness of whatever exists in that moment occurs, but within a context of gentleness, kindness, and acceptance.

Cultivating Mindfulness: Formal and Informal Practice

Mindful practice involves "practicing" or cultivating the skills of mindfulness, namely, intentionally attending with an open, accepting, and discerning attitude. Mindful practice can be categorized into *formal* and *informal* practice. Formal practices involve systematic meditation practices geared toward cultivating mindfulness skills, such as sitting meditation, body scan meditation, and walking meditation. Formal practice can involve relatively brief daily meditation practice or can be practiced as part of intensive retreat involving numerous hours of formal sitting and walking meditation in silence each day for a week, a month, and longer (see Exhibit 1.2).

Informal practice "refers to the application of mindfulness skills in every day life" (Germer et al., 2005, p. 14) and involves intentionally bringing an open, accepting, and discerning attention to whatever one is doing, whether it is mindful reading, mindful driving, or mindful eating. The purpose of the informal practice is to generalize to everyday life what is learned during the formal practice. In terms of the helping professions, all clinical work can be considered "informal mindful practice": intentionally viewing the therapy session as a time to consciously attend in a caring, open, discerning way. We discuss this more fully in chapter 2 (this volume), as we believe it is a central way of bringing mindfulness into psychotherapy and deserves significant attention.

Mindfulness and Psychotherapy

Our thesis is that mindful awareness is fundamental to all therapy and that the practice of mindfulness can help therapists cultivate and connect with this awareness. The remainder of the volume focuses on helping readers explore mindfulness as (a) an important dimension of

EXHIBIT 1.2

Mindfulness Exercise

"Mindfulness has to be experienced to be known." (Germer, Siegel, & Fulton, 2005, p. 8)

Mindfulness of Breathing. To begin, find a comfortable place to sit quietly, and assume a sitting posture that is relaxed yet upright and alert. Focus your attention on the breath as a primary object of attention, feeling the breathing in and breathing out, the rise and fall of the abdomen, the touch of air at the nostrils. Whenever some other phenomenon arises in the field of awareness, note it, and then gently bring the mind back to the breathing. If any reactions occur, such as enjoying what arose in your mind, or feeling irritated by it, simply note the enjoyment or irritation with kindness, and again return to the experience of breathing.

clinical training with unique contributions toward fostering basic therapy skills such as attention, empathy, and presence; (b) an empirically supported clinical intervention effective across a wide range of populations; (c) a means of fostering self-care for clinicians; and (d) a way to expand the profession's focus beyond pathology to include positive growth, development, and transformation.

As this volume travels more and more deeply into the territory of mindfulness, our goal is to bring greater well-being to both patients and clinicians. In fundamental terms, we view mindfulness as a natural human capacity. Seen through this lens, mindfulness helps bridge the gap between therapist and patient, offering a reminder that we are all human beings wanting health, happiness, and freedom from suffering.

The Mindful Therapist 2

A therapist has to practice being fully present and has to
cultivate the energy of compassion in order to be helpful.

—Thich Nhat Hanh (2000, p. 152)

I n chapter 1, we described mindfulness as a way of being in
the world (big *M* mindfulness) and as a specific practice
involving the conscious development of skills (little *m* mindfulness). Mindfulness may be seen as "a crucial ingredient in
the therapy relationship, and as a technology for psychotherapists to cultivate personal therapeutic qualities" (Germer,
Siegel, & Fulton, 2005, p. 9). The former involves the psychological process of *mindful awareness*—a deep abiding presence
or awareness—whereas the latter refers to skills developed
through *mindful practice*—the systematic practice of intentionally attending in an open, kind, and discerning way.
With psychotherapy in mind, Germer et al. (2005) conceptualized three ways to integrate mindfulness into therapeutic
work, collectively known as *mindfulness-oriented psychotherapy:* The first is through the personal practice of mindfulness
meditation in order to cultivate mindful presence in therapeutic work, termed *therapist mindfulness;* the second is through
the application of a theoretical frame of reference informed
by theories and research about mindfulness and Buddhist
psychology, termed *mindfulness-informed psychotherapy;* and
the third, known as *mindfulness-based psychotherapy,* is explicitly
teaching clients mindfulness skills and practices to enhance
their own mindfulness (Germer et al., 2005). In this chapter

we focus on the mindful therapist[1], expanding on previous suggestions that therapist mindfulness can enhance outcome by supporting common therapeutic factors known to be crucial to client improvement (Germer et al., 2005; Martin, 1997).

Common Therapeutic Factors

The psychotherapy literature about common factors psychotherapy can be summarized by the statement "We know that many seemingly dissimilar forms of psychotherapy work" (Seligman, 1995, as cited in Germer et al., 2005, p. 4), or "everybody has won so all shall have prizes" (Rosenzweig, 1936). This conclusion is commonly known as the "Dodo bird verdict" (Luborsky, Singer, & Luborsky, 1975) because the statement was originally made by a dodo bird judging a footrace in the novel *Alice in Wonderland;* it refers to the observation that across different therapeutic modalities there is very little difference in outcome, regardless of theoretical orientation or specific techniques applied (Seligman, 1995). Rosenzweig's original conceptualization of the reason that different therapies seemed to fare equally well was that improvements may be due to implicit common factors shared across many diverse modalities of therapy. Meta-analyses of the voluminous research engendered by this observation have largely shown that there are only small differences in outcome between bona fide treatments across a wide range of therapies and clients (Luborsky et al., 2002). Thus, the body of evidence some 8 decades later supports Rosenzweig's early conclusions from the 1930s.

This Dodo bird verdict is not unequivocally accepted by all psychotherapists and researchers, however, and a lively debate continues in the literature about the importance of specific versus common factors in psychotherapy outcome (e.g., DeRubeis, Bortman, & Gibbons, 2005; Lohr, Olatunji, Parker, & DeMaio, 2005). For example, there are cases of treatments that have been proven both efficacious and specific to certain disorders, such as exposure and response prevention for obsessive–compulsive disorder, cognitive–behavioral therapy (CBT) for panic disorder, exposure therapy for posttraumatic stress disorder, and

---

[1] There is a way in which we language things that ossifies them. The "mindful therapist" gives the impression that if you just did it right then you would be a "mindful therapist," which lends itself to a kind of idealization and reification. We are not intending this phrase to be interpreted in this way, but instead using it to describe therapists who practice and care about mindfulness.

group CBT for social phobia (DeRubeis et al., 2005). Nonetheless, while the relative importance of common versus specific factors remains unresolved and likely varies depending on which psychological disorders and symptoms are in question, few scholars deny the importance of factors that are present and common across the majority of therapeutic modalities.

Overall, the largest proportion of variance in therapy outcome (about 40%) is associated with relatively static factors related to client characteristics such as age, gender, prior history of depression, social support, and other extratherapeutic factors (Lambert, 1992). Fifteen percent of variance in change is accounted for by patient expectancies, or the placebo effect, and a similar amount, 15%, is accounted for by specific techniques unique to the treatment modality. This leaves approximately 30% of the variance in outcome, which has been attributed to common factors that are present in most therapeutic encounters (Lambert, 1992).

The finding that common factors may account for a significant part of therapy outcome, in fact, twice as much of the variance as specific techniques, has led to the search for common factors underlying seemingly distinct yet equally effective therapies. Current conceptualizations identify several essential elements. Weinberger (2002) identified five important common factors: relationship variables, expectancies, confronting problems, mastery, and the attribution of outcomes. The most important of these and the strongest predictor of therapeutic outcomes has proven to be the relationship variables factor. Relationships characterized by empathy, unconditional positive regard, and congruence between therapist and client have proven most beneficial (Bohart, Elliott, Greenberg, & Watson, 2002). It is interesting that both Carl Rogers (Rogers, 1957) and earlier Rosenzweig (1936) believed that therapist characteristics of empathy, genuineness, and unconditional positive regard (C. R. Rogers, 1961) may not be only necessary but indeed sufficient factors to stimulate change. Lambert identified a therapeutic relationship characterized by "trust, warmth, understanding, acceptance, kindness and human wisdom" (p. 856) as a common factor (Lambert, 2005). Hence, therapists who are able to create an atmosphere conducive to a good therapeutic relationship are more likely to help clients reduce their suffering, regardless of the specific modality used. In this chapter, we focus primarily on the ways that mindful awareness and mindful practice in therapists can enhance the therapeutic relationship. It is clear that mindfulness may enhance other common factors as well; however, our focus is on this most important common factor: the therapeutic relationship.

The Mindful Therapist

Mindful Reminder: Think about your most recent clinical encounter— Were you truly present with the client?

In light of the importance of therapeutic relationships characterized by presence, warmth, trust, connection, and understanding of the client, it is not surprising that a number of authors have suggested mindfulness as a common factor across all successful therapeutic encounters regardless of theoretical orientation (Germer et al., 2005; Martin, 1997) and recommended meditation training as a support to develop core clinical characteristics (Anderson, 2005; S. L. Shapiro et al., 2008). Our objective is to describe the qualities of the mindful therapist that may enhance patient outcome through strengthening the therapeutic relationship. We believe these qualities are supported by mindful awareness on the part of the therapist and that they have the potential to be acquired through mindfulness practice. A broad range of qualities may augment one's capacity for forming a strong therapeutic alliance with clients; some have been empirically investigated, whereas others are still awaiting investigation. We address (a) attentional capacity and therapist presence, (b) attitudes applied during therapy, (c) self-compassion and self-attunement of therapists, (d) therapist empathy and attunement toward the client, and (e) therapist emotion regulation and handling of countertransference.

Attention and Therapist Presence

We suggest that mindful awareness has always been an implicit part of successful psychotherapy. The abilities to pay attention and sustain attention are essential to therapeutic practice, and have been explicitly addressed by a wide range of theoretical orientations. For example, Freud's direction to apply "an evenly hovering attention" to the therapy session and Perls's statement that "attention in and of itself is curative" are the most well-known of these directives.

The application of this type of attention is clearly crucial for developing a positive therapeutic relationship and for conducting the therapy session itself. No matter how many years of training a therapist has had in a specific theoretical orientation, or how many well-learned skills he or she has in his or her toolbox, if he or she cannot sustain attention during the therapy and cannot switch attention to multiple objects (e.g., what the patient is saying, his or her own experience in his or her body), it would be difficult to create good rapport or take in all of what is occurring during the session and hence respond appropriately. The ability to focus attention and achieve or at least work toward sustained attention and concentration is crucial for truly being present in the therapy encounter.

Everyone is familiar with how it feels to interact with someone who is clearly not paying full attention to you; the person's eyes dart around the room or a glazed look appears, the person seems to be miles away in his or her own thoughts and doesn't respond appropriately to your words and actions, or maybe the person comes and goes, seeming to listen for a while and then tune out. Contrast this with what it feels like to engage with someone who is consistently attuned to your experience, who looks into your face and clearly resonates with your emotions in his or her eyes and body, who is focused on listening to what you have to say. This latter experience is one of engaging with someone who is present, who is paying attention to his or her experience of you in each moment—in short, with someone who is mindful. As anyone who has experienced this type of connection will know, this attention allows you to feel seen, heard, and understood. The capacity to be mindfully present is inherent in everyone; however, deepening this capacity and being more reliably and consistently present requires systematic practice. We suggest that mindful presence and attention can be optimally developed through formal mindfulness meditation practice.

The research literature on mindfulness and attention supports this hypothesis, with a growing number of controlled studies demonstrating that mindfulness meditation increases ability to direct and sustain attention (Jha, Krompinger, & Baime, 2007; Slagter et al., 2007). A neurobiological study showed greater cortical thickening in areas of the brain associated with sustained attention and awareness (the right prefrontal cortex and right anterior insula) in experienced mindfulness meditation practitioners compared with nonmeditating control participants (Lazar et al., 2005). In a similar way, Jha et al. (2007) found improvements in overall attention, by measuring response times on the Attention Network Test (ANT) following training in 8 weeks of mindfulness meditation for novices and after a month-long retreat for more experienced meditators. The ANT measures the alerting response (i.e., the ability to direct attention quickly to relevant stimuli) as well as the orienting response (i.e., the ability to disattend to nonrelevant information). People who were trained for 8 weeks in mindfulness-based stress reduction (MBSR) were more able to direct focused attention when required, whereas those who attended a 1-month retreat (the more advanced practitioners) showed improvements in their ability to orient, or return their focus in the face of distractions. These findings suggest that abilities to focus attention quickly and sustain this focus on the chosen object may develop over time with greater mindfulness practice.

These abilities to focus and sustain attention are essential to effective clinical work, and yet professional training programs in clinical psychology as yet do not offer systematic ways to cultivate them. All of this research demonstrates that mindfulness practice may be one effective avenue to strengthen these vital therapist qualities.

Research has also examined the effects of meditation on control over the deployment of attention. It is well documented that when a person attends closely to one thing it can prevent him or her from noticing something else (Simons & Chabris, 1999). This is believed to happen because of limited attentional resources; thus, if too much attention is allocated to the first stimulus, the second stimulus is missed. Recent longitudinal research demonstrated that intensive meditation training (a 3-month mindfulness meditation retreat) increased control over the distribution of attention so that less attention was devoted to the first stimulus, resulting in enough attention remaining to detect the second stimulus (Slagter et al., 2007). In clinical work, this ability to attend to a rapid succession of stimuli is essential; otherwise, critical information could be missed. These findings support previous research that attention is not a fixed entity but a flexible skill that can be cultivated through meditation practice. This skill of attention is crucial for therapy, allowing the therapist to attend to subtle and rapid information from the client as well as sustain attention for the entire therapy hour.

In an effort to assess the importance of attention for practicing therapy, a qualitative interview study was conducted with experienced therapists who practice mindfulness, and investigated the question "How does having a personal mindfulness meditation practice influence therapists' ability to be present with clients in the therapeutic relationship?" (McCartney, 2004). A main theme that emerged through phenomenological analysis, *counselor presence*, was enhanced by *being in the moment* with clients. Being in the moment was described as the ability to pay attention in the present moment throughout the therapy session. According to the therapists, being in the moment involved developing a still and quiet place within themselves where they felt centered, calm, and peaceful. Being fully present and aware of their level of attention allowed the therapists to connect with clients as fellow human beings and establish a nurturing therapeutic relationship. Another recent qualitative report of mindfulness training with counseling graduate students found that students reported they were more attentive in the therapy session and more comfortable with silence during the session after mindfulness training (Schure, Christopher, & Christopher, 2008). They felt this helped to support the therapeutic relationship in specific ways:

> I am more comfortable with listening, sitting in silence, and just being present. Mindfulness is after all about being present and aware. In other words the course has helped me focus more on

the client, instead of believing I have to 'do' something to change the client, or relieve their pain. (p. 52)

As can be seen from the research already described, mindfulness meditation practices have the potential to help therapists develop skills in paying close attention to both the client and his or her internal environment, as well as sustain that attention over the course of the entire therapy session. This ability to pay attention is an essential skill for psychotherapy, and it appears that mindfulness practice is one systemic approach for cultivating it in therapists.

Therapist Attitudes

The way in which therapists pay attention during the therapy encounter is also crucial. There can be a cold, hard, clinical aspect to attention, one devoid of any human warmth; this type of attention does not feel supportive and will not enhance the therapeutic relationship. Contrast this to the attitudes exemplified in mindfulness practice, summarized by Jon Kabat-Zinn as nonattachment, acceptance, letting go, beginner's mind, nonstriving, nonjudging, patience, and trust (J. Kabat-Zinn, 1990). Other mindfulness attitudes include warmth, friendliness, and kindness (Segal, Williams, & Teasdale, 2002; S. L. Shapiro & Schwartz, 2000a), which could significantly enhance the therapeutic encounter. The list provided is by no means exhaustive or rigid, but simply provides a heuristic for the general tone and quality of therapist attention. These qualities support the therapist's ability to approach the client with an open mind, to see the person freshly in each moment without judgment or attachment to outcome. Further, they explicitly cultivate warmth, friendliness, and kindness, which will enhance the therapeutic encounter and create a secure holding environment in which the clients may feel safe enough to disclose even their most shameful thoughts and experiences. Further, the attitudes of nonstriving, nonattachment, and patience create an environment that allows the patient to go at his or her own pace without pressure to achieve a certain result or follow a set protocol. Martin described the application of mindfulness in therapy as achieving a state where "such attitudes as being right, controlling the situation, or maintaining therapist self-esteem give way to a quiet, limber, nonbiased and non-reactive response" (Martin, 1997, p. 299).

We believe the attitudes cultivated during mindfulness practice will significantly enhance the therapeutic encounter by strengthening specific qualities in the therapist essential for a healing relationship. Preliminary evidence supports this hypothesis, demonstrating that mindfulness is indeed associated with increases in these proposed attitudes.

For example, Brown and Ryan (2003) demonstrated that higher levels of mindfulness are associated with greater openness to experience as measured on the NEO Five-Factor Inventory (Murray, Rawlings, Allen, & Trinder, 2003)—a measure of general personality characteristics—and Thompson and Waltz (2007) found that higher trait mindfulness was associated with less neuroticism and more agreeableness and conscientiousness on the same measure. As noted earlier, we believe this quality of openness allows therapists to cultivate unconditional positive regard and a stronger therapy relationship (C. R. Rogers, 1961) because they are open to whatever experiences the client brings to therapy. However, we are aware of no published research specifically linking the cultivation of specific mindfulness qualities as described earlier with enhanced therapeutic relationship and patient outcome. We suggest this is a particularly fruitful direction for future research.

Self-Compassion and Attunement

Mindful Reminder: When do you find it most difficult to cultivate compassion for yourself?

Mindfulness practice also helps cultivate the essential therapeutic element of *compassion*, which is a cornerstone of the therapeutic relationship. Compassion is often defined as combining two qualities: the ability to feel empathy for the suffering of the self or other, along with the wish to act on these feelings to alleviate the suffering. In mindfulness practice, the development of compassion begins with learning to relate to oneself with compassion and kindness. A person systematically attends to his or her experience with kindness and begins to observe the crippling effects of self-judgment. This continued process allows people to cultivate attunement with themselves, which is the first step toward cultivating attunement with others. As stated by Siegel (2007a)

> With mindful awareness, we can propose, the mind enters a state of being in which one's here and now experiences are sensed directly, accepted for what they are, and acknowledged with kindness and respect. This is the kind of interpersonal attunement that promotes love. And this is, I believe, the intrapersonal attunement that helps us see how mindful awareness can promote love for oneself. (pp. 16–17)

Attunement, as described by Siegel, is a precursor to compassion in that it involves being in touch with the inner experience of another (or oneself—known as *self-attunement*). Self-attunement requires the development of a *witness consciousness* or, in psychodynamic terms, the observing ego. This aspect of consciousness observes the content of one's experience from a removed distance, accepting it without judgment or interpretation, as something that just is, an element of the human experience. Development of the witness consciousness supports the development of self-attunement. In an attuned relationship with oneself, the witness (the "I") is aware of the ongoing flow of experience and of the thoughts and emotions rising and falling in this stream (the "me"—"I can see this is difficult for me"). To achieve self-attunement, therapists must practice clearly seeing their own reactions and thoughts toward themselves as they perform the role of therapists and in their everyday lives. When they find themselves being very critical and wishing or expecting they should be different in some way, they can consciously practice applying the attitudes described above to their experience, simply observing the critical thoughts without believing them or reacting to them.

Through mindfulness practice, we therapists can strengthen our self-attunement and are better able to relate to ourselves with greater acceptance and compassion. We can systematically attend to our own suffering with openhearted presence, and begin to recognize that our personal suffering is not unique. We may begin to understand in a new and more visceral way that all beings experience suffering, and we develop a deep compassion and a strong desire to alleviate this suffering in ourselves and in others. According to therapist interviews (McCartney, 2004), mindfulness practice helps the development of self-compassion through fostering the recognition of the *universality of being human*. This phrase refers to the realization that everyone suffers, and no one is immune from the human condition. Thus, everyone deserves compassion. One therapist stated it as such:

> There's a connection between us and a larger universe, whatever you want to call it, we're all in one another, we're all everybody. Anything I do to hurt you, hurts me—anything I do to hurt my environment, hurts me. . . . [W]e're all interconnected and we all suffer.

In support of the hypothesis that self-compassion aids in the development of compassion for others, Henry, Schacht, and Strupp (1990) analyzed moment-by-moment videotaped interactions between therapists and clients, rating the degree of hostile and controlling communication from the therapists. They also had therapists rate themselves in terms of their own introjects during therapy. It is not surprising that those therapists who were least accepting and more critical of themselves were also most hostile, controlling, and critical toward their clients. They concluded that therapists who were most self-accepting were far more likely to engage their clients in accepting and supportive transactions.

Some research has been done recently to determine whether self-compassion can be trained in therapists (S. L. Shapiro, Astin, Bishop, & Cordova, 2005; S. L. Shapiro, Brown, & Biegel, 2007). S. L. Shapiro and colleagues examined the effects of MBSR on health care professionals working in a veterans hospital. Results of this randomized controlled trial demonstrated significant increases in self-compassion, pre- to postintervention, in addition to decreased stress and burnout and increased life satisfaction. These results were supported by the anonymous qualitative reports from the participants, including the statements "this practice is vital to living with compassion" and "the greatest benefit is being more gentle and kind with myself."

Supporting this preliminary research, a recent study explored the effects of MBSR on counseling psychology students in a marriage and family therapist graduate program (S. L. Shapiro et al., 2007). Results demonstrated that MBSR led to significant improvements in self-compassion pre- to postintervention compared with a matched control group. It is interesting that improvements in mindfulness (measured by the Mindful Awareness Attention Scale) directly mediated changes in self-compassion following the intervention. As these students became more mindful, they were also kinder to themselves. Self-compassion is arguably an important quality for therapist well-being; however, as noted earlier, this quality appears to be important for the therapeutic relationship as well.

Empathy and Attunement With Others

Mindful Reminder: How can you apply this understanding to help develop compassion for your clients?

Empathy was defined by Carl Rogers as the ability "to sense the [patient's] private world as if it were your own, but without losing the 'as if' quality" (C. R. Rogers, 1957, p. 95). This "as if" quality also reinforces the importance of developing the witness consciousness described earlier. As discussed, empathy toward others is unlikely to occur until therapists have achieved some level of attunement and compassion toward themselves. As the Strupp study supports, a harsh, self-deprecating therapist is less likely to be able to genuinely convey feelings of nonjudgmentalness and compassion to a client. Hence, the development of self-compassion is crucial in therapists, as it sets the groundwork for the development of empathy and compassion for others.

Empathy has been posited as a necessary condition for effective therapy (Arkowitz, 2002; Rogers, 1992, as cited in Bohart et al., 2002). In fact, according to Bohart et al. (2002), "empathy accounts for as much and probably more outcome variance than does the specific intervention" (p. 96). Yet therapists and clinical training programs have been challenged to find ways of cultivating empathy (S. L. Shapiro & Izett, 2008). Research suggests that meditation can significantly enhance empathy in therapists. For example, Lesh (1970) found that counseling psychology students demonstrated significant increases in empathy after a Zen meditation intervention compared with a wait-list control group. Empathy was measured by students' ability to accurately assess emotions expressed by a videotaped client. Supporting this early research, a randomized controlled trial examined the effects of an 8-week MBSR intervention for medical and premedical students. Students were randomly assigned to the mindfulness intervention or a wait-list control group. There were significant increases in empathy levels in the meditation group compared with the control group (S. L. Shapiro, Schwartz, & Bonner, 1998). These results held during the stressful examination period and were replicated when the control group received the same MBSR intervention months later. Recent research with graduate students in counseling psychology found similar results: 8 weeks of training in MBSR led to significant improvements in empathic concern for others pre- and postintervention (S. L. Shapiro et al., 2007). Also observed were improvements in mindfulness, which directly mediated changes in empathy following the intervention. In other words, a significant reason these students improved their levels of empathic concern for others was because they became more mindful. Results of another qualitative study of counseling graduate students support these quantitative findings (Schure et al., 2008). After training in mindfulness, students described an ability to better connect with clients and feel empathy toward their suffering. One reflected on how this improves the therapeutic relationship:

> I think that this results in me being able to be more present, and
> being able to have more empathy for experiences they share with
> me. I think before this class my anxiety would override other
> feelings at times, and it was harder to be in touch with these.
> And even beyond the affective realm, I think that being mindful
> and more 'centered' allows me to look outside of myself more, and
> observe my clients and my relationship with them more.

These preliminary studies suggest that meditation is an effective intervention to cultivate empathy in therapists.

Research in neurobiology is also beginning to explain how meditation may help develop empathy. The discovery of mirror neurons (di Pellegrino, Fadiga, Fogassi, Gallese, & Rizzolatti, 1992), which allow for the ability to create an image of the internal state of another's mind, offers a window into the neurological underpinnings of empathy. Mirror neurons "ensure that the moment someone sees an emotion expressed on your face, they will at once sense that same feeling within themselves" (Goleman, 2006, p. 43). Neuroscience is demonstrating that "the ability to imagine another person's perspective and to empathize correlates with mirror neuron activity" (Siegel, 2007a, p. 137; Siegel, 2007b). The interesting thing is that mirror neurons often fire at a *subacute* level, that is, a level less intensive than that of the initial emotion in the communicator. For example, if a client is feeling sad and crying, the therapist may feel sad as well but not outwardly shed tears. In a similar way, if a client smiles or laughs, the therapist may feel the happiness or amusement but at a lower level that is not always reflected outwardly in smiling and laughing behavior. Daniel Siegel referred to this type of attunement as "the heart of therapeutic change" (Siegel, 2007a). This may be the neurobiological explanation of why training in mindfulness meditation has been shown to significantly increase measures of empathy, and once again supports the intimate intercorrelation between empathy and compassion toward oneself and others.

Emotion Regulation

There has been a great deal of research investigating how training in mindfulness might help clients who have difficulties with regulating their emotions, such as people diagnosed with borderline personality disorder and major depression. Indeed, specific interventions have been developed based on elements of mindfulness for these emotion-regulation problems: dialectical behavior therapy (Linehan, 1993a, 1993b) and mindfulness-based cognitive therapy (Segal et al., 2002), respectively. However, the importance of emotion regulation for therapists (as well as clients) should not be overlooked, as it is an essential skill necessary to develop a good working alliance and positive therapeutic relationship. Therapists must learn to regulate their emotions and be constantly aware of when it is skillful to express emotion and when it is necessary to refrain from reacting outwardly. It is often necessary to tolerate strong emotions, which frequently arise in the therapy setting, and to create a holding space for them.

This sense of holding or creating space for emotions (both the therapist's and the client's) can be illustrated by a commonly used metaphor of dissolving salt in water (Kornfield, 2003). Imagine dissolving a tablespoon of salt into a glass of water. If you drink this mixture, it will taste very salty and bitter. Pour this mixture into a larger jug and fill that with water, and the salty taste will be less; if this water is then further diluted in a pond or even a vast lake, the salty taste would be barely detectable and not at all bothersome. The same applies to holding emotions in a therapy session (Germer et al., 2005). The therapist learns to be a larger "vessel" that can hold an immense amount of emotional content while at the same time maintaining equanimity.

For example, in the qualitative study in which the researchers interviewed therapists who practice mindfulness (McCartney, 2004), therapists described using the witness to observe and hold both the client's process and the therapist's experience of the client. One therapist said,

"I can feel myself especially reaching for my witness the more dramatic it gets over there in the client's seat. It's like my witness is . . . a grounding in myself" (McCartney, 2004, p. 60). In addition to creating a larger vessel, this holding witness also serves another important purpose: to help form boundaries around the experience of the therapist and that of the client. This is necessary to prevent reactivity to what the client is generating. This therapist also stated, "There's a trust of my awareness of what is going on in me as an indication of what is going on for them, but I have to be mindful of what's going on in me in order to be able to use my organism as an instrument with them" (McCartney, 2004, p. 60). This statement illustrates how developing the witness allows therapists to manage classic therapeutic countertransference, such as their own reactions to what the client is directing their way. Because of the familiarity with their minds and bodies developed through meditation practice, they are able to see their personal response to a client's behavior and regulate this emotion, which could otherwise damage the therapeutic relationship.

Through the ability to attend to and regulate their own emotional reactions, therapists can be more present and accepting of clients across a range of emotionally charged therapy situations, and hence more likely to maintain a strong and supportive therapeutic relationship. Again, we are aware of no published studies directly linking therapist emotion regulation with the therapeutic relationship; however, this is an important direction for future research.

Preliminary Evidence for the Mindful Therapist

Earlier we highlighted the qualities of the mindful therapist we believe are conducive to enhancing the important common factor of the therapeutic relationship. Although improved client outcome is an important goal of training mindful therapists, until recently no research has investigated the impact of therapist mindfulness or therapist mindfulness training on client outcomes. However, a recent series of studies by Grepmair and colleagues in Germany examined just this question (Grepmair, Mitterlehner, Loew, Bachler, et al., 2007; Grepmair, Mitterlehner, Loew, & Nickel, 2007). They began with a nonrandomized sequential cohort pilot study comparing outcomes of 196 patients treated by therapists-in-training who either were or were not also practicing Zen meditation, and found that those patients whose therapists were practicing meditation had better self-reported outcomes on measures of understanding of their own psychodynamics, difficulties, and goals. These patients also reported making better progress in overcoming their difficulties and symptoms and in developing new adaptive behaviors they could apply in daily life (Grepmair, Mitterlehner, Loew, & Nickel, 2007).

The second study of this group employed a similar approach, but with a much tighter randomized controlled design (Grepmair, Mitterlehner, Loew, Bachler, et al., 2007). The researchers randomly assigned 18 therapists in training either to learn Zen meditation or to a control group that had training-as-usual. The therapists-in-training in the Zen group practiced meditation with a Zen master daily on weekdays for 1 hour throughout the study. The investigators assigned 124 inpatients with a range of mood and anxiety disorders to be treated by these therapists according to an integrative therapy plan that included both individual and group therapy sessions for a total of 8 hours each week. Patients were not aware of which therapists were meditating, and rated the quality of each individual therapy session and their overall well-being before and after the full course of treatment. Overall, those patients being treated by the Zen group fared better than their counterparts by higher ratings on the therapeutic processes of clarification and problem solving. They said they better understood their own psychodynamics, the structure and characteristics of their difficulties, and the possibilities and goals for their development. Their symptoms also improved more over time across a wide range of standard outcomes, including fewer symptoms of anxiety, depression, hostility, somatization, and obsessions and compulsions.

This is the first demonstration of the power of mindfulness training for therapists to enhance patient outcomes. The findings were unequivocal: On 10 of 11 outcome measures the patients treated by meditating therapists excelled. This study is a good example of the type of research needed to "connect the dots" between the mindful therapist, his or her influence on the therapy relationship, and patient outcomes. Only with this type of research can the suppositions in this chapter be thoroughly investigated.

The Mindful Therapist: Concluding Thoughts

In summary, we hypothesize that the development of an array of qualities in the mindful therapist will enhance the therapeutic relationship and hence promote beneficial therapy outcomes. The qualities of the mindful therapist include the development and refinement of an open, kind, and accepting attention, as well as self-compassion, self-attunement, and empathy for others. The mindful therapist also develops the ability to regulate emotions and hence prevent therapeutic ruptures from occurring through unconscious countertransference behavior.

We postulate that formal training in mindfulness practices can help therapists across a range of theoretical orientations develop these specific qualities that enhance the important common factor of the therapeutic relationship. We also believe that informal practice can help the therapist consciously bring these qualities to each therapeutic encounter. As noted in chapter 1 (this volume), informal practice involves intentionally bringing one's full attention to any activity of daily life. We suggest that making the therapy session itself an informal mindfulness practice is an important way to explicitly bring the qualities one is developing through formal mindfulness practice into the therapy session. At the beginning of each therapy session it is helpful for the therapist to connect with the breath and the body and to consciously form an intention to informally practice mindfulness throughout the therapeutic encounter. The therapist needs to first ground him- or herself in the present moment, acknowledging what he or she finds within him- or herself in terms of physical tension, emotions, thoughts, and expectations before engaging with the client, in order to be conscious of what he or she brings into the session. Throughout the session, the therapist applies intentional attending moment by moment to him- or herself and the client in a nonjudgmental, open, caring, and discerning way. Forming such an intention also involves periodically asking, "Am I fully present? Am I awake?" and consciously reconnecting with the breath and the body as a way of anchoring and grounding throughout the session.

We believe that formal mindfulness practice, in addition to making the therapy session an informal mindfulness practice, greatly enhances qualities essential to effective therapy. In this chapter we drew on the nascent research literature in this area, and we specifically address directions for future research in chapter 10 of this volume. We believe further investigation into the effects of the mindful therapist on therapy outcome will elucidate important insights into the potential of mindfulness training for therapists as well as the mechanisms through which therapist mindfulness affects outcome.

Mindfulness-Informed Therapy | 3

Don't turn your head.
Keep looking at the bandaged place.
That's where the Light enters you.

—Rumi (1995)

Thus far we have introduced the concept of mindfulness, proposing it as a common factor as well as a means of training therapists to become more effective. Now we turn to a second pathway for integrating mindfulness into psychotherapy: mindfulness-informed therapy. Mindfulness-informed therapy offers a framework for integrating wisdom and insights from Buddhist literature, the psychological mindfulness literature, and one's own personal practice into therapeutic work; however, the therapist does not explicitly teach mindfulness meditation practice (Germer, Siegel, & Fulton, 2005).

Often clinical psychologists and others in the helping professions believe the teachings of Buddhism and the practice of mindfulness have value for their clients, but the nature of the clinical work, the client, or the setting makes it inappropriate or impractical to explicitly teach formal mindfulness practice. Whether formal meditation practice is an appropriate intervention is an individual clinical decision made by the therapist or by the therapist and client together, which takes into account all of the variables involved in the individual case. The research literature has not definitively identified specific patient populations that are contraindicated; however, it is also clear that formal mindfulness practice should not be considered a panacea for all people, all conditions, and all circumstances. There are many situations in which meditation may not be the most effective intervention. For example, Johanson (2006) suggested that persons with personality disorders require "counseling in ordinary consciousness" before they are taught formal meditation practice that requires them to look deeply inside themselves (p. 23). He went on to suggest that persons "on the edges of psychosis do not have sufficient psychic structures in place to allow them to study themselves mindfully" (p. 23). Others have suggested that persons diagnosed with major depressive disorder may be so severely depressed that they do not have the concentration capacity to engage in formal meditation, and further, attempts at formal meditation may lead to rumination, which can perpetuate the depressive episode. Similarly, there is controversy about the application of formal meditation in cases of traumatic stress. In light of the many circumstances in which formal practice may not be effective or appropriate, it is helpful to consider applications of mindfulness-informed therapy.

Mindfulness-Informed Therapy: Clinical Examples

Mindfulness-informed therapy is a relatively new conceptualization of how to integrate mindfulness into psychotherapy. There is no manual that can delineate how to do so, nor any specific instructions to guide this nascent approach toward integrating mindfulness and psychotherapy, although excellent books such as Epstein's *Thoughts Without a Thinker* (2004) and Kornfield's *The Wise Heart* (2008) can help guide in a general sense. Later we offer clinical case examples of how we have incorporated insights and teachings from Buddhism and mindfulness into our own clinical work. This list of references is by no means comprehensive; it simply suggests potential points of exploration for both client and therapist based on insights informed by mindfulness.

IMPERMANENCE

One of the major tenets of Buddhism is impermanence, the truth that everything changes. This is one of the first insights that arises as one practices mindfulness. We recognize that everything is in constant flow. We also begin to see that we often live as if things are permanent, static, and unchanging. The mindful approach suggests that suffering arises out of this mistaken view that things are permanent. We suffer not because things are impermanent but because we resist impermanence, trying to cling to things, people, states, and experiences. This grasping and trying to make things the way they want them to be causes much suffering that often goes unrecognized. The insight of impermanence can be liberating to clients and can be offered without teaching the formal mindfulness practice.

For example, the therapist can highlight cases of impermanence and use language that acknowledges the dynamic and ever-changing nature of experience. He or she can also invite clients to observe the changing nature of their own experience; to focus specifically on changing thoughts, emotions, or body sensations; and to begin to recognize the ephemeral nature of all experience.

> Alicia, a 28-year-old woman, was experiencing significant depression and anxiety resulting from a recent breakup with her fiancé. During therapy she continued to retell her story of the breakup and remained entrenched in a belief that she would always be alone, and would never have children or a family. She believed things would always be this way. I invited her to examine the emotions beneath her static, unchanging story. Were they themselves static and unchanging? As she began to pay attention, anxiety became predominant in her experience. I asked her to stay with that feeling; what did she notice about it? She said her thoughts were racing: For example, where should she live, what should she do next, how could she live without him? I invited her to let go of these thoughts that were feeding the emotion of anxiety, and to simply be with the unadorned experience of anxiety itself. What was it like? Was it constant and unchanging? Or was it more wavelike, washing over her and then settling? As she directly experienced the anxiety, she felt how it changed within her. She noticed that it often arose when she was replaying one of her stories about the breakup. When she simply sat with the bare emotion itself, the anxiety often lasted only a few moments and then passed away. She noticed that underneath the anxiety was a deep sadness. She was able to feel into this sadness, the loss of her fiancé, the loss of a dream. She directly experienced the sadness in her body, felt its shape and texture, watched it move and change, watched the intensity of it rise and pass away. She was surprised that her emotions were so ephemeral. At first she had believed she was constantly sad and anxious. And yet she was seeing that this was not true, that her experience was changing moment by moment. She recognized that nothing stays the same, not the relationship she was clinging to, or the misery of the breakup she was trying to escape. She began to rest in the changing nature of things, experiencing the rising and passing away with greater equanimity and clarity. Yet this happened without her becoming a student of Buddhism, or even understanding these insights in explicitly Buddhist terms. The concept of impermanence itself provided a helpful way of reframing and re-experiencing what was happening.

NO SELF

The Buddhist teachings on impermanence extend to the understanding of self. Put simply, everything changes, including the self. There is no stable, solid, unchanging entity that can be labeled as *self*. As psychotherapist Thomas Bien (2006) wrote: "When you look deeply into the river of yourself, there is nothing to hold on to, nothing permanent and unchanging. Your body, your feelings, your thoughts, your perceptions—all are flowing and changing from moment to moment" (p. 150).

This is one of the most difficult teachings for Westerners to understand and accept. It is relatively easy to accept the Buddha's teachings that suffering exists, but to accept that there is no stable entity called a self can be confusing and disconcerting. And yet, this 2,600-year-old teaching is receiving support from the current scientific literature (see Davidson et al., 2003; Kornfield, 2002, 2008; Siegel, 2007a), as *TIME Magazine* reported: "After more than a century of looking for it, brain researchers have long since concluded that there is no conceivable place for a self to be located in the physical brain, and that it simply does not exist" (Lemonick, 1995, ¶ 35).

Used in appropriate circumstances, a wholehearted inquiry into the question "Who am I?" can be liberating, allowing the client to step outside the egocentric perspective and see that this fixed entity one is constantly defending does not really exist, at least not in the way one thinks it does. Exploring the nature of self requires systematic self-investigation. As therapists, we and our clients can inquire, "Am I this body? Am I the skin, the hair, the muscles and bones, or the organs? Am I this stream of ever-changing emotions? Am I these thoughts, ideas, and beliefs? If not, then who am I?" When we explore these questions with clients, we offer the possibility that the self is not what one thinks it is, and that perhaps one can experience the ever-changing and flowing reality of the self. We can explore the possibility that what one calls "self" is ephemeral and in continuous flux. We are able to see thoughts as just thoughts, that this thought is not me. We are able to see emotions as just emotions; for example, sadness is arising, as opposed to "I" am sad. We recognize that we are larger than any of these temporal, transitory experiences. We also begin to recognize that we are none of these experiences. The sage Nisargadatta put it like this: "Wisdom tells me I am nothing. Love tells me I am everything. Between these two my life flows."

> Julie, age 47, had been diagnosed with breast cancer 3 years previous. She had completed her treatment and been in remission for 2 years. However, despite her relatively good prognosis, she said she felt depressed and anxious much of the time. Since her diagnosis of cancer, Julie reported feeling afraid

of life. She spent most of her time at home and was unwilling to explore new activities or people. I asked her how she thought of herself these days and she said, "I see an old woman, a cancer patient. I feel afraid a lot, and my body feels tired." After reflecting this back, I asked, "Is this story true? Is this who you really are?" She paused, and slowly responded, "I don't know." I asked, "Who is it that is aware of these thoughts of 'I'm old' or the emotions of 'I'm afraid'? She paused and a long silence followed. "I guess that's me too." And I requested, "Tell me more about this part of you. Can you feel it right now?" She reflected, "Yes, I feel it. I feel a part of me that is bigger than these thoughts and feelings. This part of me does not feel afraid or sick. This part of me actually feels peaceful." Julie was beginning to realize that her story about who she was was not the whole story. As we continued to explore her constructed identity of the "cancer patient" she saw how limiting and restricting this story was. As she investigated her own experiences more closely over time, she came to see how ephemeral each thought, emotion, and body sensation was, and she began to hold them more lightly. After some weeks, she said she had even begun to laugh at her thoughts, saying "thank you for your opinion" as she stepped back into life. Julie was able to see that although she contained all of these experiences, they were not who she really was.

ACCEPTING WHAT IS

Another example of mindfulness-informed therapy is the insight that much suffering arises because one resists what is actually happening, wanting things to be different from how they actually are. Buddhism suggests that suffering is based not on what is happening but on one's relationship to what is happening. It is the desire for things to be different than they are that causes suffering. When one resists, and does not accept what is, one suffers.

Buddhist teacher Shinzen Young offered a helpful description of how resistance causes suffering. He differentiated pain from suffering, suggesting that pain (e.g., illness, loss, traffic) is the reality of what is happening, and is something that cannot be avoided. Suffering is determined by one's relationship to that reality. He offered a simple yet powerful equation: Suffering = Pain × Resistance ($S = P \times R$). The amount that one *resists* one's *pain* determines how much one *suffers*. For example, if a person is stuck in traffic he or she may become impatient and irritated, wanting the other cars to get out of his or her way. The "pain" of waiting in traffic can be isolated and for simplicity's sake assigned 10 units of pain. Isolating the "resistance" component, let's assume the driver is experiencing 20 units of resistance. The net suffering experienced is thus 200 units (10 pain × 20 resistance = 200 suffering)! When people resist their experience, they significantly increase their suffering. Shinzen Young aptly pointed out that from a mathematical perspective, anything multiplied by 0 is 0. Thus, if one has zero resistance to pain, one does not suffer. This does not mean we do not still experience pain; however, it means we have some control over how much one suffers.

This teaching suggests a way of openly relating to experience instead of closing down and resisting it. It involves a radical acceptance of whatever is here, because it is already here. Mindfulness teaches us to stop struggling against our experience, to stop resisting what is. When we simply rest with what is, we have an opportunity to perceive and relate to our circumstances directly, with greater clarity and freedom.

This shift in how we relate to what is present involves embracing everything that arises. As human beings we experience the entire range of emotions. Mindfulness teaches us to acknowledge and attend to them all. Often we want to push away and deny the negative thoughts and emotions. We expend a lot of energy avoiding what is already here. The mindful approach requires a courageous trust that we can face whatever is here. Through seeing clearly what is already present, we are able to consciously respond with wisdom and clarity.

> **Mindful Reminder:** Pause, breathe deeply, and connect with your body. Can you maintain this connection while reading?

Juan was a 28-year-old Latino gang member who had been transferred from the veterans hospital in New York to our veterans hospital because another gang member tried to kill him. He was experiencing panic attacks and was constantly afraid that someone was going to kill him. He had been in a gang since he was 12 and had learned not to trust anyone and to live with constant vigilance. When he came to see me he made it very clear that he just wanted the panic attacks to go away, and that he definitely did not want to talk, especially not about his anxiety. In speaking with Juan, I drew on the mindful approach that teaches that seeing the problem clearly helps one respond more effectively. I asked him: "Five guys are about to jump you from behind. Do you want to be ambushed, or would you want the chance to turn around, face them and see clearly what kind of weapons they have?" He replied, "Of course I would want to see them clearly!" To which I said, "It's the same with the panic attacks—do you want to keep getting ambushed or do you want to begin to understand and see clearly what is actually happening?" Juan hesitantly nodded. We talked about how the first step is simply acknowledging and accepting what was happening as it was happening. Juan agreed to attend to the anxiety attacks and to report back what he noticed. Although the focus of our work together consisted of cognitive–behavioral treatment for anxiety, incorporating mindfulness teachings about accepting what is actually present helped to elicit his cooperation and openness.

CONSCIOUS RESPONDING VERSUS AUTOMATIC REACTIVITY

Central to the teachings of Buddhism is the recognition that suffering arises out of habitual ways of reacting and the automatic grip of old mental habits. People often react automatically to stimuli as opposed to consciously and discerningly responding. One of the most common automatic mental habits is the belief that a person can think his or her way out of problems. This type of intellectual problem solving is understandable, given that many problems are solved by rationally approaching them. However, what often happens in the mental health arena is that this driven problem-solving mode turns into rumination, which exacerbates difficulties (Nolen-Hoeksema, Morrow, & Fredrickson, 1993). Clients end up thinking about feelings and wishing they would go away instead of directly experiencing them (Segal, Williams, & Teasdale, 2002).

Mindfulness teaches us to let go of this habitual intellectual problem-solving mode (at least temporarily) and bring our awareness to the difficult emotions underlying our experience and to the felt sense of these emotions in the body. Through this process we are able to stop and attend, centering ourselves in the body instead of automatically reacting. Through letting go of our habitual reactivity, we are able to see with greater freshness and clarity and, paradoxically, may arrive at a solution. Buddhism teaches that when we are able to see clearly, the appropriate response more naturally arises. A great ailing Zen meditation teacher was asked at the end of life to summarize all of his teachings and answer the question "What is the teaching of an entire lifetime?" He replied, "An appropriate response." By learning to stop, we can break the cycle of automatic reactions and be able to consciously and appropriately respond.

> Martha, age 46, tended to ruminate about her 17-year-old son's seeming inability to decide what to do with his life. To her he seemed aimless and unconcerned about his future. She constantly worried what would become of him. Are his grades good enough to get into college? Would he be able to survive out in the real world? Her son didn't seem to care about any of it; he was happy in the basement playing computer games. To soothe her anxiety, she constantly nagged him about his shortcomings, including his lack of effort and direction. But the more she nagged and tried to get him to take his life seriously, the less inclined he was to cooperate. Their stalemate caused tension for the whole family. I asked her if she believed her nagging was helpful. "Well, no," she replied, "but I can't seem to help it. It is my knee-jerk reaction every time I see him loafing about." We investigated her automatic reactions, bringing care and attention to the anxiety she discovered underneath them. As she

attended to her experience of anxiety, she began to see that instead of being present with her own emotions she was entrenched in the habit of nagging her son. Her conditioned reactivity to her behavior, which was based on values instilled in her from her demanding upbringing, was creating a great deal of suffering. Instead of automatically reacting, she began to pause and breathe, being with her own anxiety without needing to express her concerns immediately to her son. She learned to better tolerate unpleasant emotions and to pause before responding to her son. In this way, she was able to consciously and skillfully share her concern about him, instead of reacting out of her own anxiety.

CURIOSITY AND INVESTIGATION

Another helpful Buddhist teaching is the emphasis on curiosity and investigation into one's own experience. Peace activist and meditation teacher Thich Nhat Hanh calls this "seeing deeply," which involves close and careful exploration of the present moment. Buddhist teachings suggest four areas that are important to investigate mindfully: body, feelings, mind, and the underlying principles of experience (dharma).

This investigation invites us to become experts of our own experience and to trust our direct experience more than any teachings or teachers. The Buddha is often quoted as saying, "Be a lamp unto yourself." He taught his students not to accept anything as true just because he (or any authority) said so, but to seek and discover for themselves what was true for them. Each person is encouraged to take responsibility for developing his or her own beliefs on the basis of direct experience.

This context of curiosity and exploration can be very helpful in the therapy setting. Helping the client investigate his or her direct experience shifts the focus and allows the client to step outside of the personal, subjective relationship to experience and to take a more inquisitive, objective view. The investigation is not born out of an attempt to solve, but out of caring curiosity and interest in the self. It is only through sustained self-exploration that we can develop a deep sense of self-knowing.

As therapists, we can model this curiosity about our clients' experience. For example, if a client shares that she is feeling sad, the therapist can respond with genuine curiosity: "Hmmm . . . sadness. Tell me more. . . . How interesting. What does it feel like?" As the client learns to be curious about her interior experience and to pay careful attention, she has direct access to insights. For example, she may become aware of how rapidly she classifies incoming stimuli without really attending to the information. She may see how, on the basis of these quick categorizations, she then relates to her conceptualization of experience as opposed to the reality of what is.

The mindful approach encourages this genuine curiosity, which can help clients consciously and directly attend to and investigate experience, moment by moment, without automatically categorizing it before they fully experience it. They become interested in the direct knowing of all the details of the experience. What does it feel like to live in this body? What does it feel like to have these thoughts arise and pass away? What does this emotion feel like? Hmmm . . . interesting.

> Nicholas, a seventh grader, was having trouble in school and appeared depressed and withdrawn. He said very little in our first session, reporting simply that he was "bored." As the therapy went on, his descriptor of bored continued. During the third session, I asked, "Well, since you seem to be bored, let's explore what that really means. Tell me about 'bored.' What are all the things in your life that are boring?" We wrote them on the chalkboard. And then I asked, "What does it feel like to be bored in your body?" Again, we wrote down all of the descriptors: gray, nothing, dark, tired. This was followed by a long pause, and then "sad, all by myself." "Hmmm, what does it feel like to be sad, to be all by yourself?" He responded softly, "I'm scared no one will help me. I'm scared to ask for help." As we continued to explore with curiosity and kindness, we began to uncover the layers of sadness and fear beneath his reported boredom. Through gently investigating his experience we learned how to appropriately be with and respond to it.

PARADOX

Anyone familiar with Buddhism has no doubt come across many of its paradoxes, such as "want not to want" or "emptiness is form and form is empty." Conceptual paradox has been used in Buddhism as a means of liberation; it is an instrument of taking one beyond the usual, discursive way of viewing things to a place of greater flexibility and perspective. The idea of paradox is not new to the West; for example, paradoxes have been extensively used in psychotherapies based on cybernetics and systems theory (Bateson, Jackson, Haley, & Weakland, 1956; Watzlawick, 1990; Winnicott, 1965). T. S. Eliot, in his penetrating words "teach us to care and not to care," ("Ash Wednesday," stanza 34) captured a paradox often associated with Buddhism. Buddhism teaches the importance of deep caring as well as the importance of holding things lightly, not forcing or overlaying a pressure or "should" quality to the course of things. As Eugene Cash, meditation teacher and psychotherapist, noted, "The art of meditation is learning how to care and not to care" (Cash, 2008). Another paradox in Buddhism is the teaching of knowing things deeply and not knowing, referred to in Zen as "don't know mind." The instruction is to penetrate deeply into the nature of things and also to accept and rest in the places where one simply does not know.

Mark, a 51-year-old man, had been diagnosed with sarcoma, a rare form of cancer. Because of the rare nature of the disease, the prognosis and treatment were uncertain. Most concerning for him was not knowing what course of treatment to choose. He visited many experts; some recommended medicine X, but some asserted that this was incorrect and he should most definitely take medicine Y. Both medicine X and medicine Y had severe side effects that would significantly impair his quality of life. Mark came to therapy expressing anxiety about not making the right choice. All of his fear about the disease itself had been channeled into trying to figure out which medication to take. He and his family had spent innumerable hours searching the Internet for answers. All the evidence was contradictory. Although he had investigated thoroughly and had an abundance of information on both medications, he still did not know what to do. As we began to explore his anxiety, he shared how afraid he was of dying, and he felt if he could just figure out what the right medication was he would be okay. He had decided to begin with medication X; however, every day he worried if he should really be on medication Y. I asked him, "How does it feel to not know what to do?" As he tried to answer he began to cry and could not speak. After some moments he said, "I'm just so exhausted. I spend all of my time trying to figure it out; I just want to know." And I asked, "What is it you want to know? What is it really?" He responded softly, "I want to know I'm going to be okay." Silence. I responded, "Yes, you want to know you are going to be okay. And how would it feel to give yourself permission to rest in the 'not knowing'—to know that you have done everything you could to determine the best course of treatment, and now it is time let go into not knowing, and resting as best you can in the present moment?" After a few deep breaths I asked, "How do you feel right now?" He responded, "Okay, softer, more relaxed . . . kind of like a heaviness has been lifted." Mark continued to practice resting in "don't know mind," and although he still frequently experienced fear and anxiety, he gradually developed greater freedom and an ability to relax with uncertainty.

INTERDEPENDENCE

Buddhism teaches that everything is interdependent; all things are connected. Often people live their lives as if they were separate entities from each other. This gives rise to confusion, fear, loneliness, and despair. Mindfulness-informed therapy can offer a different view, teaching that all things are connected in a complex multidimensional web. Therapy provides a useful context in which to investigate whether things do indeed arise together in a mutually interdependent web of cause and effect. In our role as therapists we explore how thoughts, emotions, and behaviors have consequences (subtle and significant) and how these consequences inform the next moment, each moment building on the momentum of the one before it. As clients discover small examples of how things are interconnected, they begin to open to the possibility that everything in the universe is interconnected and mutually interdependent. This realization generates not only a sense of connection but also a mutual responsibility toward all beings. They recognize that everything they do has an effect, that everything is interconnected. With this increased responsibility, they also gain a sense that they are not separate or isolated, that they are intimately interconnected with all things.

> Jane, age 46, was struggling in her marriage. She felt alone and isolated and disconnected from her husband. In therapy we discussed the idea of interdependence. Out of this conversation she explored the possibility that perhaps her husband also felt alone and isolated, and that just as she wanted to be happy, so too did he want to be happy. She made a commitment to offer greater kindness and physical affection to him. She did so openheartedly, not expecting anything in return. The next week she came back filled with excitement. "You won't believe what happened! All week I woke up with the intention to treat William with kindness and love no matter what he did. I carried through on this intention most days, and kept reminding myself that just as I wanted to be happy, so too did he want happiness. Then out of the blue on Friday he brought home a bouquet of flowers and wrote on the card, 'I love you.' He hasn't done anything like that in years!" She realized that her husband also wanted connection and that one's intentions and actions, however small, have an effect. By bringing greater kindness and love to her husband she was able to change the entire system.

ESSENTIAL NATURE

A final example of a teaching we use that falls under the heading of mindfulness-informed therapy is the concept of innate goodness or essential nature. Buddhism teaches that all beings are born with a pure and noble essence: "O Nobly Born, O you of glorious origins, remember your radiant true nature, the essence of mind" (Trungpa, 1975). This teaching is especially needed in the West, where people often live in a "trance of unworthiness," (Brach, 2003, p. 5) believing they are deficient in some way. Constant self-judgment and self-recrimination create unnecessary suffering, while leaving people mired in guilt and anger, instead of working to cultivate their innate goodness.

Mindfulness offers a radically different approach, with a reassurance that our essential nature is pure and virtuous. As human beings begin to examine and question views of unworthiness and deficiency, we begin to understand the effects of our constant judgment and shame. With careful observation and loving attention we see that our delusion of unworthiness causes enormous suffering. Offered a context in which the client's essential being is virtuous, pure, and deeply lovable, the client begins to consider this possibility for him- or herself (akin to Rogers's unconditional positive regard).

Recognizing innate goodness does not mean one overlooks the need for development and change. However, this insight helps us to trust ourselves, and develop the balance of clear-sightedness and compassion. As Zen master Suzuki Roshi reportedly remarked to a disciple, "You are perfect just the way you are. And . . . there is still room for improvement!" (Jack Kornfield, personal communication, March 2, 2004). Mindfulness-informed therapy suggests that no matter the circumstances, everyone shares an inherent goodness of heart that is available in any moment. Through the genuine application of kind attention we can let go of our shame and recognize our essential nature, which is radiant and beautiful.

> **Mindful Reminder:** Reflect on how you might bring one of these insights into a current or past clinical case.

Gary, a 62-year-old Vietnam War veteran, was in a group I was facilitating for veterans with posttraumatic stress disorder. One day in the group he shared how he and his comrades had thrown cans of food off the truck at little Vietnamese children running after them. He recounted, "We were actually trying to hit them and hurt them; it was a kind of game, target practice. I was laughing when we'd take a child down. What kind of person laughs when they hurt an innocent child?" Staring at the floor, shaking his head, he softly said, "We were so cruel. So cruel." The room was quiet, and the shame and grief he felt was palpable. In the silence that followed he and I made eye contact, and I could feel his surprise when he saw no judgment or disgust on my face. I asked him to look around the room, and he saw the love and support of all the men there, looking at him with acceptance and understanding. After a long silence I offered the group an excerpt from a poem titled "Saint Francis and the Sow," by Galway Kinnell (1993), which speaks of reteaching a person his or her innate loveliness, the essential goodness that is always present. Into the silence following the end of the poem I asked, "When clouds cover the sun, does that mean the sun has stopped shining?" Gary began to cry. We all did. For a moment, the heavy burden of unworthiness was lifted, and we felt the freedom of believing in our essential goodness.

Conclusion

Mindfulness-informed therapy draws on ideas from Buddhist psychology, the Western psychological literature on mindfulness, and the therapist's personal mindfulness practice. Therapists who use mindfulness-informed therapy have direct experience with mindfulness and draw on the insights of their direct knowing as well as on mindfulness and Buddhist literature and teachings. The direct experience with mindfulness practice, however, is essential for truly understanding the nuances, paradoxes, and complexities of mindfulness and the subtleties of how to most skillfully integrate it into psychotherapy.

The intention of this chapter was to introduce the possibility of incorporating mindfulness teachings without teaching formal meditation practice and to explore possible themes the therapist can draw on as part of a mindfulness-informed therapeutic approach. The suggestions in this chapter are not comprehensive but are offered as examples for using a mindfulness-informed framework. For further exploration in this area, a number of excellent and thorough books that integrate Buddhist psychology and Western psychotherapy are available (see Appendix D), including Bien (2006), Brach (2003), Epstein (2004), Kornfield (2008), Magid (2002), Moffitt (2008), Safran (2003), and Young-Eisendrath and Muramoto (2002).

Mindfulness-Based
Psychotherapy 4

Look deeply at life as it is in the very here and now

—*Buddha* (Samyutta Nikaya, p. 326)

n chapters 2 and 3, we reviewed Germer et al.'s (2005) classi-
fication of mindfulness-oriented psychotherapy into three
types: the mindful therapist (chap. 2), mindfulness-informed
therapy (chap. 3), and mindfulness-based therapy, which is
the focus of this chapter. In this chapter, we address the definition and scope of mindfulness-based therapies and describe
the therapies that have the most empirical backing. For each
mindfulness-based therapy, we illustrate the central mindfulness practices as well as similarities and differences among
therapies. Issues of who is qualified to provide mindfulness-
based therapies are also briefly addressed. Research into the
efficacy of mindfulness-based therapies is summarized in
chapters 5 (mental health) and 6 (physical health).

Mindfulness-based therapy involves those therapies in
which mindfulness meditation practices are explicitly taught
as a key ingredient in the treatment protocol. A variety of
approaches incorporate both formal and informal mindfulness
practices into the therapy treatment protocol. The best known
of these are mindfulness-based stress reduction (MBSR;
J. Kabat-Zinn, 1990), mindfulness-based cognitive therapy
(MBCT; Segal, Williams, & Teasdale, 2002), dialectal behavior
therapy (DBT; Linehan, 1993a, 1993b), and acceptance and
commitment therapy (ACT; Hayes, Strosahl, & Wilson, 1999).

Before we review the specifics of these and other mindfulness-based therapies, it is useful to scan the research and

clinical environment to get a sense of the growing popularity of mindfulness-based approaches. For example, a cursory Internet search for the term *mindfulness-based* yielded over 134,000 hits. Most of these links appear to relate directly to mindfulness-based therapy program information, although some are more peripheral. Reflecting the inroads mindfulness-based therapies have made into mainstream psychology and medicine, searches of the scientific literature on PsycINFO and PubMed in February 2008 using the same term, *mindfulness-based*, yielded 260 and 115 published scientific articles, respectively. Many of these articles appear in both databases, but it is safe to say that there are well over 300 different published scientific articles regarding various theoretical and empirical perspectives on mindfulness-based interventions, with many more studies under way.

To assess the enthusiasm of funders, grant peer reviewers, and the scientific community for these types of approaches, we searched the CRISP (Computer Retrieval of Information on Scientific Projects) database for all studies receiving funding through the National Institutes of Health (NIH). When funded studies with the term *mindfulness-based* are plotted year-by-year across all institutions (see Figure 4.1), the trend for increasing research support is clear. In 2008, 44 funded studies were in progress; this number had increased from 0 in 1998 and only 3 in 1999. As can easily be seen from the graph, funding spiked between 2003 and 2005, when funded grant numbers jumped from 5 to 32. The total number of funded studies over the years cannot be surmised from this graph, however, as some multiyear grants are represented in more than 1 year, so total numbers are less than the sum of all years combined. Nonetheless, this growth curve is impressive, especially given that funding levels and success rates overall dropped across these years. Indeed, this assessment of funded studies is the most stringent measure of the caliber of mindfulness-based research, given that funding success rates at NIH have been dropping over the years and currently hover around 10% to 15% of all submitted applications.

What types of studies are being conducted given this influx of funds and interest in mindfulness-based interventions? The range is quite staggering. A list of mindfulness-based therapies funded by NIH (see Exhibit 4.1) and types of problems and populations being studied (see Table 4.1) tell the tale. Clinical groups being trained in mindfulness techniques range from people with common mental health problems such as mood and anxiety disorders to those with a range of physical health conditions from asthma to organ transplant. A growing number of mindfulness-training studies are also looking at such outcomes as immune system function, cognition, and attention in healthy or aging populations. In summary, there is great public and scientific interest in mindfulness-based interventions, which are being applied to a very wide range of problems and clinical populations. In addition, the quantity of scientific studies of mindfulness-based

FIGURE 4.1

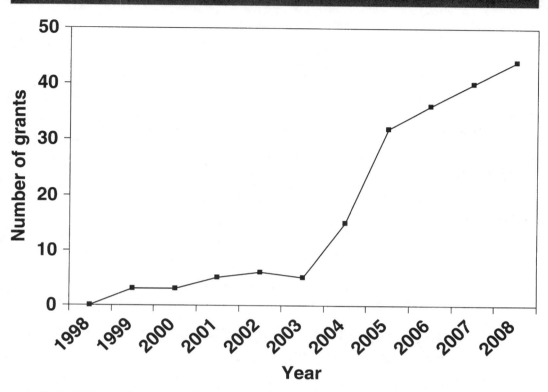

Note. National Institutes of Health (NIH)-funded mindfulness-based studies from 1998 to 2008.

EXHIBIT 4.1

Types of Published Mindfulness-Based Therapies

Mindfulness-based stress reduction (MBSR)
Mindfulness-based cognitive therapy (MBCT)
Mindfulness-based eating awareness training (MB-EAT)
Mindfulness-based art therapy (MBAT)
Mindfulness-based relapse prevention (MBRP)
Mindfulness-based relationship enhancement (MBRE)
Acceptance and commitment therapy (ACT)
Dialectal behavior therapy (DBT)

TABLE 4.1

NIH-Funded Studies Underway on Mindfulness-Based Therapies

Populations being studied		Outcomes in healthy populations
Mental health	**Physical health**	
Depression	Coronary heart	Inflammation/immune function
Anxiety	disease/hypertension	Attention
Posttraumatic stress	HIV/AIDS	Stress (acute/chronic)
disorder/trauma	Cancer	Cognition (in seniors)
Social phobia	Bone marrow transplant	Health status (in seniors)
Eating disorders	Hot flashes/menopause	
Obesity	Irritable bowel syndrome	
Personality disorders	Solid organ transplant	
Substance abuse/smoking	Chronic pain	
cessation	Asthma	
Insomnia		

interventions is steadily growing, and the caliber of these studies is consistently improving.

Common Mindfulness-Based Therapies

Mindful Reminder: Are there ways you could routinely apply mindfulness in the moments of your everyday life?

Ruth Baer, in the first chapter of the book *Mindfulness-Based Treatment Approaches,* provided an overview of a number of common mindfulness and acceptance-based therapy approaches (Baer & Krietemeyer, 2006; this book is also a good resource for more detail on these therapies). In this section we focus on MBSR as the basic model for mindfulness-based approaches and then summarize some of the similarities and differences between several other approaches. We cover MBSR and MBCT in some detail and briefly discuss other therapies emerging from the tradition of MBSR, which we refer to as *mindfulness-based (MB) therapies.* Finally we discuss DBT and ACT as modalities that stem from other therapeutic traditions but incorporate mindfulness.

MINDFULNESS-BASED STRESS REDUCTION

The first and still most popular form of mindfulness-based therapy is MBSR. Developed by Jon Kabat-Zinn and colleagues at the University of Massachusetts Medical Center in 1979, MBSR takes the form of an 8-week group program of up to 35 participants who meet weekly for

2½ to 3 hours, with a 6-hour silent retreat occurring on a weekend between classes 6 and 7. MBSR is described in the book *Full Catastrophe Living: Using the Wisdom of Your Body and Mind to Overcome Pain, Stress and Illness* (J. Kabat-Zinn, 1990). It was developed in response to a perceived need for alternative treatment for patients who were falling through the cracks of the traditional medical system. Often difficult to treat, patients with refractory pain or anxiety disorders who attended early MBSR classes began to report remarkable improvements. With the publication of the book and the emergence of empirical reports of the benefits of MBSR, it began to increase in popularity, and many health professionals sought training in this modality.

MBSR is an intensive training program in a variety of mindfulness practices, both formal and informal. Participants are required to practice meditation and gentle yoga at home for a total of 45 minutes, 6 days each week during the course of the program. The primary mindfulness techniques taught include the body scan, sitting meditation, walking meditation, gentle yoga, and informal daily mindfulness practice. Didactic teaching of mindfulness occurs each week, with time for participant processing of their experience, feedback from facilitators, and group discussion of challenges to practice and other insights that may arise. The atmosphere is collaborative and encouraging, with group facilitators implicitly embodying and outwardly encouraging the application of mindfulness attitudes of nonjudging, patience, acceptance, beginner's mind, nonstriving, letting go, nonattachment, and trust.

The program typically begins with eating one raisin mindfully; then shifts focus to the body scan, a guided somatic sensory awareness exercise in which the facilitator slowly directs participants' attention through body parts, usually from the feet to the head, encouraging them to pay close attention to whatever arises in each area moment to moment, without trying to change the experience or achieve any particular outcome (see Appendix A for guided body scan instruction). Attitudes of reverence, awe, and love are sometimes suggested, but participants are primarily encouraged to simply notice whatever arises in the practice. This can take up to 45 minutes. This practice encourages the development of several core mindfulness skills: paying close and sustained moment-by-moment attention to a specific object of awareness; flexibility of attention in moving from one body region to the next; noticing whatever sensations, thoughts, or feelings arise without trying to change them; returning to the intended focus of awareness when the mind inevitably wanders; and applying mindfulness attitudes of kindness, acceptance, and nonjudging to the experience.

Mindful yoga is also introduced within the first few sessions (this varies from program to program). The purpose of the yoga movements is to cultivate kindness for the body within the context of gentle mindful movement. It is not an athletic endeavor; rather, participants are encouraged to pay close attention to their experience and gently explore their edges in various positions while applying the same mindfulness attitudes as they did in the body scan. They are instructed not to compare themselves with others or with their own performance from one day to the next but simply to practice being fully aware of the body's capabilities in every moment as if for the first time. This mindful yoga is a way to become familiar with and "make friends" with the body, which in many cases has been the cause of a great deal of frustration, disappointment, and pain. Although not a goal of mindful yoga, many participants find themselves becoming physically stronger, more flexible, and with improved balance with regular practice of these gentle exercises.

Sitting meditation may be considered the core of the program, with practice emphasizing a constant turning toward and remembering the focus of the exercise, which usually begins with breath awareness (see Appendix B for guided sitting meditation instructions). Participants are instructed to feel the in-and-out flow of breath and notice whenever their attention strays from that focus. This point of noticing can give rise to many "aha" moments, when the participant has an opportunity to refocus on the breath and begin again. Beginning again is seen as the heart of the practice, and attitudes of curiosity, patience, and lightheartedness are encouraged. Over the course of the program, the focus of sitting will broaden from always the breath to a greater mindfulness of other aspects of moment-by-moment experience, including sounds, bodily sensations, emotions felt in the body, and passing thoughts. The practice of "bare awareness" or "choiceless awareness" is introduced through the weeks with an emphasis on accepting whatever arises as it is, learning to breathe with whatever comes up, and becoming a larger container for potentially difficult experiences. The potential for the acquisition of insight through mindful awareness is introduced, not as a goal to strive toward but as an inevitable outcome of consistent practice.

Walking meditation is also incorporated into the curriculum, with the awareness typically directed toward the bodily sensations of walking (see Appendix C for guided walking meditation instructions). The speed can be normal or fast, and often it is slowed down to allow full awareness of different parts of the step, for example, the meditator notes lifting the foot, moving it through space, lowering it toward the floor, placing it down, shifting the weight onto that foot, and subsequently lifting the opposite heel. All of this is done with the same attitude of openness and curiosity, always returning focus when the mind wanders. This practice is sometimes easier for new practitioners, who may find sitting still for extended periods to cause discomfort and restlessness. (However, in general, the core instruction in mindfulness is to face whatever is aversive and observe the shifting nature of aversions themselves.)

A final formal meditation practice included during the MBSR day-long class and throughout the concluding sessions is loving-kindness (metta) meditation (see chap. 8, this volume). Loving-kindness meditation is a type of practice that purposefully cultivates feelings of kindness and compassion toward different objects of attention. This traditionally begins with oneself or a benefactor and gradually expands to others in one's life and eventually to all beings.

Finally, informal mindfulness practices are encouraged throughout the day as ways to begin incorporating mindfulness as a way of life, rather than as an isolated formal practice. Hence, mindfulness of everyday tasks such as eating, grooming, washing the dishes, and communicating with others is encouraged. Informal practice involves intentionally attending to whatever one is doing with care and kindness. Mini meditation exercises are prescribed that can be done at any time, such as at stoplights, when waiting in line or for appointments, in traffic, or while on hold. These informal practices simply involve intentionally tuning in to the body and breath for a short time as one carries out activities of daily living.

MINDFULNESS-BASED COGNITIVE THERAPY

A newer twist on MBSR came about with the development of MBCT in the late 1990s. Cognitive therapists John Teasdale, Mark Williams, and Zindel Segal were experts on the treatment of depression using cognitive–behavioral therapy (CBT), the current gold standard. The main challenge facing clinicians and researchers in the area of depression was preventing relapse. Although there were effective treatments for acute episodes of depression, no therapy had been especially effective at preventing relapse. Most people who recovered from a major depressive episode were likely over time to have more. Segal and colleagues were interested in understanding the psychological underpinnings of depression relapse in order to design effective therapies for this problem. With the surge of interest and research into MBSR, they became familiar with the model and believed aspects of mindfulness could help recovered depressed patients steer clear of relapse. Over time, and with the help and encouragement of Dr. Kabat-Zinn and his colleagues, they developed and manualized MBCT, a formal therapy integrating MBSR and CBT (Segal et al., 2002). This therapists' manual was supplemented recently with a patient self-help book that comes with a guided meditation CD (J. M. Williams, Teasdale, Segal, & Kabat-Zinn, 2007).

MBCT is typically conducted over 8 weeks with smaller groups than in MBSR, up to about 12 participants. In terms of practices, MBCT is similar to MBSR, using the body scan, sitting meditation, walking meditation, and informal daily mindfulness. However, MBCT does not include the formal loving-kindness meditation instructions, although kindness toward oneself and one's experience is emphasized throughout MSCT.

The didactic material is focused more on understanding depression than on stress and the stress response, as in the original MBSR program. A model of understanding depression as a vicious downward spiral triggered by futile efforts to logically argue away negative thoughts is presented to participants, and an alternative way to deal with negative thoughts is offered. Participants are invited to become aware of the persistent and familiar negative patterns of thought as they begin to arise, and to change their relationship to the thoughts. Instead of ruminating over any particular thoughts of unworthiness or hopelessness, people learn to see these thoughts just as thoughts, which will come and go in their own time. They recognize that thoughts and emotions arise and pass if they are not "fed" or believed as a static reality that represents the way things are and always will be. Hence the meditation practices are directed toward noticing and allowing these types of experiences to come and go, with the same mindfulness attitudes of kindness, curiosity, and patience.

Specific techniques unique to MBCT include the "3-minute breathing space." This exercise is similar to the mini meditations practiced in MBSR, but more formalized into three distinct steps:

1. Focus on the range of internal experience, addressing the question, What is my experience right now? For this first minute no attempt is made to change the experience, just to note with acceptance what it consists of;
2. focus full attention on the movement and sensations associated with the breath, breathing in and out for a full minute; and
3. expand awareness once again to the body as a whole, including posture, facial expression, and emotions, again with acceptance and without judgment.

This process is sometimes described as an "hourglass" wherein the attention is broad at first, then narrows to the breath at the waist of the hourglass, and finally expands again. It is meant to be practiced anytime throughout the day, especially when participants begin to feel overwhelmed.

Other elements of cognitive therapy are added to the MBSR curriculum, including discussion of how one's current mood affects the automatic thoughts that arise; for example, a person in a depressed mood tends to have more depressed thoughts and is also more likely to believe these depressed thoughts are true. Participants are encouraged to see that thoughts are not truth or reality, and that they change moment to moment and day to day depending on current mood and situations. They begin to see thoughts as impermanent, as passing mind-moments that are not necessarily true. Unlike with traditional CBT, they are taught not to purposefully change any thoughts or replace distorted thoughts with healthier alternatives but just to see them for what they are. In addition, participants are encouraged to practice activities that generate feelings of mastery and pleasure, as these types of activities are known to help prevent relapse. In the last two sessions, plans for relapse prevention are discussed. Participants reflect on what they have learned in the MBCT course as well as their past experiences to determine an effective plan for how to continue to prevent relapse.

OTHER EMERGING MINDFULNESS-BASED THERAPIES

Many other therapies modeled after MBSR are emerging. These therapies have modified the MBSR curriculum in response to the needs of specific clinical groups. These pioneering therapies have appeared only recently in the published literature and an evidence base for their usefulness is just beginning to be developed. Next, we review the four most researched of these newer mindfulness-based therapies.

Mindfulness-Based Eating Awareness Training

Quite a bit of work has been conducted in the modification of the traditional MBSR curriculum to treat individuals with binge eating disorder and, more recently, obesity. First developed by Jean Kristeller (Kristeller, Baer, & Quillian-Wolever, 2006), mindfulness-based eating awareness training integrates elements of MBSR and CBT with guided eating meditations. The eating-relevant guided meditations address issues around body shape, weight, and eating-related processes such as appetite and satiety. Overeating is seen as symptomatic of larger systemic dysregulations involving disturbances of affect, cognitions, and behavioral regulation. Mindfulness training is seen as a way to increase awareness of automatic patterns and then to disengage from undesirable behaviors and reactivity. Many of the meditations use food in the group sessions, beginning with the raisin exercise, a simple exercise of mindfully eating one raisin and building up to more challenging foods such as cookies, cakes, and finally a full buffet around which the practice of making mindful food choices is incorporated. There is some body work, but the use of yoga is limited compared with traditional MBSR.

Mindfulness-Based Relationship Enhancement

Another emerging mindfulness-based therapy described by Carson and colleagues (Carson, Carson, Gil, & Baucom, 2006) is mindfulness-based relationship enhancement (MBRE), developed to enhance the relationships of couples who are relatively happy. It is closely modeled on MBSR in terms of format, techniques, and homework topics; however, several of the elements have been modified into dyadic exercises rather than individual ones. For example, in MBRE the loving-kindness meditation practice focuses on generating feelings of kindness and care toward the partner. There is a greater emphasis on loving-kindness meditation in general in MBRE than in MBSR. In MBRE, it is introduced in the first session and continued throughout the intervention, as opposed to in MBSR, where it is only formally introduced during the daylong retreat. There is also emphasis on practicing mindful communication and listening skills within the sessions that may transfer into daily life for the couples. Yoga exercises are modified to allow for more partner involvement, referred to as a "dyadic dance" wherein partners physically support and facilitate one another in the postures. Other mindful couples' exercises include a mindful touch exercise and back rub, and discussion of how mindfulness can enhance sensual intimacy. Overall, the focus is on bringing mindfulness to the relationship both during the class sessions and in daily life.

Mindfulness-Based Art Therapy

Another example of mindfulness-based therapies is mindfulness-based art therapy (Monti et al., 2005), which has been developed for use in medical populations and piloted specifically in women with breast cancer. It incorporates elements of the creative process as a means for expressing emotions around the meaning of the illness, health, and healing. It incorporates art-making with traditional elements of MBSR, with the goal of enhancing both the supportive and expressive aspects of treatment. Participants use multiple artistic modalities and exercises designed to help outwardly express feelings identified through mindful awareness practices, including pain and fear.

Mindfulness-Based Relapse Prevention

Other mindfulness-based therapies gaining a foothold in addiction research and treatment circles are collectively known as mindfulness-based relapse prevention (Marlatt & Gordon, 1985; Marlatt & Witkiewitz, 2005), which is patterned after MBCT. Mindfulness-based relapse prevention integrates mindfulness with the principles of a well-established therapy for prevention of relapses to substance abuse based on cognitive and behavioral theories of risk avoidance (Daley & Marlatt, 1997). The authors hypothesized that improvements made in preventing relapses to alcohol and drug abuse may be due to changes in metacognitive processes (i.e., the ability to act as the observing witness) as well as the acquisition of specific skills to cope with urges, cravings, and negative affect. It has been applied not only to alcohol and drug abuse but also to smoking cessation (Wetter, 2008).

These are some examples of MB therapies that have been published and are the subject of funded research activity investigating their efficacy. Many more, emerging on a regular basis, will require similar investigation.

DIALECTICAL BEHAVIOR THERAPY

Turning to other therapies that incorporate mindfulness but stem from different theoretical roots, we first address DBT, then ACT. DBT was developed by Marsha Linehan (Linehan, 1993a, 1993b) specifically as a treatment modality for borderline personality disorder, although more recently it has been adapted to various other disorders. The central tenet of DBT is the balance and integration of opposing ideas: the dialectic. As an example, DBT incorporates elements of both acceptance and change. DBT therapies teach formal mindfulness practices as one of four central modules, although the exercises are typically shorter than those practiced in MBSR or MBCT and focus on specific targets of mindful awareness in addition to the breath and body. The other three modules of interpersonal effectiveness, emotion regulation, and distress tolerance are influenced by the core mindfulness skills such that the four modules are intimately interconnected.

Within the mindfulness module, three "states of mind" and six "mindfulness skills" are introduced. The states of mind are *reasonable mind,* the logical rational part of the mind that makes intellectual decisions; *emotional mind,* which is the reactive mind wherein emotions control thoughts and behaviors; and *wise mind,* the integration of the former two modalities that balances the intellect with intuition and emotions. These three states of mind can be seen as the balance between the opposing dialectic of emotion and reason, and is developed through the practice of mindfulness skills.

The six mindfulness skills are broken down into three "what" skills and three "how" skills. The what skills specify just what one does during mindfulness training, specifically: *observing, describing,* and *participating.* Observing and describing are similar to the mindfulness practices in the other MB therapies previously described; participating refers to attending completely and immersing oneself in the present moment, as well as acting with spontaneity and without self-consciousness. The three "how" skills—*nonjudgmentally, one-mindfully,* and *effectively*—parallel the mindfulness attitudes. One-mindfully typically refers to focusing undivided attention on one thing at a time. This component as defined in DBT refers to a practical skill involving recognizing the limitations of a situation, identifying one's goals, and using skillful means to achieve them, rather than attending to one thing at a time as in other MB therapies. There is a very robust body of studies (see Lynch, Trost, Salsman, & Linehan, 2007; Ost, 2008) demonstrating clinical effectiveness with borderline personality disorder.

ACCEPTANCE AND COMMITMENT THERAPY

The roots of ACT are also different than those of MBSR and MBCT. ACT stems from relational frame theory, a very broad theory that attempts to account for all of human language and cognition by positing that relationships within and between individuals are learned associations reinforced through behavioral contingencies (Hayes et al., 1999). ACT stems from this context and applies acceptance and mindfulness strategies in conjunction with commitment to certain goals and values along with behavior change strategies. The goal is to increase psychological flexibility by learning how to contact the present moment fully and consciously, based on demands of specific situational circumstances.

ACT is usually delivered in an individual rather than group format and can be applied to a broad range of psychological problems. A central tenet of ACT is that clients often use language in futile attempts to control their inner lives; this is similar to the idea in MBCT of trying to argue with or change dysfunctional thoughts, which tends to be counterproductive. Through metaphor, paradox, and experiential mindfulness exercises, clients learn how to contact and identify thoughts, feelings, and sensations that have previously been feared and avoided. They learn to accept these inner events, develop greater clarity about values, and commit to changing behavior in service of these deeply held values. Hence, the idea of experiential avoidance is a central concept, and many of the therapy exercises are designed to facilitate exposure to feared inner experiences through the use of various mindfulness practices.

A key concept in ACT that will be familiar to practitioners of mindfulness is termed *cognitive fusion*. This idea illustrates the belief that thoughts are true and factual, and hence are signposts that dictate feelings, reactions, and behaviors; in effect, the cognitive, affective, and behavioral aspects of a person can become "fused." In cognitive "defusion," the antidote to this problem, clients learn to observe passing thoughts without assuming they are true or important and without having to act on their content. They can be seen as just mind events that come and go, no matter how aversive their content. Attempts to eliminate or change these thoughts are not made, and a simple observational stance is assumed. Hence, when a person is fused with cognitions, thoughts (e.g., "I'm going to screw this up and be so embarrassed") become truth to the person and are accompanied by bodily reactions (tension, flushing, sweating) and feelings (dread) that lead to corresponding behaviors (avoiding the situation, stammering). In cognitive defusion, the thought can be recognized as just a thought and allowed to pass without triggering the associated feelings and behaviors, so the person can engage in the feared behavior without mishap. The witness consciousness is used in ACT as a way of helping to achieve cognitive defusion, so that instead of noting the thought "I'm a failure" an individual would learn to say to him- or herself, "I'm having the thought that I'm a failure." This distancing aids the process of separating the self from passing thoughts and feelings and frees the observer-self from being influenced by these passing mental events.

Finally, similar to DBT, ACT includes explicit attention to the client's values and goals in life, and seeks to promote committed action in areas such as relationships, health, personal growth, career, and citizenship. Goals relevant to the client's values are set in therapy, and obstacles that stand in the way of committing to these goals (which often result from anxiety, avoidance, fear, etc.) are examined. Plans are made to help overcome these obstacles and ultimately align actions with core beliefs and values.

Similarities and Differences Among Therapies

Mindful Reminder: Stop for a moment and scan your body. Are there areas of tension, holding, tightness? Are you able to release some of this right now?

As summarized throughout this chapter, many of the mindfulness-based therapies share common theoretical underpinnings and specific exercises. DBT and ACT use shorter, less formal, and more focused mindfulness exercises than do the MB therapies, and also include explicit focus on both acceptance and change-based strategies, whereas the MB modalities mostly rely on acceptance. Most of the mindfulness-based interventions are offered in group formats, whereas ACT is typically an individual therapy and DBT contains both individual and group components. Specific modifications of mindfulness-based modalities add exercises relevant to the population being treated, whether these include focused eating exercises for binge eaters or awareness of cues for relapse in substance abusers. The duration of the treatments also varies: The group mindfulness-based techniques are usually about 8 weeks in duration, whereas ACT can be for a short or longer period, depending on the client. DBT typically lasts for 1 year or longer.

ROLE OF MINDFUL MOVEMENT

Another difference among therapies is in the importance placed on the role of mindful movement. Formal practice of mindful movement and stretching is not included in DBT or ACT. In terms of the other MB therapies, the role of mindful movement has not received much attention in the literature. The originators of MBSR would argue that this component is crucial to the program as a whole; however, the practitioners now being trained in program delivery are largely health care professionals, many of whom do not have extensive experience or training in mindful movement and may be reluctant to risk teaching these movements for fear of causing harm or injury. They may also not as readily see the benefit of incorporating these mindful body movements and stretching into the more cerebral practices of formal meditation. The benefit of mindful movement versus sitting and body scan meditation practices in MB therapies remains an empirical question, but our belief is that for certain patient populations in particular, the mindful movement is a crucial element of success. For example, in studies involving thousands of patients with cancer over the last 10 years, patients reported equal benefit from the mindful movement and from the formal meditation practices. Only empirical investigation will be able to show the extent to which mindful movement is helpful and for which populations it is most beneficial.

THERAPIST QUALIFICATIONS

With the growing public interest in MB therapies, many professionals wish to know how to become properly qualified to deliver these interventions in a safe and ethical manner, and potential program participants wish to determine how to find a qualified instructor. This issue of who is qualified to deliver these types of therapies has been somewhat controversial. The Center for Mindfulness in Medicine, Healthcare, and Society is the only professional body that provides certification for MBSR teachers, whereas other professional bodies provide professional licenses to practice therapy in each jurisdiction. Practitioners and developers of MBSR and MBCT strongly believe that in order to teach these modalities instructors need to have their own daily practice of meditation. This is not a requirement for other therapies developed outside this tradition, such as DBT and ACT.

The guidelines suggested by the Center for Mindfulness for MBSR teacher certification are quite stringent and include (a) professional experience and graduate degree or equivalent in the fields of health care, education, or social change; (b) ongoing daily meditation and body-centered awareness practice and commitment to the integration of mindfulness into everyday life; (c) regular participation in 5- to 10-day silent, teacher-led mindfulness meditation retreats; and (d) experience teaching a minimum of four 8-week MBSR courses. In addition to these elements, they require specific training in MBSR as provided though a series of professional development opportunities. The first exposure is typically a 7-day professional retreat where professionals are introduced to the theoretical foundations and curriculum of MBSR. This is followed by participation in a full 8-week program with supervision; and participation in a longer practicum in MBSR with opportunities for coteaching with feedback and individual supervision; and finally a teacher development intensive during which a group of teachers practice teaching one another with feedback. All of these courses are offered through the teaching arm of the Center, Oasis. Equivalencies with proof of teaching on videotapes or CDs are sometimes accepted (Santorelli, 2008).

Many professionals deliver MBSR programs without this certification, as it is an informal requirement and not required by most professional licensure bodies. Therapists practicing other forms of mindfulness-based therapies generally have adopted these guidelines as the gold standard. Specific training workshops for MBCT are routinely offered over the course of a few days or a weekend, but no specific teacher requirements are detailed. The philosophy of the ACT community is to foster

> an open and responsible scientific culture that is non-hierarchical, self-critical, and that makes it easy for everyone to play a role. In furtherance of these values the ACT Community has decided not to formally certify therapists, trusting an open process of development to weed out problems. (Hayes, 2005)

Hence, although many ACT training opportunities are provided, no certifying body exists. For DBT, which has been an established therapy modality for a longer time, training is provided in many graduate programs but not actively certified by any central body.

The issue of teacher certification is likely to remain controversial as practitioners attempt to find a balance between protecting the integrity of the practice but not overly limiting opportunities to offer mindfulness-based interventions to populations in need.

Conclusions and Future Directions

This chapter highlighted the emerging field of mindfulness-based interventions, both the well-established MBSR and MBCT as well as the newer MB therapies that are being developed and applied to a broad array of disorders and populations. The development of MB therapies is quite exciting, opening seemingly unlimited possibilities for the applications of mindfulness. The danger, however, is that as mindfulness gains in popularity it faces possible harm through the potentially unskillful application of its tenets. There is great debate in the field of mindfulness-based psychotherapy regarding how to protect the sanctity and purity of the modalities as they have been originally conceptualized and applied, while at the same time remaining open to new and potentially very useful applications. This debate is by no means closed, and it will likely continue as mindfulness continues to enter the mainstream of medicine and mental health care.

Some purists are deeply concerned by the removal of the concept of mindfulness from its traditional Buddhist roots, which are the implicit basis of *all* the mindfulness-based interventions, including MBSR. These purists suggest that the application of mindfulness in a secular treatment has resulted in a watering down of its potential power and intended applications. Others believe that if a "secularized mindfulness" can be of benefit and is more accessible to a wide range of populations, then by all means it should be used. Our belief is that a clear understanding and some experience of the traditional context of mindfulness is helpful to teachers and therapists applying its tenets. Reading of the original Buddhist texts is useful to deepen one's ability to convey important concepts to clients, even if the traditional Buddhist vocabulary to describe the concepts is not used. This does not imply that all mindfulness-based therapists must spend years or even months at meditation retreats, but it does seem essential to have a regular mindfulness practice and to read some translations of Buddhist psychology and basic philosophy regarding the nature of suffering, its root causes, and recommended methods to end suffering.

Our hope is that practitioners and researchers involved in the development, investigation, and application of mindfulness-based interventions will have a deep personal experience to inform their clinical work and empirical investigations. As S. L. Shapiro, Walsh, and Britton (2003, pp. 85–86) noted

> Without direct experience, concepts (and especially transpersonal concepts) remain what Immanuel Kant calls "empty" and devoid of experiential grounding. Without this grounding we lack adequatio: the capacity to comprehend the deeper "grades of significance" of phenomena (Schumacher, 1977), which Aldous Huxley (1944) refers to in *The Perennial Philosophy* as "knowledge is a function of being . . . ." Without direct practice and experience we may be in part blind to the deeper grades of significance of meditation experiences, and blind to our blindness.

We believe that our direct experience with mindfulness will best inform clinical interventions as well as research investigations. We also believe that further, rigorous evaluation of all newly introduced MB therapies is essential. As helping professionals, our ethical duties are to provide the most appropriate form of intervention for each client who crosses our threshold. We can do this only from a deeply informed position, drawing from both personal experience and evidence-based science.

DOES IT HELP? AND HOW DOES IT HELP? | II

Mindfulness-Based Interventions for Mental Health

5

Seek not to have that everything should happen as
   you wish,
But wish for everything to happen
as it actually does happen,
and you will be serene.

—*Epictetus* (Melden, 1950, p. 151)

The growing interest in mindfulness-based interventions described in chapter 4 (this volume) has been paralleled by scientific research investigating the effects of these types of programs on a wide variety of patient populations, as well as in healthy individuals. In this chapter, we focus on research studies that have investigated the effects of mindfulness-based (MB) interventions on people with psychological problems such as depression and anxiety. We also cover psychological outcomes measured in groups of healthy individuals. Distinguishing between all studies investigating the efficacy of meditation itself and those that have focused on what we termed *mindfulness-based interventions* in chapter 4 (this volume) is useful in structuring the review. Here we focus on reviewing only the latter category; a comprehensive review of the former (all meditation studies) was released in 2007 in a detailed report of 400-plus pages commissioned by the National Center for Complementary and Alternative Medicine (Ospina et al., 2007). It can be accessed electronically through the Agency for Healthcare Research and Quality (http://www.ahrq.gov/clinic/tp/medittp.htm). Within the body of mindfulness-based stress reduction (MBSR) research, we focus on important published research reports that have moved the field forward, as well as the most recent research, rather than striving to be completely comprehensive. Other thorough reviews are available that address outcomes in both psychological and medical populations (Baer, 2003; Bishop, 2002; Grossman, Niemann, Schmidt, & Walach, 2004).

Clinical Populations

We begin our review by examining the effects of mindfulness-based interventions across diverse clinical populations.

MINDFULNESS-BASED STRESS REDUCTION

In historical terms, clinical research on MBSR began with Jon Kabat-Zinn, who conducted basic program evaluation research on participants through his early MBSR classes. This type of research was typically uncontrolled, employing pre–post designs, which is usual for initial research investigating the efficacy of a new intervention. Jon Kabat-Zinn et al. (1992) found that in a group of 22 participants diagnosed with generalized anxiety disorder, improvements were seen over the course of the program in anxiety levels, depressive symptoms, and generalized fears, measured with reliable objective scales. These improvements were still evident 3 years after intervention participation (Miller, Fletcher, & Kabat-Zinn, 1995); compared with a similar cohort from the program, the magnitude of improvements in this smaller sample was typical. The majority of the group reported still practicing mindfulness techniques at a 3-year follow-up. Another early study of 20 long-term psychotherapy clients with anxiety and depression symptoms also found improvements after participation in a MBSR intervention on mood and psychiatric symptoms (Kutz et al., 1985).

These early studies did not use randomized comparison groups to control for effects of the simple passage of time, which is important because of the tendency for symptoms to remit on their own given enough time (known as regression toward the mean). Randomization is also important to ensure baseline comparability between groups, on both qualities that can be measured (e.g., age, gender, baseline psychopathology) and those that are more elusive yet may be important for outcome (e.g., motivation, personality characteristics). Symptoms may also remit over time as a result of nonspecific factors, such as attention from a caring professional, social support from a group, or a feeling that one is doing something beneficial to help oneself, which can lead to expectancies for improvement (i.e., the placebo effect). Studies with wait-list control groups, a common design in mindfulness research, control for the first two issues (remission over time and baseline comparability of groups) but do not control for nonspecific factors of therapy such as attention and expectancy for improvement, as the wait-list group typically undergoes no treatment during the waiting period. In fact, wait lists can foster the opposite of positive expectancy effects while one is waiting for a desired treatment; that is, participants may not expect any improvement over the waiting period (or expect to get worse) until they finally get the treatment. Study designs with active comparison groups that control for attention, time in a group, and social support and foster positive expectations are the most stringent test of the efficacy of a therapy.

Recent work in MBSR has used these more controlled types of designs. One study compared MBSR with the gold-standard treatment of 12 weekly sessions of cognitive–behavioral therapy (CBT) in 53 patients with social anxiety disorder (Koszycki, Benger, Shlik, & Bradwejn, 2007). Both interventions resulted in improved mood, functionality, and quality of life, but CBT proved superior in terms of improving specific measures of the severity of social anxiety. This result is not surprising considering the focus of CBT is specifically on alleviation of symptoms associated with the disorder, whereas the MBSR program targets general overall well-being and quality of life.

Anxiety reduction has continued to be a focus of MBSR work. Weiss et al. (M. Weiss, Nordlie, & Siegel, 2005) added MBSR training to psychotherapy for a group of outpatients with primarily anxiety and depressive symptoms. When compared with a group that received psychotherapy only, both groups improved similarly on psychological distress, but those in MBSR showed greater gains on a measure of goal achievement and were able to terminate therapy sooner. Another randomized controlled trial looked at MBSR as an adjunct to pharmacotherapy in anxiety disorders, compared with an anxiety disorder education program (S. H. Lee et al., 2007). Patients in the MBSR program improved more than their counterparts on several self- and clinician-rated measures of anxiety and on hostility, but there were no group differences on measures of depression.

In 1999 Kristeller and Hallett published the first study of the application of an adapted form of MBSR (later to be called MB-EAT) specifically designed for persons with binge-eating disorder; (for extensive discussion of MB-EAT program development, see Kristeller, Baer, & Quillian-Wolever, 2006). This pilot work showed a significant decrease pre- to postintervention on measures of mood and bingeing frequency. Currently a large randomized controlled trial funded by the National Institutes of Health is under way to examine the effects of MB-EAT for binge-eating disorder; however, results are not yet published.

Another adapted application of MBSR is mindfulness-based therapy for insomnia (MBT-I), an intervention using a mindfulness-based approach combined with cognitive–behavioral therapy for insomnia (CBT-I). The overall goal of the MBT-I program is to help individuals reduce wakefulness at night and to manage emotional reactions that arise in response to chronic insomnia. Components of this program include (a) skill acquisition, with awareness of bodily sensations, thoughts, and feelings as the primary skill; and (b) bringing mindful awareness to work with thoughts and feelings that arise during the course of insomnia. Together, participants are taught to make significant changes in the way they approach both sleeping and waking stress, with the goal of bringing mindfulness into all aspects of their lives (Heidenreich, Tuin, Pflug, Michal, & Michalak, 2006).

In a recent pilot study, 30 participants with insomnia participated in a 6-week multimodal intervention integrating mindfulness meditation and CBT-I. Results demonstrated statistically and clinically significant improvements in several nighttime symptoms of insomnia pre–post intervention (Ong, Shapiro, & Manber, 2008). Further testing of this innovative intervention using a randomized controlled design is currently under way.

Mindfulness approaches have also been applied to addictions research (Bowen et al., 2006; Bowen, Witkiewitz, Dillworth, & Marlatt, 2007; Marlatt & Chawla, 2007). In the best-known and largest study, a sample of 173 incarcerated individuals completed a 10-day course in mindfulness (Vipassana[1]) meditation and provided follow-up data 3 and 6 months postintervention. Although not in the same format as MBSR, the mindfulness meditation practices were similar. Participants' postrelease behavior was compared with that of inmates who had chosen not to participate in the meditation program. Despite the lack of randomization, at baseline no significant differences between the groups were found on substance use or demographic variables, including gender, income, education, or ethnicity. Over the course of follow-up, participants in the meditation program showed significantly greater reductions in alcohol, marijuana, and crack cocaine use and had decreases in alcohol-related problems and psychiatric symptoms. They also had larger increases in internal drinking-related locus of control and optimism. In addition, mediational analyses showed that course participants had decreased use of thought suppression about substance use, which is thought to backfire in preventing relapse. This decrease in avoidance of thoughts about abusing substances was found to partially mediate the use of alcohol after prison release.

Finally, pilot work on a number of applications of MBSR to different psychological and behavioral disorders has appeared in the literature. For

---

[1] Vipassana, or "insight meditation," refers to meditation techniques practiced by many branches of modern Theravada Buddhism. Vipassana is often referred to simply as "mindfulness meditation."

example, a mindfulness intervention with a focus on the soles of the feet was helpful in controlling aggressive behavior in a case study of three patients with developmental disabilities and anger management problems. The meditation exercises helped each to maintain community placements over the course of 4 years of community follow-up (Singh, Lancioni, Winton, Adkins, et al., 2007). Another study targeted anxiety reduction in people with schizophrenia and has thus far reported positive results only on a case basis (Davis, Strasburger, & Brown, 2007). A feasibility pre–post study of mindfulness meditation training with 32 adults and adolescents with attention-deficit/hyperactivity disorder (ADHD) found self-reported improvements in ADHD symptoms of inattentiveness and hyperactivity, as well as decreases in anxiety and depressive symptoms (Zylowska et al., 2007). Participants also demonstrated enhanced performance on tasks measuring attention and cognitive inhibition (the Attention Network Test). The skills that improved—filtering conflicting attentional demands and set-shifting—are thought to play an important role in the development of inhibition and self-regulation, which are the key deficits in individuals with ADHD (Zylowska et al., 2007).

In summary, despite much enthusiasm and some promising findings, relatively few stringently designed clinical trials have been conducted in MBSR for psychological problems. As is seen in chapter 6 (this volume), the research base for efficacy in medical populations is currently much stronger. There continues to be a need to investigate the efficacy of MBSR compared with other gold-standard treatments for patients with anxiety and other mental health issues.

MINDFULNESS-BASED COGNITIVE THERAPY

Mindful Reminder: What is the quality of your heart right now? Can you keep it open even as we examine the scientific literature with an analytical mind?

Most mindfulness-based cognitive therapy (MBCT) studies originate from experienced psychotherapy researchers; because of this, in general the MBCT research tends to be quite strong methodologically. Studies evaluating the efficacy of MBCT first addressed the issue of prevention of relapse in patients who formerly were depressed, and have largely been conducted by Teasdale, Williams, and colleagues in the United Kingdom. The first of these appeared in 2000, with a small study comparing the autobiographical memory of patients with major depressive disorder (MDD) in remission who participated in MBCT with that of those randomly assigned to a treatment-as-usual (TAU) control group (J. M. Williams, Teasdale, Segal, & Soulsby, 2000). MBCT patients were less likely after treatment to retrieve very generic negative memories than were the control participants, a process thought to contribute to depression relapse. This group was followed with a larger sample of 132 patients whose depression had remitted, this time with depression relapse monitored as the primary outcome (Teasdale et al., 2000). In patients who had three or more previous episodes of depression, MBCT halved the rate of relapse over 1 year of follow-up; in the TAU group, only about 35% remained depression-free after this time period, but that number was close to 70% in the MBCT group.

Additional work by this group replicated this finding in a trial of 75 patients who were in remission from depression, at least 12 weeks free of antidepressant medication use, and had two or more previous episodes of depression, and hence were at high risk of relapse (Ma & Teasdale, 2004). Similarly, for those with three or more (but not two) previous episodes of MDD, MBCT in addition to TAU, compared with TAU only, resulted in significantly fewer relapses over a 1-year follow-up period (36% vs. 78% relapse).

MBCT may also have applications in those who are currently depressed, not just those in remission. A nonrandomized clinical audit study by the same group showed that for patients with current MDD who were treatment-resistant, depression scores improved by an effect size of approximately 1.0 over the course of MBCT treatment, bringing them into the nonclinical range of symptomatology (Kenny & Williams, 2007).

Other research groups have also initiated MBCT research for the treatment of depression with small uncontrolled trials. A trial of 19 patients by Kingston, Dooley, Bates, Lawlor, and Malone (2007) used a nonrandomized design to compare MBCT plus TAU with TAU alone in patients with three or more previous episodes of MDD who still had some residual depressive symptoms. For those who attended five or more of the MBCT sessions, greater reduction pre- to posttreatment on depression symptom scores on the Beck Depression Inventory was seen, although rumination was not significantly different between groups. In a group of 13 patients recruited from a primary care practice with recurrent depression or recurrent depression and anxiety, 72% showed improvements in depression symptoms and 63% reported less anxiety (Finucane & Mercer, 2006). Qualitative interviews revealed that participants felt being part of a group was a normalizing and validating experience, and they continued to use the mindfulness techniques 3 months after the course. Most thought some form of follow-up would be useful in order to maintain practice after the group.

A qualitative study of 30 people over the age of 65 with recurring depression who completed the MBCT program revealed interesting themes (A. Smith, Graham, & Senthinathan, 2007). Participants described having more awareness of themselves and their environment, and feeling more vividly alive. They had more acceptance of the self and of things that could not be changed, as well as feeling more in control, both over what is attended to and over one's emotional reactions and responses. They described better coping, letting go of attachments, and more awareness of the breath, as well as changes in identity and lifestyle. They were able to enjoy life more, felt calmer, and felt others could also see the differences. In terms of symptoms, they felt more relaxed, calm, and energetic; had less pain and spent less energy ruminating; and could take things more lightly. When asked about the benefit of the program to their lives, those who described it as providing major benefit increased over a year of follow-up from 48% at the end of the course to 62% a year later. This growing body of work speaks to the potential for MBCT not only to help patients with a history of recurrent depression stay depression-free but also alleviate mood symptoms in patients still struggling with moderate to mild levels of depression.

Recently the UK group has applied MBCT to bipolar disorder as well as unipolar MDD (J. M. Williams et al., 2008). For a small group of people with bipolar disorder in remission, MBCT improved anxiety and depressive symptoms compared with a wait-list control group, and also improved anxiety more than for it did those with unipolar MDD who also participated in MBCT. J. M. Williams et al. also investigated the usefulness of MBCT for patients with suicidal behaviors, theorizing that the techniques of MBCT should be useful in reducing suicidal thoughts (J. M. Williams, Duggan, Crane, & Fennell, 2006). So far this idea has been supported only by case conceptualizations and theory, but clinical trials are investigating these effects (J. M. Williams & Swales, 2004; J. M. Williams et al., 2006).

Although the bulk of the research supporting MBCT to date has been in patients with depressive and other mood disorders, MBCT has also been applied in the treatment of generalized anxiety disorder (GAD). A small group of 11 patients with GAD showed improvements pre- to post-treatment on scores of anxiety and depression symptoms (Evans et al., in press), but this work is still in its infancy, as no controlled trials have yet been performed. Other diverse applications of MBCT are beginning to emerge as abstracts, dissertations, or small case reports but have not been published as full papers. Some of these applications use MBCT for the treatment of insomnia (Heidenreich et al., 2006), behavioral problems and anxiety in children (J. Lee, 2006; Semple, Lee, & Miller, 2006), road rage (Diebold, 2003), and anger and domestic violence in married men (Silva, 2007).

DIALECTICAL BEHAVIOR THERAPY

Dialectical behavior therapy (DBT) was developed as a therapy to be applied to people with borderline personality disorder (BPD; Linehan, 1987, 1993a), so it is not surprising that the bulk of the evidence supporting its efficacy is from that treatment population. A 2007 review of DBT in BPD summarized seven randomized controlled trials (RCTs) for DBT and four RCTs for non-BPD diagnoses (Lynch, Trost, Salsman, & Linehan, 2007). Another 2008 review identified 13 RCTs of DBT (9 of which were for patients with BPD; Ost, 2008). The first trial of a full year of therapy was conducted by Marsha Linehan and colleagues, and different aspects of the study were published in multiple papers (Linehan, 1993a; Linehan, Armstrong, Suarez, Allmon, & Heard, 1991; Linehan et al., 2006). A group of 44 patients with BPD and a history of recent and repeated intentional self-injury or suicide attempts were randomized to either DBT or TAU and followed for 1 year. Patients in DBT showed greater reductions in intentional self-injury rate, total psychiatric inpatient hospital days, self-rated anger, and greater improvements in global and social role functioning. These researchers went on to focus specifically on BPD patients with substance abuse problems, showing improvements in illicit drug use, opiate use, and overall social and global adjustment. They also showed better treatment retention in small groups of women diagnosed with BPD and drug dependence compared with either TAU (Linehan et al., 1999) or another active therapy and medication to help with opiate withdrawal (Linehan et al., 2002). Other groups have also investigated the efficacy of DBT for women with BPD, showing similar improvements in impulsiveness, anger, depression, global adjustment, and decreases in suicide attempts (Koons et al., 2001; Turner, 2000; van den Bosch, Koeter, Stijnen, Verheul, & van den Brink, 2005; van den Bosch, Verheul, Schippers, & van den Brink, 2002; Verheul et al., 2003), primarily compared with TAU. Two studies compared DBT with antidepressant medication only (Simpson et al., 2004; Soler et al., 2005). Overall, in the review by Ost (2008), the average effect size of the DBT interventions was 0.58, which is considered to be a medium-sized effect and likely clinically significant.

DBT has also been modified from its original version and applied to other groups, primarily people with symptoms of depression. A small study of 34 older patients (over the age of 60) found that after 28 weeks remission rates from major depression were higher after DBT than with medication alone (Lynch, Morse, Mendelson, & Robins, 2003), and in patients over 55 with both depressive symptoms and personality disorders, improvements in interpersonal skills were seen after DBT compared with medication alone (Lynch, Chapman, Rosenthal, Kuo, & Linehan, 2006). In another study, 24 patients with ongoing depressive symptoms resistant to antidepressant medication were randomly assigned to DBT or a wait-list group (Harley, Sprich, Safren, Jacobo, & Fava, 2008). Those in DBT showed significantly greater improvements in depressive symptoms on both clinician and self-ratings after 16 sessions. Effect sizes in this study were large for both measures of depression (between 1.3 and 1.5). An open trial of 10 adolescents with bipolar disorder who received a full year of DBT showed significant improvements from pre- to posttreatment in suicidality, self-injurious behavior, emotional dysregulation, and depressive symptoms (Goldstein, Axelson, Birmaher, & Brent, 2007). Finally, in women with binge-eating disorders, DBT skills training decreased the number of binge episodes and days on which bingeing occurred (Safer, Telch, & Agras, 2001) and, in another group, also decreased anger and concerns about body weight and body image (Telch, Agras, & Linehan, 2001).

The issue of the efficacy of DBT and the quality of the studies may still be debated (Ost, 2008), but in general the treatment appears to show benefit, particularly for women with DBT who exhibit suicidal behavior or substance abuse and for those with depressive symptoms and potentially eating disorders. Because DBT is a multimodal treatment (as described in chap. 3, this volume), the question of how important a role mindfulness skills and practice play in the observed benefits is pivotal. In a review of mechanisms of change in DBT, Lynch et al. (2006) described the mindfulness component of DBT as "observing, describing, and participating fully in one's actions and experiences, in a nonjudgmental and one-mindful manner (i.e., attending to one thing at a time), with a focus on effective behavior." They went on to state "In DBT, the ultimate goals of mindfulness skills are to help patients (1) increase their conscious control over attentional processes, (2) achieve a 'wise' integration of emotional and rational thinking, and (3) experience a sense of unity or oneness with themselves, others, and the universe." With these goals in mind, they proposed several mechanisms of change through mindfulness practice: (a) behavioral exposure and learning new responses; (b) emotion regulation; (c) decreasing literal belief in rules (this is similar to the concept of cognitive defusion in acceptance and commitment therapy [ACT]: seeing thoughts as just thoughts and not necessarily true); and (d) attentional control. This proposed model of mechanisms of change has yet to be tested in DBT research, so for the time being the centrality of these mindfulness mechanisms remains theoretical.

ACCEPTANCE AND COMMITMENT THERAPY

A 2008 review of RCTs of ACT described 13 RCTs in which ACT, singly or in combination with another treatment, was compared with a control group or another active treatment (Ost, 2008). Two studies focused on depression, two on psychotic symptoms, and two on stress symptoms. Five additional studies focused on different psychological disorders including BPD (Gratz & Gunderson, 2006), opiate dependence (Hayes et al., 2004), smoking cessation (Gifford et al., 2004), math anxiety (Zettle, 2003), and trichotillomania (Woods, Wetterneck, & Flessner, 2006), and two examined medical populations with epilepsy (Lundgren, Dahl, Melin, & Kies, 2006) and diabetes (Gregg, Callaghan, Hayes, & Glenn-Lawson, 2007), which are discussed in chapter 6 (this volume). The overall effect size on a variety of psychosocial and symptom-related outcome measures when combined in a meta-analysis was 0.68, a medium- to large-sized effect.

It is interesting to note that the effect sizes in the various meta-analyses that have been conducted (for MBSR, DBT, and ACT; Baer, 2003; Grossman et al., 2004; Ost, 2008) are all in a similar range from 0.5 to 0.7. This represents a medium-sized effect overall on a very wide range of outcomes and is typically in the range considered to represent clinically significant change: That is, with an improvement on outcomes of half of a standard deviation, most patients show improvements that would be meaningful in terms of real-life functioning.

Healthy and Community Samples

Astin et al. (1997) examined the effects of an MBSR intervention for healthy college students and found improvements on symptoms of anxiety and depression, spirituality, and sense of control in the intervention group compared with the wait-list control group. Similar results were confirmed in a larger sample of medical and premedical students using a wait-list design by S. L. Shapiro et al. (1998). Another study using a wait-list control group of community volunteers showed similar-sized improvements after MBSR on measures of stress and general psychiatric symptoms (K. A. Williams, Kolar, Reger, & Pearson, 2001). In a community group of largely Hispanic inner-city residents compared with a nonrandomized group with similar demographics, MBSR was feasible and resulted in greater improvement on measures of general health, physical role functioning, vitality, social functioning, and emotional functioning (B. Roth & Robbins, 2004).

A well-designed RCT compared MBSR with relaxation training or no intervention in college students (Jain et al., 2007). Both active interventions were successful in decreasing levels of distress and improving positive moods compared with the control condition, but greater effect sizes were seen in MBSR for its effect on enhancing positive mood states. Mediational analyses showed that the benefits of MBSR were partially mediated by decreases in rumination, which were not seen in the relaxation-only group. In another group of healthy university students, six individual sessions of mindfulness training were compared with two guided-imagery sessions (Kingston, Chadwick, Meron, & Skinner, 2007). Students who had the mindfulness training showed significant increases pre- to posttreatment in their pain tolerance compared with those in the other condition, although there were no differences on mood or blood pressure.

Carson, Carson, Gil, and Baucom (2004) evaluated the preliminary efficacy of mindfulness-based relationship enhancement using a randomized wait-list trial in a group of relatively happy, nondistressed couples. Couples participating in the intervention reported improvements in their relationship's satisfaction, autonomy, relatedness, and closeness, as well as improvements in their acceptance of each other and a lessening in distress about their relationship. As individuals they were also more optimistic and relaxed and reported less distress than did those in the wait-list group. Benefits were maintained at a 3-month follow-up, and the amount of meditation practice was related to the magnitude of the benefits reported.

The research investigating psychological outcomes in healthy community populations is currently quite minimal; future research investigating the enhancement of positive outcomes and delving into the possibilities for personal growth and transcendence would be welcome. This area is further discussed in chapter 9 (this volume).

Summary

The research investigating the efficacy of mindfulness-based interventions for the treatment of psychological symptoms and disorders is continuing to grow at a fast pace; undoubtedly the next decade will see the publication of many more large randomized trials investigating the efficacy of mindfulness-based interventions for a variety of populations. As it stands, there is solid evidence that mindfulness-based treatments can be successfully applied to the treatment of symptoms of anxiety and depression, whether MBSR, MBCT, or ACT is applied. Mixed-modality intensive treatments, such as DBT, that incorporate mindfulness training are also useful for treating more complex personality disorders, which often include substance abuse and self-harming behaviors. Despite the growth in studies investigating the usefulness of mindfulness training in various types of mental health conditions, the field is still quite young. Well-designed future research is necessary to determine the details of what is effective for whom, for treating which symptoms, in what setting, and over what time period. Furthermore, the mechanisms by which these multimodal interventions are helping individuals have only begun to be explored, and this area merits significant future attention. As can be seen, there are numerous fruitful directions for future research, which we discuss in greater detail in chapter 10 (this volume).

Mindfulness-Based Interventions for Physical Health

6

We will try today to find the source of healing, which is
in our minds. . . . It is not farther from us than ourselves.

—*Vaughan and Walsh* (1992, p. 89)

In chapter 5 (this volume), we reviewed seminal and current
studies investigating the effects of mindfulness-based interventions on outcomes in populations with psychological disorders and in healthy individuals. In this chapter, we use a
similar strategy to summarize the important research investigating the effects of mindfulness-based interventions that
have focused on physiological or medical outcomes in a variety of medical populations and in healthy populations. Of
note, many of the investigations of medical populations
focus on outcomes similar to those described in chapter 5,
such as stress levels, depression, mood states, anxiety, and
other psychological reactions to illness. A minority of the
studies looked at the direct impact of mindfulness-based
interventions on disease pathology or progression. Both types
of studies are summarized in this chapter. Populations studied
range widely from people with chronic pain and fibromyalgia
to people with heart disease, organ transplant, and cancer,
to mention just a few. The bulk of the research in this chapter
examined the effects of mindfulness-based stress reduction
(MBSR) interventions, so it is organized by disease type rather
than by type of intervention.

Clinical Populations

PAIN

The earliest reports from J. Kabat-Zinn and colleagues focused on patients with a broad mix of chronic pain syndromes (J. Kabat-Zinn, 1982; J. Kabat-Zinn, Lipworth, & Burney, 1985; J. Kabat-Zinn, Lipworth, Burney, & Sellers, 1987). The 1982 report evaluated 51 patients before and after MBSR participation, documenting improvements in pain levels as well as mood and other psychiatric symptoms on the Symptom Checklist–90–R (SCL-90-R), a commonly used measure of psychological symptomatology. A similar pre–post design was used in a larger sample of 90 patients (including the original 51) and showed similar improvements pre- to postintervention. J. Kabat-Zinn and colleagues also compared these MBSR participants with a treatment-as-usual (TAU) group from a pain clinic, finding that the MBSR patients had improved more than the TAU group did on measures of mood, pain symptoms, and general psychiatric distress. They then conducted a series of follow-up assessments in 1987 with 225 patients with chronic pain who had completed MBSR over a several-year period, showing that although pain ratings themselves had returned to baseline within about 6 months, other ratings of general distress, psychological symptoms, and adherence to the mindfulness practices were maintained. The majority of the participants rated their overall outcomes and the importance of the program to them as high.

Another report of MBSR for chronic pain appeared in 1999, also using a pre–post assessment design (Randolph, Caldera, Tacone, & Greak, 1999). The 78 patients evaluated showed improvements on measures of ratings and beliefs about pain, as well as improved mood on the Profile of Mood States and fewer psychiatric symptoms on the SCL-90-R General Severity Index.

One more recent study evaluated MBSR and massage for the management of chronic musculoskeletal pain in 30 pain patients randomly assigned to MBSR, massage, or a no-intervention control condition (Plews-Ogan, Owens, Goodman, Wolfe, & Schorling, 2005). Immediately postintervention, the massage group had more pain reduction and improved mental health status compared with usual care, while the MBSR group showed greater longer term (1 month) improvements in mental health outcomes compared with usual care and the massage condition. Thus, MBSR was more effective for enhancing mood in the long term, but massage provided more immediate pain relief.

McCracken, Vowles, and Eccleston (2005) applied principles of acceptance and commitment therapy (ACT) to a group of 108 chronic pain patients who participated in a 3- to 4-week residential pain program. Overall, participants reported increases in emotional, social, and physical functioning, and decreases in health care use. This team also found that a measure of mindfulness (the Mindful Attention Awareness Scale, or MAAS) was correlated with multiple measures of pain functioning in 105 patients with chronic pain (McCracken & Vowles, 2007). Beyond measures of pain itself, mindfulness accounted for significant variance in depression, pain-related anxiety, and physical and psychological disability, such that patients with higher levels of mindfulness had fewer symptoms. This group further analyzed the same data and found that changes in acceptance accounted for unique variance in outcomes beyond improvements due to changes in pain intensity and catastrophic thinking (Vowles, McCracken, & Eccleston, 2007). In their most recent study, this team replicated their findings in a new sample of 171 patients with chronic pain, offering 3 to 4 weeks of ACT and mindfulness-based treatment in a group format, 5 days per week for 6 ½ hrs each day. Significant improvements were reported pre- to posttreatment on measures of pain, depression, pain-related anxiety, disability, medical visits, work status, and physical performance. The process variable of acceptance of pain was associated with improvements in all outcome measures (Vowles & McCracken, 2008).

MBSR has been applied to the treatment of chronic lower back pain. Carson et al. (2005) applied a variant of MBSR with an extended focus on loving-kindness practice with 43 patients. Participants were randomly assigned to the loving-kindness program or TAU; treatment participants showed improvements in pain perception and psychological distress, whereas there were no improvements in the control group. More loving-kindness practice on a given day was associated with lower pain ratings on that day and lower anger the following day. In older adults, Morone, Greco, and Weiner (2008) recruited 37 participants with an average age of 75 years who were randomized to MBSR or a wait-list control condition. Compared with the wait list, the MBSR participants showed significantly greater improvements on measures of chronic pain acceptance, engagement in activities, and overall physical functioning. Another application to chronic low back pain used an intervention called "breath therapy," which combines body awareness, breathing, meditation, and movement, similar to the MBSR program (Mehling, Hamel, Acree, Byl, & Hecht, 2005). Thirty-six patients with chronic low back pain were randomized to breath therapy or standard physical therapy, and assessed at baseline, posttreatment, and 6 months later. Both groups of patients reported lower levels of pain, and those in breath therapy had greater improvements in functional, physical, and emotional role performance, while those in physical therapy improved more in vitality.

Although sample sizes in the randomized controlled trials (RCTs) conducted in this area remain small, support for MBSR as a helpful intervention for improving coping with pain symptoms and overall adjustment in patients with chronic pain continues to mount. The growing number of randomized comparison studies with either TAU or other active treatments should result in more robust and convincing evidence of the efficacy of mindfulness-based approaches for the treatment of pain.

Fibromyalgia (FM) is another pain-related condition associated with overall bodily stiffness, soreness, and pain trigger points located throughout the body, in which symptoms seem to be exacerbated by stress. Other symptoms include fatigue and sleep disturbance, and FM is considered notoriously difficult to treat. An early report in 1993 with pre–post assessments of 59 participants in MBSR showed improvements on scales of well-being, pain, fatigue, sleep, coping, and FM symptoms, as well as general symptomatology on the SCL-90-R (Kaplan, Goldenberg, & Galvin-Nadeau, 1993). Patients were classified as "responders" if they showed moderate to marked overall improvement. By this definition, 51% of the sample responded to the treatment. In 1994 another study of patients with FM emerged (Goldenberg et al., 1994). In this case, although the trial was not randomized, 79 participants in the MBSR program were compared with two groups: those on a waiting list for the program and those who had declined participation in the group. MBSR participants showed greater improvements than both groups on measures of pain and sleep as well as FM impact and global severity of psychological symptoms.

Weissbecker et al. (2002) were interested in investigating the effects of MBSR on sense of coherence (which they describe as a disposition to experience life as meaningful and manageable) in women with FM. Ninety-one women with FM were randomly assigned to MBSR or a wait-list control group. Compared with the control participants, program participants reported a significant increase in their sense of coherence after MBSR participation, and stronger sense of coherence was related to lower levels of perceived stress and less depression.

Another large RCT was conducted by Astin et al. in 2003. The researchers randomly assigned 128 patients with FM to a group combining mindfulness meditation plus Qigong movement therapy or an education support group control condition. A large number of outcome measures including pain, disability, depression, and coping were assessed, but although patients did improve over time, neither group proved superior. This test of an active and likely efficacious control condition, combined with a mind–body group somewhat different from traditional MBSR, may account for these results.

A research group in Germany has also been studying the efficacy of MBSR for FM (Grossman, Tiefenthaler-Gilmer, Raysz, & Kesper, 2007). In a quasi-experimental design, 58 women were assigned to either MBSR or an active support condition based on date of entry into the study. The women in the MBSR condition showed greater improvement pre–post on measures of pain, coping, quality of life, anxiety, depression, and somatic complaints, which were maintained 3 years later. Finally, a recent RCT assessed the effects of MBSR on depression symptoms in 91 women with FM (Sephton et al., 2007). Women were randomized to ether MBSR or a wait-list control group, and assessed pre–post and 2 months later with the Beck Depression Inventory. Those in the MBSR group showed significantly more improvement on depression symptoms across all three time points.

Hence, MBSR seems to be an effective intervention for alleviating symptoms common in FM such as pain, depression, and a range of psychological outcomes, although it has yet to be tested against proven efficacious active control conditions that would provide a tougher test of overall efficacy.

CANCER

There is a fairly significant body of work investigating the efficacy of MBSR for patients with various types of cancer. In fact, this literature itself has been reviewed on several occasions since 2005 (Carlson & Speca, 2007; Lamanque & Daneault, 2006; Mackenzie, Carlson, & Speca, 2005; Matchim & Armer, 2007; Ott, Norris, & Bauer-Wu, 2006; J. E. Smith, Richardson, Hoffman, & Pilkington, 2005). Because of the large number of these studies, this section is organized by type of outcomes studied.

Psychological Outcomes

Mindful Reminder: Are you mindfully reading right now, bringing your full presence to what you are reading, or do you notice yourself to be distracted or rushing to get through the chapter?

The bulk of the experimental work has been conducted by Carlson and colleagues in Canada, beginning with an RCT in which 89 patients with a variety of cancer diagnoses were randomized to MBSR or a wait-list control condition (Speca, Carlson, Goodey, & Angen, 2000). Patients in the MBSR program improved significantly more on mood states and symptoms of stress than did those in the control condition, with large improvements of approximately 65% on mood and 35% on stress symptoms. They specifically reported less tension, depression, anger, concentration problems, and more vigor, as well as fewer peripheral manifestations of stress (e.g., tingling in hands and feet), cardio-pulmonary symptoms of arousal (e.g., racing heart, hyperventilation), central neurological symptoms (e.g., dizziness, faintness), gastrointestinal symptoms (e.g., upset stomach, diarrhea), habitual stress behavioral patterns (e.g., smoking, grinding teeth, overeating, insomnia), anxiety and fear, and emotional instability compared with those still waiting for the program. These patients, as well as the control group, were assessed 6 months after treatment completion, and similar benefits were seen in both groups over the follow-up period (Carlson, Ursuliak, Goodey, Angen, & Speca, 2001). In the combined group more home practice was associated with greater decreases in overall mood distur-bance, and the greatest improvements were seen on anxiety, depression, and irritability.

Tacon, Caldera, and Ronaghan (2004) also investigated the effects of MBSR on psychological outcomes in patients with cancer, conducting a small pre–post study with 27 women diagnosed with breast cancer. These women showed improvements over the MBSR course on measures of stress and anxiety, as well as less hopelessness and anxious preoccu-pation about cancer and greater internal locus of control. Bauer-Wu and Rosenbaum (2004) adapted MBSR for individual use in isolated hospitalized bone-marrow transplant (BMT) patients, finding immediate effects on levels of pain and anxiety. Bauer-Wu and Rosenbaum (2004); and Horton-Deutsch, O'Haver Day, Haight, and Babin-Nelson (2007) also investigated MBSR in 24 BMT patients; they provided six to eight biweekly 20- to 40-minute individual sessions consisting of one-on-one training in mindfulness with an experienced instructor, based on an adaptation of the group MBSR curriculum. In 15 patients who completed postassessments, less negative affect was reported after the intervention despite increasing symptoms of nausea and appetite loss, and patients found the program feasible, though they felt that train-ing in mindfulness before hospitalization would have been optimal. In the largest study, Hebert et al. (2001) randomly assigned 157 women with breast cancer to MBSR, a nutrition education program, or usual care groups. The outcome measures included dietary fat, complex carbohydrates, fiber, and body mass. Not surprisingly, only the dietary nutrition education program resulted in changes in body mass and fat consumption postintervention. Results on the psychological measures were not reported.

A unique modification on MBSR that has been applied to cancer patients is mindfulness-based art therapy (MBAT), which combines the principles of MBSR with other creative modalities. In an RCT ($N = 111$), researchers compared the 8-week MBAT intervention with a wait-list control in a heterogeneous cohort of women with mixed cancer types receiving usual oncology care. Compared with the usual care group, the MBAT participants had less depression, anxiety, and hostility as well as fewer somatic symptoms of stress (Monti et al., 2005). Hence, mount-ing evidence from both uncontrolled and a small number of controlled studies supports the usefulness of MBSR for reducing psychological symptoms such as stress, anxiety, irritability, and depression in a broad range of individuals coping with cancer.

A recent qualitative and quantitative study was conducted with 13 women who had completed breast cancer treatment, with a focus on exploring process variables related to changes over the course of MBSR (Dobkin, 2008). The women experienced decreases in perceived stress and medical symptoms as well as improvements on mindfulness as measured with the Mindful Attention Awareness Scale (MAAS). They became more mindful, took better care of themselves, and tended to view life as more meaningful and manageable. Themes identified by the women in focus groups reflecting on their experience with MBSR were (a) acceptance, (b) regaining and maintaining mindful control, (c) taking responsibility for what could change, and (d) cultivating a spirit of openness and connectedness. In identifying the processes at work for these women, alterations in levels of mindfulness and worldview were highlighted.

Another process study using participants from the Calgary, Alberta, program was reported by Brown and Ryan (2003). They found that increases in MAAS scores in 41 patients with early-stage breast or prostate cancer who participated in MBSR predicted decreases in psychological distress and a decline in stress and stress-related symptoms. Carlson and Brown (2005) also compared MAAS scores in 122 patients with cancer with 122 matched community control participants, and showed that similar associations between higher mindfulness and lower mood disturbance and stress symptoms were found in both samples, enforcing the validity of the construct and measure of mindfulness in this patient population.

In sum, the studies in patients with cancer investigating the alleviation of suffering from psychological symptomatology such as anxiety and depression, and the enhancement of outcomes such as greater mindfulness and coping skills, support an important role for mindfulness-based interventions.

Biological Outcomes

Thus far we have focused on the effects of MBSR in improving psychological outcomes in patients with cancer, but a number of studies have also been conducted investigating biological outcomes and health behaviors, such as sleep. Carlson and colleagues (Carlson, Speca, Patel, & Faris, 2007; Carlson, Speca, Patel, & Goodey, 2003, 2004) conducted a pre–post MBSR intervention with 59 survivors of early-stage breast or prostate cancer who were all at least 3-months posttreatment. Outcomes included biological measures of immune, endocrine, and autonomic function in addition to psychological variables. Similar to previous studies, significant improvements were seen in overall quality of life, symptoms of stress, and also in sleep quality. Immune function was investigated by looking at the counts of a number of lymphocyte subsets, including T cells and natural killer (NK) cells. In addition to cell counts, their function was also assessed by measuring how much of four different cytokines were secreted by the T and NK cells in response to an immune challenge. Cytokines were either of the pro-inflammatory or anti-inflammatory variety; pro-inflammatory processes have been associated with several poorer outcomes in both cardiovascular and cancer patients. Although there were no significant changes in the overall number of lymphocytes or cell subsets, T cell production of interleukin (IL)-4 increased and interferon gamma decreased, whereas NK cell production of IL-10 decreased. These results are consistent with a shift in immune profile from one associated with depressive symptoms to a more normal profile. Patterns of change were also assessed over a full year following program participation. Although complicated, the pattern of change in cytokines over 1 year of follow-up supported a continued reduction in pro-inflammatory cytokines (Carlson et al., 2007).

This study also looked at salivary cortisol, because daily salivary cortisol levels have been related to stress and health and are often dysregulated in cancer survivors; such dysregulation has been associated with poorer disease outcomes. Salivary cortisol was assessed three times daily both before and after program participation, and the shape of the pattern of cortisol secretion throughout the day was assessed; abnormal profiles have been associated with shorter survival in metastatic breast cancer patients (Sephton, Sapolsky, Kraemer, & Spiegel, 2000). It is interesting that these hormone profiles also shifted pre- to postintervention, with fewer evening cortisol elevations found post-MBSR and some normalization of abnormal diurnal salivary cortisol profiles occurring (Carlson et al., 2004). Over the year of follow-up, continuing decreases in overall cortisol levels were seen, mostly because of decreases in evening cortisol levels (Carlson et al., 2007). This is significant because higher cortisol levels, particularly in the evening, are considered to be an indicator of dysregulated cortisol secretion patterns and poorer clinical outcomes.

Measures of autonomic system function have also been of interest because cancer survivors are at high risk of cardiovascular disease because of the toxicity of their cancer treatments. Hence, Carlson et al. (2007) looked at the effects of MBSR on resting blood pressure and heart rate. In a group of breast and prostate cancer survivors, overall resting systolic blood pressure decreased significantly from pre- to post-MBSR. This result is desirable as high blood pressure (hypertension) is the most significant risk factor for developing cardiovascular disease.

In other work with biological outcomes, an innovative study by J. Kabat-Zinn's group looked at the effects of combining a dietary intervention with MBSR on prostate-specific antigen (PSA) levels, an indicator of the level of activity of prostate cancer cells in men with biochemically recurrent prostate cancer (Saxe et al., 2001). They found that the combined program resulted in a slowing of the rate of PSA increase in a pilot sample of 10 men, and they are currently conducting a larger RCT to verify this significant impact on such an important marker of biochemical recurrence in prostate cancer.

One other study applied MBSR to low-income ethnic minority women with abnormal Pap smears; Pap tests screen for early indications of mutations that are precursors to cervical cancer (Abercrombie, Zamora, & Korn, 2007). In this study Spanish- and English-speaking women participated in a 6-week MBSR program, but although 51 women initially enrolled, only 13 attended one or more classes, and only 8 women attended four or more classes and provided data. Those who did complete the study showed a significant reduction in anxiety pre- to postintervention and evaluated the program positively. In focus group interviews they stated they were able to decrease stress in everyday life and better able to cope with health problems.

Sleep Outcomes

In terms of sleep outcomes, an RCT by S. L. Shapiro et al. examined the relationship between participation in an MBSR program and sleep quality and efficiency in a breast-cancer population (S. L. Shapiro, Bootzin, Figueredo, Lopez, & Schwartz, 2003). They did not find statistically significant relationships between participation in an MBSR group and sleep quality; however, they did find that those who practiced more informal mindfulness reported feeling more rested. Carlson and Garland (2005) found a very high proportion of cancer patients with disordered sleep (approximately 85%) in a general sample of 63 patients before attending the MBSR program . In these patients, sleep disturbance was closely associated with levels of self-reported stress and mood disturbance, and when stress symptoms declined over the course of the MBSR program, sleep also improved. Improvements were seen on the Pittsburgh Sleep Quality Index subscales of subjective sleep quality, sleep efficiency, and hours of sleep. On average, sleep hours increased by ½ to 1 hour per night. The change in fatigue scores was also statistically significant, and associations were found between fatigue and sleep at both pre- and postintervention, such that more sleep difficulty was associated with greater fatigue. These results were similar to previous ones regarding sleep, where Carlson et al. (2003) found the percentage of patients who reported their sleep as "good" improved from 40% before the program to 80% afterward, reinforcing the more recent finding.

In summary, the MBSR research in cancer is perhaps the most developed of all the different medical populations, but although a number of outcome domains have been assessed, there is nonetheless a need for large-scale trials comparing MBSR with other active interventions in these populations. There is also a need for studies of mediation and dismantling studies to investigate which components of the program are most active, and through which mechanisms they are producing change.

CARDIOVASCULAR DISORDERS

A good deal of meditation research using the transcendental meditation (TM) approach has looked at patients with hypertension (high blood pressure) and coronary heart disease and reported positive findings (e.g., Jayadevappa et al., 2007; Schneider, Alexander, Staggers, Orme-Johnson, et al., 2005; Schneider, Alexander, Staggers, Rainforth, et al., 2005). This research has been reviewed elsewhere (Ospina et al., 2007; Walton, Schneider, & Nidich, 2004), so here we focus only on recent applications of mindfulness-based interventions.

One study applied MBSR to 22 women with cardiovascular disease in a small RCT comparing MBSR with a wait-list control group (Tacon, McComb, Caldera, & Randolph, 2003). Compared with controls, women in the MBSR group showed greater reductions in anxiety, better emotional regulation, and less use of reactive coping styles after the intervention. This group then went on to randomize 18 women with heart disease to either an MBSR or no-treatment control group, and measured resting levels of stress hormones, physical functioning, and cardiovascular responses to an exercise test before and after participation (McComb, Tacon, Randolph, & Caldera, 2004). Although there were no statistically significantly effects of the program on measures of stress hormones or physical functioning, there was a trend toward better outcomes in the MBSR group, and the women in the MBSR group did show slower breathing frequency. The authors felt these trends may prove significant in a larger study and that MBSR showed promise for improving physiological markers in women with cardiovascular disease.

A well-designed study of 52 patients with hypertension randomized participants to contemplative meditation practice or a no-treatment control and found decreases in heart rate and both systolic and diastolic blood pressure as measured during 24-hour ambulatory monitoring and in reaction to mental stress testing (Manikonda et al., 2008). In another study, 19 very ill elderly patients with congestive heart failure were randomized to a meditation group that participated in weekly sessions and listened to a meditation tape at home for 30 minutes, twice daily, for 12 weeks, or a control group that attended only weekly meetings (Curiati et al., 2005). The meditation group showed significantly greater improvements on measures of quality of life, lower levels of norepinephrine (an excitatory steroid), and better cardiopulmonary performance on exercise testing.

Although the research on strictly mindfulness-based approaches to treating cardiovascular disease is quite preliminary, it does show promise for improving both psychological and biological outcomes that may be important for disease progression.

EPILEPSY

There remains an active debate in the literature about possible negative effects of meditation in people with epilepsy (Jaseja, 2006a, 2007; St. Louis & Lansky, 2006). On the positive side, studies primarily of TM in epilepsy have documented beneficial changes in brain activity on electroencephalogram monitoring, as well as improvements in epilepsy symptoms (Fehr, 2006; Orme-Johnson, 2006; Swinehart, 2008). The alternative hypothesis is that meditation practice may cause increased neural synchrony in the brain, which may result in cognitive kindling and hence a lower threshold for epileptic seizures (Lansky & St. Louis, 2006). This viewpoint is also supported with case studies of adverse effects (Jaseja, 2006b).

Despite this interest in meditation and epilepsy and some controversy around the topic, no studies of MBSR have been published. However, one group recently applied ACT to the treatment of patients with epilepsy, beginning with an RCT comparing ACT with a usual care treatment in 27 South Africans (Lundgren, Dahl, Melin, & Kies, 2006). After 9 hours of individual and group therapy, seizure frequency was significantly reduced in the ACT group. One month after the intervention, 57% were seizure free in the ACT group compared with none in the control group. Twelve months later, 86% were seizure free in the ACT condition and only 8% in the control group, and quality of life, personal well-being, and life satisfaction measures improved more in the ACT group. When they looked at potential mediators of this large improvement, changes in seizures, quality of life, and well-being were found to be partially mediated by epilepsy-related acceptance or defusion, values attainment, and persistence in the face of barriers (Lundgren, Dahl, & Hayes, 2008). Hence, patients had learned to be more psychologically flexible, accepting of things as they were with their illness, and not so tied into believing passing thoughts. They were also more focused on persistently engaging in activities that were highly valued and living in accordance with their own values.

This group then compared the ACT intervention with a yoga intervention in patients with epilepsy (Lundgren et al., 2008; Lundgren, Dahl, Yardi, & Melin, in press). A small group of 18 patients with confirmed drug-refractory epilepsy were randomly assigned to 12 sessions of ACT or yoga and followed up for 1 year. Frequency and duration of seizures were found to be reduced in both groups, and ACT did so significantly more than did yoga. In addition, both groups improved significantly on quality of life. Finally, another group, this one in India, tested a combined yoga and meditation program in 20 patients who practiced twice daily for 3 months (Rajesh, Jayachandran, Mohandas, & Radhakrishnan, 2006). For the 16 patients who continued practice beyond 3 months, 14 responded with 50% or greater reductions in seizure frequency, and 6 of these were seizure-free for 3 months.

The research in mindfulness treatments for epilepsy is very preliminary, but research does show potential for ACT in particular to be helpful with this patient population.

HIV/AIDS

Two studies have been conducted with people infected with the HIV virus, and one with AIDS patients in palliative care. A pilot study of MBSR in HIV-infected youth sought to determine the feasibility of this type of intervention in 13- to 21-year-olds (Sibinga et al., 2008). Of 11 African American youth who initially signed up, 7 attended at least one class and 5 finished the program. Interviews with those who completed the program identified five themes: (a) improved attitudes (less negativity); (b) decreased reactivity and impulsivity; (c) improved behavior, less lashing out; (d) improved self-care; and (e) the value of being in a group. On average, they rated the importance of the group to them at 9.6 on a scale from 1 to 10, indicating that although attrition was high, those youth infected with HIV who were able to complete the program did benefit.

Another study investigated the impact of MBSR on immune and endocrine measures in patients with HIV (Robinson, Mathews, & Witek-Janusek, 2003). Using a nonrandomized design, researchers recruited 46 HIV-infected patients for either the MBSR or comparison groups (assigned by patient preference), but only 24 completed the study. Compared with the controls, participants in the MBSR group showed an increase in NK cell activity and number, an important measure in HIV infection. NK cells represent the main type of innate immunity in the body and help to fight off opportunistic viral infections. There were, however, no significantly different changes in mood or stress measures, although they trended toward improvement in the MBSR group and worsening in the control condition. In the final study, 58 patients with late-stage AIDS in a palliative care setting were randomized to 1 month of loving-kindness (metta) meditation, massage, both, or neither (A. L. Williams et al., 2005). The meditation was self-administered through an audiotape. The combined meditation and massage group showed the most benefit in terms of greater overall quality of life and spirituality compared with either treatment alone.

OTHER DIAGNOSES

A handful of studies have investigated the potential efficacy of mindfulness-based interventions in a wide variety of other medical conditions. This section summarizes this eclectic group of studies to give a further idea of some of the avenues of investigation that are being pursued.

A well-designed study by J. Kabat-Zinn et al. (1998) investigated whether listening to guided mindfulness meditation recordings during phototherapy treatment for psoriasis lesions could speed the healing process. Psoriasis is a disease characterized by rashlike lesions that can occur anywhere on the body, and it is typically treated with photo-therapy in what resemble upright tanning beds; symptoms are also known to worsen during periods of high stress. Thirty-seven patients were randomly assigned to the mindfulness or control conditions, and psoriasis status was assessed objectively throughout treatment by direct inspection by both unblinded clinic nurses and blinded physician inspection of patients, both in person and through evaluation of photographs of the skin lesions. Several time points were determined: the first response to treatment, the turning point where treatment was judged as working, the halfway point, and the final clearing point. The patients in the mindfulness condition reached the halfway point and the clearing point significantly more rapidly than did those in the control condition, demonstrating that simple mindfulness practice could enhance the treatment response.

Two studies to date have investigated the effect of MBSR on rheumatoid arthritis, a painful autoimmune condition caused by swelling of the joints (Pradhan et al., 2007; Zautra et al., 2008). In the first, 63 participants were randomized to MBSR or a wait-list control condition. Self-report questionnaires evaluated depressive symptoms, psychological distress, well-being, and mindfulness, and rheumatoid arthritis disease activity was evaluated by a physician masked to treatment status. After 2 months, there were no differences between the groups, but at 6 months, there were significant improvements in psychological distress, well-being, depressive symptoms, and levels of mindfulness in the MBSR group. The most recent study used multimodal outcome measures and compared 144 participants randomly assigned to one of three conditions: cognitive–behavioral therapy (CBT) for pain; mindfulness meditation and emotion regulation therapy; or education only, which served as an attention placebo control (Zautra et al., 2008). The greatest improvements in pain control and reductions in inflammatory cytokines were observed in participants in the CBT pain group, however, both the CBT and mindfulness groups improved more in coping efficacy than did the education control group. It is most striking that patients with a positive history of depression benefited more from mindfulness on outcomes of both negative and positive affect and physicians' ratings of joint tenderness, suggesting that MBSR might be preferable to CBT for treating individuals who struggle with depression.

A pilot study in 11 patients with Type II diabetes investigated the impact of MBSR on indices of gylcemic control, given that stress has been related to poorer control of blood sugar levels in this group (Rosenzweig et al., 2007). At 1 month following the program, glycosylated hemoglobin A1C (HbA1c), the measure of blood sugar levels, was significantly reduced, as were measures of blood pressure, depression, anxiety, and overall psychological distress. Another study compared ACT plus a 1-day educational workshop with education only for managing Type II diabetes in 81 patients (Gregg, Callaghan, Hayes, & Glenn-Lawson, 2007). Those who participated in ACT therapy and learned how to apply acceptance and mindfulness skills to difficult diabetes-related thoughts and feelings were more likely to use adaptive coping and report better self-care behaviors. They were also more likely to have HbA1c values in the target range. Through mediational analyses, changes in acceptance coping were shown to be partially responsible for the impact of the ACT treatment on changes in HbA1c. These studies are promising in that they show benefit not only in terms of psychological outcomes but also on an important measure of disease progression in diabetes.

An innovative new application of MBSR has been reported for people with multiple sclerosis (MS) and their partners (Hankin, 2008). In a nonrandomized design, 25 couples received MBSR and another 10 acted as a comparison group. The treatment group showed significant decreases in anxiety as well as an increase in tolerance of uncertainty, while the control group showed no changes in psychological outcomes. Control participants reported a significant increase in MS-related symptoms whereas the MS symptoms for the treatment group remained stable. This result suggests that MBSR training might not only help couples cope with the difficulties of a remitting and recurring disease like MS, but also help to control symptom severity.

Rehabilitation for tinnitus, a constant ringing in the ears, was also attempted through the use of four 1-hour sessions modeled on MBCT (Sadlier, Stephens, & Kennedy, 2008). Twenty-five tinnitus sufferers were consecutively allocated to either MBCT or a wait-list control. Decreases were seen posttherapy as well as over a 4- to 6-month follow-up on a measure of tinnitus severity in the MBSR group.

A number of small pilot studies have also been conducted with a variety of different diseases and conditions. For example, Carmody, Crawford, and Churchill (2006) investigated the potential for MBSR training to help reduce the discomfort associated with menopause-related hot flashes. A pilot study of 15 women experiencing several moderate to severe daily hot flashes showed 40% reductions in the severity of hot flashes as well as improved overall quality of life. A case study of an adolescent with Prader-Willi syndrome, which is characterized by overeating and delay in the satiety response, showed decreases in weight that were sustained over 3 years through a combination treatment of exercise, healthy eating, and mindfulness training (Singh et al., 2008). The improvements seen with the addition of the mindfulness training were reported to be greater than with exercise and nutrition alone. There is also interest in the application of MBSR to patients suffering from chronic hepatitis C, but as yet no research data have been published (Koerbel & Zucker, 2007).

MIXED MEDICAL DIAGNOSES

A number of studies have conducted mindfulness-based interventions on mixed groups of medical patients. A pre–post study by Reibel, Greeson, Brainard, and Rosenzweig (2001) investigated MBSR in a group of 121 patients with a variety of different medical diagnoses and saw improvements on the usual measures of health-related quality of life and physical and psychological symptomatology. There was a 28% reduction in physical symptoms, a 44% reduction on the anxiety subscale of the SCL-90-R, and a 34% reduction on the depression subscale, and improvements were maintained over the course of a year of follow-up. Another smaller German study of 21 patients with a variety of medical diagnoses found improvements after MBSR on measures of emotional, physical, and general well-being, and qualitative interviews confirmed high satisfaction and lasting symptom reduction (Majumdar, Grossman, Dietz-Waschkowski, Kersig, & Walach, 2002).

A series of studies have been conducted with patients who were recipients of organ transplants (Gross et al., 2004; Kreitzer, Gross, Ye, Russas, & Treesak, 2005). Pilot work with 19 kidney, lung, or pancreas transplant recipients showed improvement from baseline scores after MBSR on measures of depression and sleep, and the beneficial effects on sleep were maintained at a 3-month follow-up assessment, when improvements in anxiety also became significant. Improvements on sleep and anxiety were related to the amount of home mediation practice (Gross et al., 2004). Further follow-up assessment at 6 months post-MBSR found continued improvements in sleep quality and duration as well as for anxiety and depression (Kreitzer et al., 2005). A larger ongoing RCT is under way in this same population but the results have not yet been reported.

Physiological Outcomes in Healthy Participants

The final section of this chapter summarizes studies that have investigated the effects of mindfulness practices on physiological outcomes that may have some potential bearing on disease outcomes but were conducted largely on healthy individuals.

Massion et al. investigated differences between women who had taken MBSR classes and continued to meditate regularly and non-meditators on a measure of melatonin in the urine (Massion, Teas, Hebert, Wertheimer, & Kabat-Zinn, 1995). Melatonin is the primary hormone secreted by the pineal gland and controls cycles of sleeping and waking;

it has also been implicated in diseases such as cancer (Vijayalaxmi, Thomas, Reiter, & Herman, 2002) and overall immune functioning (Guerrero & Reiter, 2002). They found higher amounts of melatonin metabolites in the urine of the meditators compared with the non-meditators, speculating this might have health implications.

Another group investigated the impact of brief training in the mindfulness body scan on important cardiovascular measures in the lab (Ditto, Eclache, & Goldman, 2006). In the first of two studies, 32 healthy university students were randomly assigned to a body scan meditation, progressive muscle relaxation, or a wait-list control condition, and practiced the assigned technique in two lab sessions 4 weeks apart. Those who practiced the body scan showed increases in parasympathetic cardiovascular activity compared with the other conditions, indicating a greater relaxation response. In the second study, 30 different students participated in two lab sessions in which they either practiced the body scan or listened to an audiobook. In this study, women showed a larger decrease in diastolic blood pressure during meditation, whereas the men had increased cardiac output during meditation. The authors concluded that there are both similarities and differences between the meditation technique and other relaxing activities.

Heart rate variability is another prognostic measure for cardiovascular health, which was measured in a group of 35 experienced meditation practitioners from Thailand (Phongsuphap, Pongsupap, Chandanamattha, & Lursinsap, in press). The expert meditators were compared with 70 matched control participants. Cardiovascular parameters were recorded during meditation practice for the experts or during quiet rest for the control participants over a period of 4 weeks. Analysis of the frequencies of heart rate variability showed synchrony of oscillations in certain specific frequencies during meditation. The authors concluded from this analysis that meditation may have health benefits such as increasing parasympathetic nervous system tone (associated with the relaxation response) and improving efficiency of gas exchange in the lungs.

Finally, Davidson et al. (2003) provided MBSR training to healthy workers from a biotechnology firm in a wait-list controlled trial, and measured the impact of the intervention on the production of antibody titres in response to a standard influenza vaccine, a common measure of the robustness of the immune response. The flu shot was given at the end of the 8-week MBSR program, and antibody production was measured 4 months later. Participants in the MBSR group showed significantly higher increases in antibody titres to the vaccination, indicating a stronger immune response.

This eclectic body of work on a handful of outcomes that may be important in terms of disease progression is just the beginning of exploration into the potential benefits of mindfulness-based interventions on physiological, endocrine, and immune outcomes.

Mindful Reminder: Pause and ask yourself what you just read. Can you remember it in detail, or was your mind wandering?

Summary

This chapter provided a whirlwind tour of the great variety of research studies conducted on a wide range of different medical conditions. Quality and depth of the research base across different conditions vary significantly, with the most evidence compiled in cancer and pain conditions, but continued work is being conducted across many domains. This body of research is still very young and over the next 20 years, the number, quality, and breadth of medical applications of mindfulness-based interventions will only increase as researchers become more knowledgeable and sophisticated in terms of design for these types of studies.

How Is Mindfulness Helpful?
Mechanisms of Action

7

> This does not belong to me; this am I not; this is not
> my Self.

—*Buddha (Jack Kornfield, personal communication, March 15, 2007)*

The previous two chapters responded to the question, "Is mindfulness helpful?" The conclusion was "Yes." This line of research is clearly fundamental to validating mindfulness as an efficacious psychological intervention, and controlled clinical trials across diverse populations should continue. However, an equally important direction for future research is to address the question, "How is mindfulness helpful?"

Investigating questions concerning the mechanisms of action underlying the transformational effects of mindfulness requires a testable theory of mindfulness. The objective of this chapter is to present a theory (developed by S. L. Shapiro, Carlson, Astin, & Freedman, 2006) aimed at understanding the mysterious and complex process of mindfulness. It is an attempt to search for common ground on which to build a more precise understanding of the primary mechanisms of action involved in mindfulness practice.

This chapter incorporates material from "Mechanisms of Mindfulness," by S. L. Shapiro, L. Carlson, J. Astin, and B. Freedman, 2006, *Journal of Clinical Psychology, 62*, pp. 373–386. Copyright 2006 by John Wiley & Sons, Inc. Reprinted with permission.

Proposing a *Theory*

How is mindfulness helpful? In developing a theory it is essential to have a clear definition of the construct. In chapter 1 (this volume), we developed a definition of mindfulness involving three elements: intention, attention, and attitude (IAA). We continue to use this definition here as we explore the mechanisms of mindfulness.

Our theory posits that mindfulness practice leads to a shift in perspective, termed *reperceiving:* the capacity to dispassionately observe or witness the contents of one's consciousness. We suggest that reperceiving is a significant factor contributing to the transformational effects of mindfulness. We believe reperceiving is a metamechanism of action, which overarches additional direct mechanisms that lead to change and positive outcome. We highlight four of these additional mechanisms: (a) self-regulation; (b) values clarification; (c) cognitive, emotional, and behavioral flexibility; and (d) exposure. These variables can be seen as potential mechanisms for other outcomes such as psychological symptom reduction, or as outcomes in and of themselves. Furthermore, this pathway is by no means a linear one; each variable supports and affects the others.

REPERCEIVING AS METAMECHANISM

Mindful Reminder: Notice the quality of your awareness right now without judging it; simply notice.

Through the process of mindfulness, a person is able to disidentify from the contents of consciousness (i.e., one's thoughts, emotions, value judgments) and view his or her moment-by-moment experience with greater clarity and objectivity. We term this process *reperceiving* because it involves a fundamental shift in perspective. Rather than being immersed in the drama of one's personal narrative or life story, a person is able to stand back and simply witness it. As Goleman (1980) suggested, "The first realization in 'meditation' is that the phenomena contemplated are distinct from the mind contemplating them" (p. 146).

Reperceiving is akin to the Western psychological concepts of decentering (Safran & Segal, 1990), deautomatization (Deikman, 1982; Safran & Segal, 1990), and detachment (Bohart, 1983). For example, Safran and Segal (1990) defined *decentering* as the ability to "step outside of one's immediate experience, thereby changing the very nature of that experience" (p. 117). Deikman (1982) described *deautomatization* as "an undoing of the automatic processes that control perception and cognition" (p. 137). And according to Bohart (1983), *detachment* "encompasses the interrelated processes of gaining 'distance,' 'adopting a phenomenological attitude,' and the expansion of 'attentional space'" (see Martin, 1997, for review). All of these concepts share at their core a fundamental shift in perspective. This shift, we believe, is facilitated through mindfulness—the process of intentionally attending moment by moment with openness and nonjudgmentalness (IAA, which is detailed in chap. 1, this volume). It allows a person to realize that one's "*awareness* of sensations, thoughts, and feelings is different from the sensations, the thoughts and the feelings themselves" (J. Kabat-Zinn, 1990, p. 297, italics in original). This awareness, this shift from subject to object, allows a deep equanimity and clarity arises (see clinical example in Exhibit 7.1).

REPERCEIVING AS DEVELOPMENTAL PROCESS

Reperceiving can be described as a rotation in consciousness in which what was previously "subject" becomes "object." This shift in perspective (making what was subject, object) has been heralded by developmental psychologists as key to development and growth across the life span (Kegan, 1982). Therefore, if reperceiving is in fact a metamechanism

---

EXHIBIT 7.1

Case Study

Cathy is a 48-year-old woman in remission from stage II breast cancer. She has completed chemotherapy and radiation treatment. She enrolled in the mindfulness-based stress reduction (MBSR) program because she felt like she had to do "something" now that her medical treatment was complete. She said she cried on her last day of chemotherapy as she walked out of the hospital; she felt like the umbilical cord had been cut, now she was on her own . . . and what if the cancer came back.

Below is dialogue that occurred during the fourth session of the 8-week MBSR program.

Cathy: I am just so afraid the cancer will return. I think about it all the time. And a fear grips me, deep inside my stomach.

Therapist: You're noticing a lot of fear. Fear of the cancer returning.

Cathy: Yes, the fear feels like it is consuming me.

Therapist: It feels like it is consuming you, like it is taking over all of you who are?

Cathy: Yes, exactly.

Therapist: And when you sit with that fear—in fact, let's take a moment to sit with it right now—how do you know you are afraid?

Cathy: I feel tightness, gripping in my stomach. My breath becomes tense and short.

Therapist: And what part of you *knows* that you are afraid?

Cathy: I don't know . . .

Therapist: Is the awareness that knows you are afraid, *afraid?*

Cathy: Hmmm. . . . No, I guess the part of me that sees the fear is simply noticing and not fearful itself.

Therapist: Yes, the fear is here, but there is also something larger, the awareness that holds the fear with kindness and acceptance, the awareness that *knows* the fear without being caught up in it. Can you feel into that place?

Cathy: Yes. It feels like I can rest here. The fear is still present, but I realize that it is not all of me, and it doesn't have to consume me.

---

underlying mindfulness, then the practice of mindfulness is simply a continuation of the naturally occurring human developmental process whereby one gains an increasing capacity for objectivity about one's own internal experience.

This natural developmental process is illustrated in the classic example of a mother's birthday, in which her 8-year-old son gives her flowers and her 3-year-old gives her his favorite toy. Although the action was developmentally appropriate, the 3-year-old is basically caught in the limits of his own self-centered (i.e., narcissistic) perspective. For him, the world is still largely subjective, that is, an extension of his self. And as a result, he cannot clearly differentiate his own desires from those of another. However, as he develops, a shift in perspective occurs such that there is an ever-increasing capacity to take the perspective of another (e.g., "my mother's needs are different from mine"), precisely because what was previously subject (identification with the mother) has now become an object that he subsequently realizes he is now separate from (no longer fused with). This is the dawning of empathy, the awareness of his mother as a separate person with her own needs and desires. The example demonstrates that as individuals are able to shift their perspective away from the narrow and limiting confines of their own personal points of reference, development occurs.

MINDFULNESS PRACTICE CONTINUES DEVELOPMENTAL PROCESS

This shift in perspective, which we have termed *reperceiving*, naturally occurs in the developmental process. We suggest, however, that mindfulness practice continues and accelerates this shift. Reperceiving, in which there is increasing capacity for objectivity in relationship to one's internal and external experience, is in many ways the hallmark of mindfulness practice. Through the process of intentionally focusing nonjudgmental attention on the contents of consciousness, the mindfulness practitioner begins to strengthen what Deikman referred to as "the observing self" (Deikman, 1982). To the extent that a person is able to observe the contents of consciousness, he or she is no longer completely embedded in or fused with such content. For example, if a person is able to see *it*, than that person is no longer merely *it*; that is, that person must be *more* than *it*. Whether the *it* is pain, depression, or fear, reperceiving allows one to disidentify from thoughts, emotions, and body sensations as they arise, and simply be with them instead of being defined (i.e., controlled, conditioned, determined) by them. Through reperceiving one realizes that "this pain is not me," "this depression is not me," "these thoughts are not me," as a result of being able to observe them from a metaperspective.

The shift in perspective we are describing is analogous to our earlier example of the young toddler who over time is eventually able to see himself as separate from the objective world in which he had previously been embedded. However, in this case, the disidentification is from the content of one's mind (e.g., thoughts, feelings, self-concepts, memories) rather than from one's physical environment. Through reperceiving, the stories (e.g., about who we are, what we like or dislike, our opinions about others) that were previously identified with so strongly become simply "stories." In this way, there is a profound shift in one's relationship to thoughts and emotions, the result being greater clarity, perspective, objectivity, and ultimately equanimity.

This process is similar to Hayes et al.'s (Hayes, Strosahl, & Wilson, 1999) concept of cognitive defusion, in which the emphasis is on changing one's relationship to thought rather than attempting to alter the content of thought itself. As Hayes et al. noted, as one strengthens the capacity for mindful observing of mental activity, there is often a corresponding shift in the self-sense. The "self" starts to be seen through or deconstructed—that is, it is realized to be a psychological construction, an ever-changing system of concepts, images, sensations, and beliefs. These aggregates, or constructs that were once thought to compose the stable self, are eventually seen to be impermanent and fleeting. According to the Buddha

> All formations are transient; all formations are subject to suffering; all things are without a self. Therefore, whatever there be of form, of feeling, perception, mental formations, or consciousness, whether past, present or future, one's own or external, gross or subtle, lofty or low, far or near, one should understand according to reality and true wisdom: 'This does not belong to me; this am I not; this is not my Self.' (Goddard, 1994, p. 27)

Through reperceiving, not only does a person learn to stand back from and observe his or her inner commentary about life and the experiences encountered, a person also begins to stand back from his or her "story" about who and what *he* or *she* ultimately is. Identity begins to shift from the contents of awareness to awareness itself. Hayes et al. (1999) described this as the shift from "self as content" (that which can be witnessed or observed as an object in consciousness) to "self as context" (that which is observing or witnessing, i.e., consciousness itself). It is this shift that may, in part, be responsible for the transformations facilitated through mindfulness practice (S. L. Shapiro et al., 2006).

It is important to note, however, that the developmental process does not end at this subject–object shift but continues until the separate sense of self is seen through and all conceptualization of subject versus object ends. Then, experience becomes simply knowing or perceiving: There is no one perceiving and nothing being perceived, but simply awareness happening (J. Kabat-Zinn, personal communication, 2007).

Mindful Reminder: Can you observe when your mind wanders and when it is concentrated, when your interest peaks and wanes, when you feel urgent and when you are relaxed?

This is the essence of the nondual nature of mindfulness, exemplified by the beautiful Hindu saying:

When I forget who I am I serve you.
Through serving I remember who I am
And know I am you. (Hindu saying)

REPERCEIVING VERSUS DETACHMENT

Reperceiving can easily be confused with an attempt to detach from one's experience, distancing to the point of apathy or numbness. However, this is in sharp contrast with the actual experience of reperceiving, which engenders a deep knowing and intimacy with whatever arises moment by moment. Reperceiving does indeed facilitate greater distance in terms of clarity. And yet, this does not translate as disconnection or dissociation. Instead, reperceiving simply allows one to deeply experience each event of the mind and body without identifying with or clinging to it, allowing for "a deep, penetrative non-conceptual seeing into the nature of mind and world" (J. Kabat-Zinn, 2003, p. 146). Through this process one is actually able to connect more intimately with one's moment-to-moment experience, allowing it to rise and fall naturally with a sense of nonattachment. A person experiences what *is* instead of a commentary or story about what is. Therefore, reperceiving does not create apathy or indifference but instead allows one to experience greater richness, texture, and depth, moment by moment—what Peters referred to as "intimate detachment" (C. Peters, personal communication, April 5, 2004).

Additional Mechanisms

Reperceiving, and the "shift in perspective" it fosters, may lead to additional mechanisms that in turn contribute to the positive outcomes produced by mindfulness practice. We highlight four mechanisms in this section: (a) self-regulation and self-management; (b) emotional, cognitive, and behavioral flexibility; (c) values clarification; and (d) exposure.

SELF-REGULATION AND SELF-MANAGEMENT

Self-regulation is the process whereby systems maintain stability of functioning and adaptability to change. Self-regulation is based on feedback loops. According to S. L. Shapiro and Schwartz (2000a, 2000b) both intention and attention function to enhance these feedback loops and create health:

intention→attention→connection→regulation→order→health

Intentionally cultivating nonjudgmental *attention* leads to connection, which leads to self-regulation and ultimately to greater order and health. Through the process of reperceiving, we are able to attend to the information contained in each moment. We gain access to more data, even those data that may have previously been too uncomfortable to examine. As Hayes asserted, "experiential avoidance becomes less automatic and less necessary" (Hayes, 2002, p. 104). Through this process, dysregulation and subsequent disease can be avoided. In addition, reperceiving interrupts automatic maladaptive habits. People become less controlled by particular emotions and thoughts that arise, and in turn are less likely to automatically follow them with habitual reactive patterns. For example, if anxiety arises, and a person strongly identifies with it, there will be a greater tendency to react to the anxiety unskillfully and subsequently regulate it by some behavior such as drinking, smoking, or overeating. Reperceiving allows a person to step back from the anxiety, to see it clearly as simply an emotional state that is arising and will in time pass away. Thus, this knowledge of the impermanence of all mental phenomena allows a higher level of tolerance for unpleasant internal states.

By developing the capacity to stand back and witness emotional states such as anxiety, people increase their "degrees of freedom" in response to such states, effectively freeing themselves from automatic behavioral patterns. Through reperceiving, they are no longer controlled by states such as anxiety or fear but are instead able to use these states as information. They are able to attend to the emotion and choose to self-regulate in ways that foster greater health and well-being. Through consciously (intention) bringing awareness (attention) and acceptance (attitude) to experience in the present moment, they will be better able to use a wider, more adaptive range of coping skills. Preliminary support for this hypothesis can be found in a study by Brown and Ryan (2003) in which people who scored higher on a valid and reliable measure of mindfulness reported significantly greater self-regulated emotion and behavior.

VALUES CLARIFICATION

Reperceiving may also help people recognize what is meaningful for them and what they truly value. Often values have been conditioned by family, culture, and society, so that people may not realize whose values actually drive their choices in life. They become the value, instead of the one who observes the value. People are frequently pushed and pulled by what they believe (based on cultural or familial conditioning) is most important, but they fail to reflect on whether it is truly important in the context of their own lives. However, when they are able to separate from (observe) their values and reflect on them with greater objectivity, they have the opportunity to rediscover and choose values that may be truer for them. In other words, they become able to *reflectively* choose what has been previously *reflexively* adopted or conditioned. The literature suggests that automatic processing often limits considerations of options that would be more congruent with needs and values (Brown & Ryan, 2003; Ryan, Kuhl, & Deci, 1997). However, an open, intentional awareness can help people choose behaviors that are congruent with their needs, interests, and values (Brown & Ryan, 2003; Ryan & Deci, 2000). A study found that when subjects are "acting mindfully," as assessed by the Mindful Attention Awareness Scale state measure, individuals act in ways that are more congruent with their actual values and interests (Brown & Ryan, 2003).

COGNITIVE, EMOTIONAL, AND BEHAVIORAL FLEXIBILITY

Reperceiving may also facilitate more adaptive, flexible responding to the environment in contrast to the more rigid, reflexive patterns of reactivity that result from being overly identified with one's current experience. If people are able to see a situation and their own internal reactions to it with greater clarity, they will be able to respond with greater freedom of choice (i.e., in less conditioned, automatic ways). As Borkovec (2002) pointed out, research from cognitive and social psychology demonstrates that "existing expectations or beliefs can distort the processing of newly available information" (p. 78). Learning to see clearly (and learning in general) depends on the ability to disidentify from prior patterns and beliefs.

Reperceiving facilitates this capacity to observe one's mental commentary about the experiences encountered in life. It enables a person to see the present situation as it is in this moment and to respond accordingly, instead of with reactionary thoughts, emotions, and behaviors triggered by prior habit, conditioning, and experience. Reperceiving affords a different place from which to view the present moment. For example, when people are caught on the surface of the ocean, and the waves are thrashing them about, it is difficult to see clearly. However, when they drop down beneath the surface of the waves (which is analogous to observing and disidentifying from the movement of one's thoughts and emotional reactions), they enter a calmer, clearer space (Deikman's [1982] "observing self," or what contemplative traditions refer to as "the Witness"). From this new vantage point, people can look up to the surface and see whatever is present more clearly—and therefore respond with greater consciousness and flexibility. Reperceiving enables the development of this capacity to observe one's ever-changing inner experience and thereby see more clearly one's mental–emotional content, which in turn fosters greater cognitive–behavioral flexibility and less automaticity or reactivity.

EXPOSURE

The literature is replete with evidence of the efficacy of exposure in treating a variety of disorders (Barlow & Craske, 2000). Reperceiving enables a person to experience even very strong emotions with greater objectivity and less reactivity. This capacity serves as a counter to the habitual tendency to avoid or deny difficult emotional states, thereby increasing exposure to such states. Through this direct exposure, one learns that one's emotions, thoughts, or body sensations are not so overwhelming or frightening. Through mindfully attending to negative emotional states, one learns experientially and phenomenologically that such emotions need not be feared or avoided and that they eventually pass away (Segal, Williams, & Teasdale, 2002). This experience eventually leads to the "extinction of fear responses and avoidance behaviors previously elicited by these stimuli" (Baer, 2003, p. 129). Goleman suggested that meditation provides a "global desensitization" because meditative awareness can be applied to all aspects of one's experience (Goleman, 1971).

Baer provided an example of this process with patients with chronic pain:

> Prolonged exposure to the sensations of chronic pain, in the absence of catastrophic consequences, might lead to desensitization, with a reduction over time in the emotional responses elicited by the pain sensations. Thus the practice of mindfulness skills could lead to the ability to experience pain sensations without excessive reactivity. (Baer, 2003, p. 128)

Indeed, one of the first successful clinical applications of mindfulness was in the context of chronic pain (J. Kabat-Zinn, 1990). Another example of how facilitation of exposure to internal stimuli can help therapeutically comes from the literature on interoceptive exposure to physical sensations in panic disorder. Reperceiving allows one to explore and tolerate a broad range of thoughts, emotions, and sensations, which may in turn positively impact a number of debilitating conditions.

Building on Previous Models

Other theorists have developed models of the role of attention and metacognition in the development and maintenance of mental disorders; these models include Wells's self-regulatory executive function (S-REF) model (S. G. Myers & Wells, 2005; Wells, 1999) and Teasdale's differential activation hypothesis (DAH; Lau, Segal, & Williams, 2004; Sheppard & Teasdale, 1996; Wells & Cartwright-Hatton, 2004).

In specific terms, Wells described a cognitive–attentional syndrome characterized by heightened self-focused attention, threat monitoring, ruminative processing, and activation of dysfunctional beliefs. These are measured by the Metacognitions Questionnaire (Cartwright-Hatton & Wells, 1997; Wells & Cartwright-Hatton, 2004). Wells and colleagues have shown that dysfunctional metacognitions are associated with disorders and symptoms including psychosis, generalized anxiety disorder, obsessive–compulsive disorder, hypochondriasis, and posttraumatic stress disorder. The S-REF model emphasizes the importance of self-directed attention in potentially enhancing anxiety by focusing attention on internal sensations associated with the experience of anxiety. This internal focus might engender fears of losing control, fear of the anxiety symptoms themselves, heightened awareness of dissatisfaction with the self, and negative cognitive activity (Wells, 1990). Wells suggested that an external attentional focus, rather than an internal focus as one would use in mindfulness training, might help people with anxiety disorders. His intervention consists of external attentional monitoring and attention switching in an auditory mode.

Unlike the IAA model we have been describing, the S-REF model of therapy applies attentional abilities of focusing, switching, and divided attention externally, rather than internally. An obvious empirical test of this would be to directly compare the efficacy of treatments based on the IAA model of mindfulness to the S-REF model in patients with anxiety disorders.

Another model that emphasizes attention is Teasdale's DAH theory, which describes vulnerability to depressive relapse by activation of dysfunctional negative cognitions, many of which may be comparable to the dysfunctional metacognitions described by Wells. This model of relapse to depression posits that transient negative moods evoke these characteristic negative thought patterns, which can spiral and trigger a relapse. Teasdale and colleagues have developed mindfulness-based cognitive therapy focusing on the idea of "decentering" from the cascade of automatic negative thoughts associated with negative moods, a concept very similar to reperceiving. In their model, as described in chapter 4 (this volume), practicing mindfulness allows people to become aware of negative thoughts and feelings that signify potential relapse and to relate to them in a new way. Participants learn, through mindfulness practice, to disengage from ruminative processing, observing thoughts as simply thoughts, thereby increasing metacognitive awareness. In this respect, the target is not the content of the thoughts per se but is instead the relationship of the individual to the process of thinking. In Wells's terminology, through mindfulness practice the metacognitions shift from evaluating thoughts as personal and dangerous to seeing thoughts as impersonal and part of the passing show, from a decentered perspective.

The IAA model is not contradictory to either of these models; in fact, the richness of the S-REF and DAH models helps to elucidate the manner in which attention is important in engendering the positive effects of mindfulness practice in the context of mental health. Indeed, the attentional component of the IAA model could be tested using the Metacognitions Questionnaire in participants in mindfulness-based stress reduction programs, investigating changes that may occur over the course of mindfulness training. This type of empirical study could help to determine whether, in fact, a shift in metacognitive awareness is occurring, as postulated.

Although IAA is not in contradiction with these two models, it is distinct from them. IAA emphasizes a triaxiomatic model, as opposed to a purely attentional model. IAA defines mindfulness as a way of involving the simultaneous arising of a particular intention, attention, and attitude. The S-REF and the DAH models do not explicitly discuss intention. Further, although the DAH does talk about a "friendly" attitude toward one's experience, the IAA model makes the attitudinal component of mindfulness more explicit and essential. IAA can be seen as an expansion of the above two models, an attempt to continue the process of developing a theoretical model of mindfulness (S. L. Shapiro et al., 2006).

Preliminary Evidence and Future Directions

Through mindfulness practice, reperceiving occurs, facilitating a shift in perspective. This shift, we suggest, is at the heart of the change and transformation affected by mindfulness practice. Preliminary evidence supports this theory that the ability to shift perspectives from an egocentric to a more objective view is salutary (Orzech, Shapiro, Brown, & Mumbar, in press). For example, Kross, Ayduk, and Mischel (2005) found that facing negative emotions from a "self-distanced," "ego-decentered" perspective rather than a "self-immersed perspective" allowed for reflection on the negative situation without reactivating negative affect and rumination.

Further, recent research confirms that mindfulness training does indeed increase this ability to reperceive. A prospective longitudinal study examined the effects of a 1-month intensive mindfulness meditation retreat on reperceiving, as assessed by the recently developed Experience Questionnaire (Fresco et al., 2007). This reliable and valid measure captures the essence of reperceiving. Results demonstrated that retreat participants showed significant increases in reperceiving after 1 month of intensive mindfulness training compared with matched controls (people attending the following 1-month retreat). These results are encouraging and provide preliminary confirmation that mindfulness leads to the ability to shift perspective in a profound and meaningful way.

Future research can address the pathways by which change occurs. We hypothesize that this shift can facilitate multiple mechanisms, including (a) self-regulation, (b) values clarification, (c) cognitive–behavioral flexibility, and (d) exposure. Future research could examine whether any of these proposed mechanisms do indeed account for a significant amount of the variance in change observed. Models linking mindfulness practice to outcomes of interest such as reduction in psychopathological symptoms and cultivation of positive psychological qualities could investigate the role of the proposed direct mechanisms using statistical tests of mediating and moderating effects. Discussion of future directions is continued with greater refinement in chapter 9 (this volume).

Conclusion

The investigation of mindfulness is still in its infancy and requires great sensitivity and a range of theoretical perspectives and methodologies to illuminate the richness and complexity of this phenomenon. We have attempted to provide a first formulation of a model to describe how mindfulness might be fostering transformation and change. This model is clearly preliminary and is merely *a* model, not *the* model. Numerous other possibilities and pathways may play a role in this mysterious and complex process. The next step is to develop testable hypotheses that can be empirically examined. From these results new hypotheses could be developed and new, more fully elaborated theories derived.

EXPANDING THE PARADIGM | III

Mindfulness and Self-Care for Clinicians

8

The helping profession can be extremely hazardous to your physical and mental health.

—*Gill* (1980, p. 24)

The vast majority of research and clinical attention has focused on how mindfulness can benefit patients. However, the health care paradigm is expanding to include the well-being of the clinician as an essential part of the system. With this recognition, the question of how mindfulness can enhance self-care for the clinician as well as the patient has begun to receive attention and interest.

As health care professionals, we often forget to "care" for ourselves. I (Shapiro) learned this during my first clinical position at the veterans hospital in Tucson, Arizona. I was eager to help and believed I was responsible for "saving" all of the people I encountered who were suffering from post-traumatic stress disorder, major depression, suicidal ideation, schizophrenia, and other significant psychiatric diagnoses. I threw myself into my work, scheduling patients after hours and at lunch breaks, taking home notes to review, and thinking about "my" patients all the time. After about 2 months, my clinical supervisor called me into his office and said, "How do you think you're doing?" I responded, "Okay . . . "

This chapter incorporates material from "Self-Care for Health Care Professionals: Effects of MBSR on Mental Well Being of Counseling Psychology Students," by S. L. Shapiro, K. Brown, and G. Biegel, 2007, *Training and Education in Professional Psychology, 1(2)* pp. 105–115. Copyright 2007 by the American Psychological Association. Reprinted with permission.

waiting to hear praise for all of my hard work. There was a pause. Then he responded, "Well, I've noticed you are taking on extra patients, staying late, have no social life, always seem to be rushing, and seem chronically exhausted. Although I believe you are an excellent clinician, I don't think you are serving yourself or others as well as you could." I was surprised, and responded, "What? I don't understand. What else can I do? There are over 40 people on our clinic waiting list. I *need* to be doing all of this." At this point, my supervisor offered me a metaphor that I have carried with me. He said, "The heart pumps blood first to itself, before pumping blood to the rest of the body. If it didn't, it would die, and then the rest of the body would die. The art of caring for others is learning how to first care for yourself. Remember this."

> **Mindful Reminder: What are the things you do to care for yourself?**

As health care professionals, we recognize the privilege of sharing so deeply in the lives of our clients. We devote considerable energy, resources, love, and time to relieving their suffering. Yet often we do not devote similar care and attention to ourselves. To put patients' welfare above our own is not skillful and can lead to deleterious consequences.

For example, health care professionals commonly experience compassion fatigue (Figley, 2002; L. Weiss, 2004) resulting from the emotional labor that comprises a significant part of therapeutic work (Mann, 2004). Stress-related psychological problems are especially widespread among health care professionals employed in high-demand settings such as hospitals (Vredenburgh, Carlozzi, & Stein, 1999) and among those working with populations that present special emotional challenges to caregivers, including clients who have experienced abuse (Coppenhall, 1995) or trauma (Arvay & Uhlemann, 1996) or have personality disorders (Linehan, Cochran, Mar, Levensky, & Comtois, 2000). Research suggests that psychological impairment affects a significant proportion of health professionals at some point in their careers (Coster & Schwebel, 1997; Guy, Poelstra, & Stark, 1989).

The negative consequences of stress on helping professionals include increased depression, emotional exhaustion, anxiety (Radeke & Mahoney, 2000; Tyssen, Vaglum, Grønvold, & Ekeberg, 2001), psychosocial isolation (Penzer, 1984), decreased job satisfaction (Blegen, 1993), reduced self-esteem (Butler & Constantine, 2005), disrupted personal relationships (M. F. Myers, 1994), and loneliness (Lushington & Luscri, 2001). Stress may also harm professional effectiveness in that it appears to negatively impact attention and concentration (Skosnik, Chatterton, Swisher, & Park, 2000), impinge on decision-making skills (Klein, 1996; Lehner, 1997), and reduce providers' ability to establish strong relationships with patients (Enochs & Etzbach, 2004; Renjilian, Baum, & Landry, 1998). Further, stress can increase the likelihood of occupational burnout (Rosenberg & Pace, 2006), a syndrome that involves depersonalization, emotional exhaustion, and a sense of low personal accomplishment.

Over 2 decades ago, the field identified these problems and called for change, advocating better care for health professionals (Butterfield,

1988). Despite this awareness, dissatisfaction and distress have continued to increase (S. L. Shapiro, Shapiro, & Schwartz, 2000). It is clear that health care professionals still need support in addressing the numerous stressors inherent in their work.

Why Do We Need to Care for Ourselves?

Part of the territory of the helping profession is encountering extraordinary amounts of suffering and stress. Thus, it is critical that we care for ourselves so that we have the strength and clarity to care for others. When we put others' needs before our own, we are strengthening our delusion of separateness, widening the gap between self and other. We strengthen our idea that "they" are really suffering and need more care and help than "I" do. When we begin to see our deep interconnectedness, often through the practice of meditation, we can let go of false views of separation. We are able to see that our clients' suffering is no different from our own. We recognize that we are all human beings. We all suffer. We all yearn for health, safety, happiness, and love. And yet, often, we in the helping professions do not believe we deserve to take time for ourselves. It seems selfish in the face of the misery and anguish we see around us. This view prevents us from seeing that at the deepest level "us" and "them" are the same, and each of us is equally deserving of kindness and attention. According to the Buddha,

> you can search the whole world for someone who is more deserving of your love and affection than you are yourself, and that person is not to be found anywhere. You, yourself, as much as anyone in the entire universe, deserve your love and affection.

His teaching requires us to see that everyone is equally deserving of kindness, attention, and care, including ourselves. There is no one more or less deserving, because we are all interconnected. If your left hand pulls a thorn out of your right hand, you don't thank your left hand for its kindness; it is simply the appropriate response. When we see pain, within ourselves or others, the appropriate response is to relieve it.

Despite the wisdom of this insight, when it comes to ourselves, many of us in the helping profession do not attend to our own pain and stress with care and attention. In his compelling book, *The Resilient Clinician*, Dr. Robert Wicks (2007) wrote about the clinician's silent psychological defenses of denial and avoidance, pointing out the significant negative consequences that arise from our lack of mindfulness and self-care.

Learning to manage stress and enhance self-care should be an essential dimension of clinical training as well as professional development (Newsome, Christopher, Dahlen, & Christopher, 2006; Shapiro,

Brown, & Biegel, 2007). However, the demand of patient loads as well as the curricular demands of graduate programs seldom leave space for explicit self-care and stress management intervention.

Programs designed to teach self-care skills to trainees as well as professionals currently in the field may represent an important form of "preventive treatment" for professionals at risk of later psychological problems (cf., Coster & Schwebel, 1997). However, the responsibility for self-care is unfortunately typically left to the individual initiative of the student or professional (Newsome et al., 2006), and specific means to develop self-care practices are not offered. This is a noteworthy limitation of our current health care system and training programs, with significant consequences for those in the helping profession and those with whom they work.

Mindfulness Training As Self-Care

Mindful Reminder: What is the quality of your breath right now?

As demonstrated in chapters 5 and 6 (this volume), a growing body of research indicates that the cultivation of mindfulness may enhance psychological well-being, mental health, and physical health (see Baer, 2003, and Grossman, Niemann, Schmidt, & Walach, 2004, for meta-analytic reviews). The majority of research has focused on mindfulness as a therapeutic intervention for patients; however, training in mindfulness may be especially relevant for health care professionals and trainees as a means of managing stress and enhancing self-care.

Although there are many options for stress management and self-care interventions, we believe mindfulness is particularly pertinent for health care professionals. First, mindfulness practice offers an opportunity to explore deeply our own pain and suffering and the causes and conditioning that lead to it. Mindfulness practice is not intended to magically take away our stress, but to help us understand and know our experience more intimately and to relate to it in a different way. It teaches us to become interested in the inner workings of our own minds, bodies, and hearts, with kindness, and in this way discover what it means to be human. Mindfulness practice helps us reduce our own stress and suffering as well as prepares us to help others reduce their stress and suffering. As Cozolino (2004) adroitly noted in his book *The Making of a Therapist*, helping another requires

> a simultaneous exploration of one's inner world and private thoughts. . . . When we begin training, we embark on two simultaneous journeys: one outward into the professional world

and the other inward, through the labyrinths of our own psyches. . . . The more fearless we become in the exploration of our inner worlds, the greater our self-knowledge and our ability to help clients. (pp. xv, xvi)

Mindful practice is an invaluable tool for engaging in this "exploration of our inner worlds" with consciousness, presence, and intention. When we are able to plumb our own psyches, we become less anxious and afraid about engaging in a similar exploration of our patients' psyches.

The attitudinal qualities of mindfulness, including nonstriving, acceptance, and self-compassion, also make it particularly pertinent intervention for helping professionals. These qualities are vital to meeting the demands and stressors inherent in the healing professions. For example, the quality of striving toward the singular goal of "fixing" patients is all too prevalent among the helping professions. We experience an enormous responsibility to "fix" patients. This pressure leads to unrealistic goals and losing sight of the present encounter with the person we are engaged with. Mindfulness explicitly teaches us how to let go of this goal-oriented stance and dwell completely in the present moment. As we practice nonstriving, we begin to see all the ways our pushing and pulling things to be a certain way in therapy—"my way"—hurt ourselves and the people we are trying to help. We recognize the unnecessary suffering we are adding to each situation, and we are able to relax into the moment as it is. Through mindfulness practice we are able to accept things as they are, recognizing that all we can do is respond as consciously and compassionately as possible.

Mindfulness also explicitly teaches self-compassion, giving us permission to be "imperfect" or, put a better way, "perfectly human." Mindfulness helps us recognize when we are not acting skillfully, without condemning or shaming ourselves. We are able to note with compassion those times when we are stressed, hungry, or exhausted, holding ourselves with the same compassion and care we bring to our patients. We practice being with "*ourselves* in the same way that we wish to be with the clients or patients" (Wicks, 2007, p. 6, italics in original). Learning to treat ourselves with kindness is an important way of practicing kindness toward others (see Exhibit 8.1 for a loving-kindness meditation).

A final reason mindfulness practice may be particularly beneficial for health care professionals is that it is not simply a technique to be used while stressed, but a way of being that can be applied during all moments of one's life. Mindfulness not only helps us respond to difficult situations with greater consciousness but also allows us to be more present for beautiful, joyful moments. Not only is this personally beneficial, but it reminds us to notice and be attuned to the moments of insight, transformation, and growth that occur in therapy. The work of

EXHIBIT 8.1

Loving-Kindness (Metta) Meditation

The loving-kindness meditation explicitly cultivates caring, kindness and love for ourselves and others. The feelings it evokes have been likened to the love a mother has for her only child, a deep and selfless love filled with benevolence. This practice is a beautiful way to cultivate care and friendliness toward ourselves and others.

Begin by sitting in a comfortable position. Connect with the body and the breath, and if it is comfortable place one or both hands over your heart center. If you can, feel the movement and vibration of your heart beating, sending blood carrying oxygen and nutrients to every cell in your body. Take a moment to consciously set an intention for this practice—for example, "to open my heart," "to cultivate loving-kindness" "to care for myself."

Begin to send loving-kindness toward yourself. You can see if certain phrases emerge that express what you wish most deeply for yourself. These phrases should be general enough that you can eventually send them to all beings everywhere. Traditional phrases include "May I be safe. May I be happy. May I be healthy. May I live with ease. May I be free from suffering." Gently and silently repeat these phrases on your own, wishing yourself well over and over again. Allow the phrases to flow through your being; allow your mind to rest and your body to be at ease. When you become aware that your mind has wandered from the phrases and the present moment, gently yet firmly begin reciting the phrases again.

"May I be safe. May I be happy. May I be healthy. May I live with ease."

If you become aware of the arising of any resistance to accepting these wishes for yourself, simply note these thoughts and feelings in the body, then gently return to the practice of repeating the phrases. Even if they feel like hollow words, simply continue with patience and kindness and observe your reactions.

When you feel ready, shift the focus from sending the phrases to yourself, to sending them to somebody you care about, such as a good friend, a benefactor, someone who inspires you. Call them to mind as clearly as possible, visualizing them or silently repeating their name. And when you sense their presence, softly direct the phrases of loving-kindness to them.

"May *you* be safe. May you be happy. May you be healthy. May you live with ease."

Imagine your wishes traveling across space and time and being received by this loved one, feeling the sensations in your own heart as you continue sending your wishes for his or her well-being.

When you feel ready, let go of this person and call to mind a neutral person, someone whom you don't know well, and about whom you feel neither positively nor negatively. You don't even have to know the person's name. Simply choose someone who plays some role in your life, such as the bus driver or the checkout person at the supermarket. See if you can visualize that person, and begin to offer the same phrases of loving-kindness to him or her:

"May *you* be safe. May you be happy. May you be healthy. May you live with ease."

EXHIBIT 8.1 (*Continued*)

Loving-Kindness (Metta) Meditation

When you feel ready, allow a difficult person to come into your field of awareness. This does not need to be your *most difficult* person. Choose someone with whom you have had some challenges, and begin to send the phrases of loving-kindness to them. It is okay if you do not feel overwhelming love for the person, and if the phrases feel rote. Simply intend the phrases toward the person as best you can, noticing with your mindfulness all of the things that come up that impede the phrases, such as thoughts, body sensations, and distractions. If you notice you are becoming too uncomfortable, then go back to sending loving-kindness to yourself or to someone you love. The goal is to aim the heart toward opening ourselves to the possibility of including, rather than excluding; of connecting, rather than overlooking; of caring, rather than being indifferent. However, you cannot force this process. Trust that your heart will open in its own time.

"May *you (difficult person)* be safe. May *you (difficult person)* be happy, healthy. May *you (difficult person)* live with ease."

Ultimately, our intention is to open our hearts and wish all beings well. We attempt to direct the phrase of loving-kindness to all beings everywhere, without distinction, without separation.

May all beings live in safety, be happy, be healthy, live with ease.

the helping profession is both challenging and uplifting, and mindfulness helps us be present for all of it.

Review of Research

Here we review a growing body of research that demonstrates the benefits of mindfulness-based stress reduction (MBSR) for health care professionals and trainees (Cohen-Katz, Wiley, Capuano, Baker, Deitrick, et al., 2005; Rosenzweig, Reibel, Greeson, Brainard, & Hojat, 2003; S. L. Shapiro, Astin, Bishop, & Cordova, 2005; S. L. Shapiro, Schwartz, & Bonner, 1998).

For example, in a randomized, wait-list controlled study with 78 medical and premedical students, S. L. Shapiro et al. (1998) examined the effects of an 8-week MBSR program on symptoms of anxiety and depression, empathy, and spiritual experience. Results indicated decreased levels of anxiety and depression and increases in empathy and spiritual experience in the MBSR group as compared with the wait-list control group. These reductions were maintained even during a stressful final exam period, and findings were replicated when participants in the wait-list control group received the MBSR intervention. The conclusions of this research were supported by four recent studies. In a controlled trial, Jain and colleagues (2007) found significant increases in positive mood states and significant decreases in stress and rumination in premedical students receiving an MBSR intervention compared with a control group. In addition, Rosenzweig et al. (2003) found that medical students participating in an MBSR course demonstrated significant decreases in total mood disturbance and distress compared with a control group. Another pre–post study examining the effects of MBSR on nursing students found significant improvements on two dimensions of empathy as well as on measures of stress (Beddoe & Murphy, 2004).

A recent study examining the effects of an MBSR course on stress and mental health symptoms in graduate counseling psychology students lends further support to the work already cited (S. L. Shapiro, Brown, & Biegel, 2007). This semester-long, 10-week course followed the MBSR program model and included weekly instruction in a variety of mindfulness meditative techniques and home-based practice. Relative to matched-cohort control participants taking didactic courses, students in the MBSR course showed significant pre–post declines in perceived stress, negative affect, rumination, and state and trait anxiety, and significant increases in positive affect and self-compassion. These findings indicate that MBSR may not only lower stress and distress but also enhance the ability to regulate emotional states, as reflected in the declines in rumination. This may be important in warding off depressive states (Nolen-Hoeksema, Morrow, & Fredrickson, 1993). In addition, the increases in self-compassion are particularly relevant to the field of counseling and therapy, as compassion for self, as well as for clients, has been posited as an essential part of conducting effective therapy (Gilbert, 2005). Research demonstrates that therapists who lack self-compassion and are critical and controlling toward themselves are also more critical and controlling toward their patients and have poorer patient outcomes (Henry, Schacht, & Strupp, 1990).

Extending this research to professionals currently engaged in clinical work, S. L. Shapiro and colleagues examined the effects of MBSR with health care workers at a Department of Veterans Affairs hospital. Results from this prospective controlled study concluded that an 8-week MBSR intervention was effective in reducing stress and increasing quality of life and self-compassion in this population of health care professionals (S. L. Shapiro et al., 2005). Supporting this research, a series of studies investigating the effects of MBSR to reduce nurse stress and burnout found positive effects of MBSR training (Cohen-Katz, Wiley, Capuano, Baker, & Shapiro, 2004, 2005; Cohen-Katz, Wiley, Capuano, Baker, Deitrick, et al. 2005). Participants were randomly assigned to MBSR or a wait-list control group. Those in the MBSR group reported significant improvements in aspects of burnout (personal accomplishment and emotional exhaustion) compared with the wait-list control group, which were maintained up to 3 months postintervention (Cohen-Katz, Wiley, Capuano, Baker, Deitrick, et al., 2005; Cohen-Katz, Wiley, Capuano, Baker, & Shapiro, 2005). Qualitative results indicated that nurses found the MBSR program helpful for promoting relaxation, self-care, and improvements in relationships at work and at home (Cohen-Katz, Wiley, Capuano, Baker, Deitrick, et al., 2005; Cohen-Katz, Wiley, Capuano, Baker, & Shapiro, 2005). They specifically identified feelings of increased relaxation and calmness, self-acceptance and self-compassion, self-awareness, self-care, and self-reliance, as well as decreased physical pain and improved sleep. Their relationships were improved through better communication, being more present and empathic, and being less reactive. They also identified challenges to the meditation practice including restlessness, pain, and dealing with difficult emotions.

Adding further support to this research Mackenzie and colleagues also investigated MBSR for nurses and nursing aids by evaluating a brief 4-week program in 16 nurses randomized to MBSR compared with 14 wait-listed control participants (Mackenzie, Poulin, & Seidman-Carlson, 2006). Findings indicated improvements in measures of burnout, relaxation, and overall satisfaction in life.

Overall, the research supports the benefits of mindfulness training for health care professionals and those in training. The next step is to explore how to incorporate mindfulness training into graduate curricula.

Integrating Mindfulness Into the Curriculum

Christopher and colleagues noted, "Faculty in counseling training programs often give voice to the importance of self-care for students during the training period and into practice after training is completed. However, few programs specifically address this issue in their curricula" (Christopher, Christopher, Dunnagan, & Schure, 2006, p. 494). In an attempt to fill this void, a few pioneering programs are developing courses that explicitly integrate self-care into their curricula.

For example, faculty in the Montana State University counseling psychology program developed a course titled "Mind/Body Medicine and the Art of Self-Care" to provide students with self-care practices through training in MBSR (Christopher et al., 2006). Results from a focus group, qualitative reports, and quantitative course evaluations suggested positive physical, emotional, mental, spiritual, and interpersonal changes in students who participated in the course. Further, students reported significant benefits in their clinical training and therapeutic relationships, such as increased comfort with silence and strong emotions, increased clarity, increased empathy and compassion, and increased ability to pay attention and listen (Newsome et al., 2006).

In the counseling psychology master's program at Santa Clara University (SCU), we offer a course, "Stress and Stress Management," that provides rigorous training in mindfulness meditation in addition to academic instruction on the negative mental and physical effects of stress and the value of a diverse array of stress management interventions. Students report significant benefits from the personal mindfulness training. Data from anonymous responses to the question "On a scale from 1–7 how important has this course been for you personally; how important professionally?" show that 95% of the participants rate the course a 6 or 7 on both professional and personal importance.

In response to students' interest and reported benefit, an advanced seminar was recently developed and implemented in the counseling psychology curriculum at SCU, titled "Mindfulness and Psychotherapy: Theory, Research and Practice."[1] This advanced seminar delves into the applications of mindfulness for psychotherapy, focusing on its unique applications both as a means to develop clinical skills and as a process of therapist self-care. Results from the first offering of this course indicated significant interest and a positive response from students, especially regarding self-care implications. Students reported that learning to apply the mindfulness practices to themselves significantly affected their clinical skills, and equally important, affected the way they related to themselves. They reported an increased awareness, empathy, compassion, and clarity in their clinical work and in their relationship to life (see Exhibit 8.2 for anonymous student reports).

Conclusions and Future Directions

Although academic knowledge and skills form the core of clinical graduate programs, an explicit focus on self-awareness and self-care is also critical. This focus on self-care is also important for professionals in the health care field. Courses that integrate training in mindfulness and meditative techniques provide one means for those in the helping profession to learn about self-care. Through this process we learn to attend

[1] The development of this course was supported by the Contemplative Practice Fellowship awarded to Shauna Shapiro by the American Council of Learned Societies and the Center for Contemplative Mind in Society.

EXHIBIT 8.2

Anonymous Written Statements From Health Care Professionals Participating in the MBSR Program in Response to the Question: "What Effects Did the MBSR Program Have on Your Life?"

- "This practice is vital to living with compassion . . . "
- " . . . opened my mind to the destructive thought patterns I have and to various ways of addressing them"
- "I can accept that I can't control everything"
- "Even in the midst of stress, I can still breathe"
- "Forgiveness!"
- " . . . helped me learn how to better manage painful emotions"
- " . . . increased sense of living more fully"
- "I will always be able to access this method of stress reduction especially in times of emotional difficulty"
- "I am more mindful of the beauty in nature and in each person I come in contact with"
- "The best benefit is being more gentle and kind with myself . . . "
- "I learned how to love"

---

to ourselves in a kind and healing way, and gain greater ability to extend this attention, kindness, and care to the patients whose lives we touch.

There is an extensive literature indicating that clinician stress and burnout negatively affect patient care, in such ways as decreased patient satisfaction, decreased compliance, and decreased recovery (Halbesleben & Rathert, 2008; Shanafelt, Bradley, Wipt, & Back, 2002). As Halbesleben and Rathert (2008) concluded, "organizations that take proactive steps to reduce burnout through system wide intervention programs will see greater benefits in terms of patient satisfaction and recovery" (p. 29).

Further attention to self-care for health care professionals and trainees is clearly needed, for the sake of both the therapist and the patient. The preliminary research reviewed here suggests the cultivation of mindfulness significantly enhances the well-being of health care professionals and trainees. Future research could explore the usefulness of MBSR and other awareness-based self-care programs as a complement to trainee curricula and professional development. It is hoped that by teaching those in the helping profession to care for themselves, they will be better able to care for others.

Exploring the Farther Reaches of Human Potential | 9

I am large, I contain multitudes.

—*Walt Whitman* ("Song of Myself", 1891)

Exploring the original goals of mindfulness meditation may help Western psychology examine and reevaluate the current definition of "normal" and expand the concept of mental health. According to S. L. Shapiro and Walsh (2007), "As we expand our models to include positive psychological, transpersonal and spiritual variables, we will begin to understand the farther reaches of human potential" (p. 69).

As reviewed in chapters 5 and 6 (this volume), several hundred research studies have demonstrated numerous significant findings of mindfulness-based interventions, including decreases in psychological and physiological pathology. However, the original intentions of mindfulness meditation reach far beyond the paradigm of the medical model, emphasizing the potential for increased positive qualities and spiritual development. This chapter attempts to expand the focus from a predominantly reductionistic, biomedical model to one that includes positive psychological domains.

Mindfulness and the meditative disciplines offer three important assumptions that speak to vital aspects of our nature and potential as human beings that lie outside most health

This chapter incorporates material from "An Analysis of Recent Meditation Research and Suggestions for Future Directions," by S. L. Shapiro and R. Walsh, 2003, *The Humanistic Psychologist, 31*, pp. 86–114. Copyright 2003 by Taylor & Francis.

care paradigms (Shapiro & Walsh, 2003). The first is that our usual psychological state is suboptimal and not well developed. As William James put it,

> Most people live, whether physically, intellectually or morally, in a very restricted circle of their potential being. They make use of a very small portion of their possible consciousness. We all have reservoirs of life to draw upon, of which we do not dream. (S. L. Shapiro & Walsh, 2003, p. 86)

The second assumption is that higher states and stages are available as developmental potentials. "What we call normality and have regarded as the ceiling of human possibilities is increasingly coming to look like a form of arbitrary, culturally determined, developmental arrest" (S. L. Shapiro & Walsh, 2003; Walsh & Vaughan, 1993). This assumption has been supported by mainstream developmental psychology, suggesting that beyond conventional, personal stages of development await post-conventional, transpersonal stages and potentials (Fowler, 1995; Kohlberg, 1981; Loevinger, 1997; Maslow, 1971; Wilber, 1999, 2000).

Mindful Reminder: What aspects of this expanded paradigm for human potential excite you?

The third assumption is that positive psychological development and transpersonal states and stages can be catalyzed by a variety of psychological and spiritual practices, including mindfulness practice (S. L. Shapiro & Walsh, 2003). It is therefore crucial to examine the impact of mindfulness-based therapies on these positive psychological and spiritual developments.

Foundational Research Studies

Researchers have examined the effects of mindfulness-based therapies primarily as a self-regulation strategy for stress management and symptom reduction. Over the past 3 decades, considerable research has examined the psychological and physiological effects of mindfulness for both psychological and medical disorders, and mindfulness-based therapies are now being used in a variety of health care settings (see chaps. 5 and 6, this volume).

However, the original intentions of mindfulness practices reach far beyond the reduction of pathology. Walsh (1983) identified traditional aims of mindfulness and meditative practice as including "the development of deep insight into the nature of mental processes, consciousness, identity, and reality, and the development of optimal states of psychological well-being and consciousness" (p. 19). Mindfulness practice seeks to help people to become free of a limited egocentric perspective and to develop greater empathy, compassion, awareness, and insight.

And yet, research exploring the effects of mindfulness meditation to attain these goals has been scarce, missing the deeper levels of meditation's original intent and focusing instead on traditional psychological variables. It is essential to rigorously examine the original intentions of meditation to cultivate positive qualities and spiritual development. This exploration, we believe, will help us uncover what Maslow (1971) called "the farther reaches of human nature."

Although basic research in mindfulness is important and should continue, "we can also examine the foci and goals of the meditative traditions themselves, assess their accompanying psychologies and philosophies, and explore their many implications for our understanding of human nature, pathology, therapy and potentials" (S. L. Shapiro & Walsh, 2007, p. 60). This expansion of the paradigm may offer far-reaching benefits, including facilitating emerging movements such as positive psychology as well as integrative movements such as cross-cultural psychology, integral psychology, and integrative psychotherapy (Arkowitz & Mannon, 2002; Snyder & Lopez, 2005).

Recent Research

A small number of pioneering studies provide a valuable foundation for expanding the paradigm of research. Below we review a sample of recent, well-designed studies on the effects of mindfulness practice on positive psychological and spiritual variables.

ATTENTION

Attention has often been conceptualized as a fixed neurological capacity with little ability to change through practice. However, recent investigation into the effects of mindfulness training on a range of attentional abilities using neuropsychological measures including functional magnetic resonance imaging (fMRI) scans, skin conductance, and electroencephalograms has suggested otherwise. Jha and colleagues (Jha, Krompinger, & Baime, 2007) compared a range of attentional skills in participants with no meditation training, participants enrolled in an 8-week mindfulness-based stress reduction (MBSR) class, and others participating in a month-long mindfulness retreat. Results indicated that participants in the MBSR group had improved abilities to quickly orient their attention on a chosen stimulus compared with both other groups. In contrast, those completing the month-long meditation retreat improved their receptive attention, which is the ability to return focus to chosen stimuli when distracted by external events, significantly more than did those in the MBSR and no-treatment groups.

Recent mindfulness meditation research has also investigated another aspect of attention referred to as the *attentional blink*. The attentional blink is the tendency to miss some stimuli in a stream because one is attending to previous stimuli. The competition of the two stimuli for limited attentional resources is what causes the attentional blink. The duration of the blink was thought to be unalterable, but one study showed that after 3 months of intensive mindfulness meditation training, people were able to decrease the size of the attentional blink. They were able to attend less to the first stimuli and more to the previously missed second stimuli, demonstrating improved control over limited brain resources (Slagter et al., 2007). The authors contend these results support the existence of plasticity in mental functions throughout life, which can be cultivated through mindfulness training.

Other neuroscience research studies investigating anatomical differences between attentional systems in the brains of meditators and non-meditators have provided another line of evidence that mindfulness training may change the actual structure of the brain in positive ways. Recent research found that brain regions associated with attention and sensory processing were thicker in long-term meditation practitioners than in matched control participants. Further, cortical thickness correlated with meditation experience: Those who had been practicing the longest also had the most gray matter in these areas (Lazar et al., 2005). In addition, the differences between meditators and control participants were most pronounced in older individuals, suggesting that meditation practice may offset the known detrimental effects of normal aging on cortical thickness. This speculation was confirmed by another study that compared attention performance and gray matter volume in various brain regions between experienced Zen practitioners and matched non-meditating control participants (Pagnoni & Cekic, 2007). They too found that the usual age-related decrease in gray matter volume in attention areas of the brain and attention skills was seen in the control participants but not in the meditators. Taken together, these research studies suggest that meditation may play a role in maintaining youthful attentional abilities into older ages.

However, these results must be considered as preliminary because they are correlational and do not conclusively demonstrate causation. It is possible that those who chose to learn meditation were physiologically different to begin with from those who had not pursued this practice. Therefore, it is impossible to conclude that meditation directly caused the observed differences in brain structure and function and yet these preliminary studies are intriguing and set the stage for further research exploring the effects of mindfulness training on the brain.

INTERPERSONAL RELATIONSHIPS

Carson, Carson, Gil, and Baucom (2004) integrated mindfulness-based intervention with the practices of loving-kindness (see chap. 4, this volume) into a mindfulness-based intervention for couples. Forty-four couples that were in well-adjusted relationships and had been married an average of 11 years were randomly assigned to a waiting-list control or the meditation intervention. The program consisted of eight 2½-hour sessions and a 6-hour retreat. In addition to components modeled on the MBSR program (J. Kabat-Zinn, 1990), a number of elements related to enhancing the relationship were added, including loving-kindness meditation, partner yoga exercises, focused application of mindfulness to relationship issues, and group discussions. Results demonstrated that the couples in the meditation intervention significantly improved relationship satisfaction as well as relatedness to and acceptance of the partner. In addition, individuals reported significant increases in optimism, engagement in exciting self-expanding activities, spirituality, and relaxation. It is interesting that increases in engagement in exciting self-expanding activities significantly mediated improvements in relationship quality (Carson et al., 2004, 2006).

Wachs and Cordova (2007) also assessed the relationship between mindfulness and emotional repertoires in intimate relationships. In their sample of married couples, higher trait mindfulness was related to better marital quality. In addition, skills in identifying and communicating emotions as well as the ability to regulate the expression of anger mediated the relationship between mindfulness and marital quality. That is, greater mindfulness skills allowed the couples to better communicate and control expression of their emotions, which led to happier marriages.

Finally, Nielsen and Kaszniak (2006) studied whether mindfulness training improved the ability to discriminate subtle emotional feelings using both self-report and physiological monitoring. When conducting a task that required identification of one's physiological reactions to emotionally ambiguous stimuli, experienced meditators were more able to discriminate emotions and were less physiologically reactive to ambiguous stimuli than were a control group of nonmeditators. They also felt more emotional clarity than did the control participants. This suggests that meditation experience may help to develop more accurate skills in internal information processing that could aid in communication and interpersonal relationships.

SELF-CONCEPT

Using a cross-section study design, Haimerl and Valentine (2001) investigated the effect of mindfulness meditation on intrapersonal (self-directedness), interpersonal (cooperativeness), and transpersonal (self-transcendence) levels of the self-concept. Subjects included prospective meditators ($n = 28$) with no experience, beginners ($n = 58$) with less than 2 years of experience, and advanced meditators ($n = 73$) with more than 2 years of experience. Advanced meditators scored significantly higher than did prospective meditators on all three subscales, and higher than beginners on the interpersonal subscale. The beginners also scored significantly higher than did prospective meditators on the transpersonal subscale. Only the advanced meditators scored higher on the transpersonal than on the intrapersonal subscale within their group. The authors concluded that scores on the intrapersonal, interpersonal, and transpersonal levels were a positive function of meditation experience, suggesting that progress in Buddhist meditation leads to significant and sequential growth in these components of personality.

Another intriguing study used fMRI of the brain to investigate the differences between brain activation when people were asked to shift between self-awareness of enduring traits and awareness of a constantly changing self in the present moment (Farb et al., 2007). Participants who completed an 8-week MBSR program were compared with meditation-naive participants. When the nonmeditators were asked to focus only on their present-moment experience, the brain areas associated with personal traits and history were also activated. However, participants who were trained in mindfulness were able to truly focus only on their present-moment experience, and thus the areas associated with personal traits and history were not activated. These results suggest that these brain areas can be "decoupled" through mindfulness practice, allowing participants to separate their awareness of present-moment self from their awareness of their personal traits and history. The meditators were better able to distinguish the self across time as an enduring entity from the self in the present moment, which is constantly changing, and the brain areas that are associated with these different types of self-awareness followed suit. This result suggests that mindfulness training may allow individuals to "objectify" the mind and disidentify from mental activities as being the totality of who they are (Siegel, 2007a).

POSITIVE AFFECT

Positive emotions are an important part of human flourishing. Noted psychologist Barbara Fredrickson (2001), for example, posited that positive emotions are indicators of well-being and causes of it. Positive emotions are thought to help broaden one's thought-action repertoire and build one's intellectual and psychological resources. Preliminary evidence demonstrates that mindfulness increases positive affect as measured by self-report and physiological indicators. An example of compelling research in this area by neuroscientist Richard Davidson shows the effects of intensive compassion meditation on brain activity. When Davidson's team scanned electrical activity of the brains of very experienced Tiebetan Buddhist monks who were generating a state of nonreferential compassion, they found that the activation in brain areas connected with the generation of positive emotions was much higher than that in the brains of normal people not trained in meditation (Lutz, Greischar, Rawlings, Ricard, & Davidson, 2004). They speculated that this intensive meditation practice may result in actual changes in brain functioning in the direction of more positive emotional states and ability to feel compassion toward others (Goleman, 2003). In a study by this same group on the effects of MBSR in employees of a high-tech company, compared with a randomly assigned wait-list control group, MBSR participants showed both greater decreases in self-rated negative affect and corresponding increases in brain activation in areas previously identified with positive affect (left-side anterior frontal activation; Davidson et al., 2003). This line of research shows that both intensive training in meditation and introductory practice in beginners can alter brain activation to support more positive emotional states.

Supporting these findings, recent controlled research by Jain and colleagues (2007) found that mindfulness intervention significantly increased positive mood states in medical students, nursing students, and premedical undergraduates.

EMPATHY

Empathy is considered an essential aspect of mental health and a fundamental part of human relationships. As noted in chapter 2 (this volume), preliminary research supports that empathy can be cultivated through the practice of mindfulness. For example, S. L. Shapiro and colleagues (1998) conducted a randomized controlled study of the effects of MBSR on 78 medical and premedical students. Participants in the MBSR group reported increased levels of empathy and decreased levels of anxiety and depression as compared with the wait-list control group. These findings were supported when participants in the wait-list control group received the MBSR intervention and demonstrated the same results of increased empathy and decreased anxiety and depression.

The findings of this study are supported by a recent study examining the effects of MBSR on counseling psychology students' empathy. Counseling students who participated in an 8-week MBSR course demonstrated significant pre–post increases in empathic concern for others as compared with a matched control group (S. L. Shapiro & Izett, 2008). Results of another qualitative study of counseling graduate students support these quantitative findings (Schure, Christopher, & Christopher,

2008). After training in mindfulness, students described an ability to better connect with clients and feel empathy toward their suffering, simply through the process of focusing on the present moment rather than being preoccupied with their own anxiety or how to fix the problem.

Recent research by Lutz, Brefczynski-Lewis, Johnstone, and Davidson (2008) investigated brain activity associated with empathy and compassion by using fMRI while novice and expert meditation practitioners generated a loving-kindness–compassion meditation state. While the participants were meditating and also while they were in a neutral state, the researchers tested affective reactivity by presenting either emotional or neutral sounds. The hypothesis was that concern for others cultivated during compassion meditation enhances affective processing, particularly in response to sounds of distress in others. They also hypothesized that the response to emotional sounds would be modulated by the degree of meditation training. Indeed, activity in regions of the brain previously associated with empathic processes (the insula and cingulated cortices) was modulated through the practice of compassion meditation; all the participants showed stronger neural responses to the sounds of distress in others during compassion meditation than when at rest. In addition, the expert meditation practitioners showed stronger responses than novices to negative emotional sounds during compassion meditation in brain areas known to participate in affect and feelings. The strength of the activity in several brain regions was associated with the degree to which participants perceived that they had successfully entered into the meditative state. Hence, this study shows that the practice of compassion meditation is associated with activation of brain areas previously linked with empathy and the wish to help others in distress.

SELF-COMPASSION

Self-compassion can be defined as the awareness that one is suffering and a genuine care and kindness for oneself to end that suffering (Neff, Kirkpatrick, & Rude, 2007). Recent research found that self-compassion is significantly predictive of other positive psychological variables, including wisdom, personal initiative, curiosity and exploration, happiness, optimism, and positive affect (Neff et al., 2007). Further, self-compassion remained a significant predictor of psychological health after controlling for shared variance with positive affect and personality.

Recent research demonstrates that participation in an MBSR program is associated with improvements in graduate counseling psychology students' mental health and self-compassion (S. L. Shapiro, Brown, & Biegel, 2007). Compared with cohort controls, students in the MBSR program reported significant pre–post course declines in perceived stress, negative affect, state and trait anxiety, and rumination, and significant increases in positive affect and self-compassion. As noted in chapter 2 (this volume), the increases in self-compassion are particularly relevant to the field of counseling and therapy, as compassion for self, as well as for clients, has been posited to be an essential part of conducting effective therapy (Gilbert, 2005). Further, MBSR participation increased levels of mindfulness, which mediated increases in self-compassion. These findings support previous controlled research demonstrating increases in self-compassion in health care professionals after MBSR intervention (S. L. Shapiro, Astin, Bishop, & Cordova, 2005).

SPIRITUALITY AND POSTTRAUMATIC GROWTH

Spirituality is complex, meaning different things to different people, and is experienced in unique ways. Current research demonstrates that mindfulness meditation may help cultivate spiritual experiences.

A recent study by Carmody, Reed, Merriam, and Kristeller (2008) found that participation in MBSR intervention significantly increased spirituality and that increases in spirituality were associated with improvements in psychological and medical symptoms. In the study by Carson and colleagues (Carson et al., 2006) noted previously, the couples who received the mindfulness-based relationship enhancement intervention reported significant increases in spirituality compared with the control group. This supports earlier findings that an MBSR intervention significantly increased spiritual experience in medical students as compared with wait-list control participants (S. L. Shapiro et al., 1998). These results were replicated when the control group received the same mindfulness intervention. Further, Astin (1997) demonstrated significant increases in spiritual experience in a randomized controlled study comparing an MBSR intervention with a control group of undergraduate students.

Work in the area of spirituality and posttraumatic growth following the traumatic experience of diagnosis and treatment for cancer supports the potential role of mindfulness in enhancing positive growth. Cancer is a major life event that can serve as a psychosocial transition that causes individuals to gradually change their worldview, expectations, and plans. People may make sense of their diagnosis by finding positive benefit in their situation. This process has been described as posttraumatic growth, benefit finding, adversarial growth, positive change, thriving, personal growth, positive adjustment, or transformation (Brennan, 2001; Helgeson, Reynolds, & Tomich, 2006). It is also similar to spirituality, which is defined as including dimensions such as meaning making, faith, purpose, and connection with others and with a higher power (Mytko & Knight, 1999). Spirituality differs from religiosity in that it relates to one's own personal experience of transcendence or relationship with a larger whole rather than specific faith-based structures or practices; hence, it is more inclusive.

In a recent study, Garland, Carlson, Cook, Lansdell, and Speca (2007) assessed posttraumatic growth and spirituality in 60 MBSR class participants with mixed cancer diagnoses an average of about 1½ years since diagnosis, before and after program participation. Stress-specific symptoms and mood disturbance were also assessed. Participants' scores on the spirituality measure and posttraumatic growth improved significantly over time, as did symptoms of stress and mood disturbance, depression, and anger. Compared with a nonrandomized comparison group of patients who were participating in a creative arts therapy class, improvements were greater in MBSR on spirituality, anxiety, anger, stress reduction, and mood symptoms.

To investigate the phenomenon of enhanced spirituality and posttraumatic growth in greater depth, researchers conducted qualitative interviews with a specific subgroup of MBSR participants (Mackenzie, Carlson, Munoz, & Speca, 2007). Nine cancer patients who had participated in the 8-week MBSR program and who continued to attend weekly drop-in MBSR sessions were interviewed for the study. Through qualitative grounded theory analysis, five major themes were identified: opening to change, self-control, shared experience, personal growth, and spirituality. This information was used to develop specific theory concerning mechanisms whereby MBSR effects change for cancer patients. In this theory the initial participation in the 8-week program is seen as only the beginning of an ongoing process of self-discovery, a slight shift in orientation that begins the growth process. At that time patients feel isolated, scared, and unsure of what to do in the face of a cancer diagnosis. The MBSR program helps to meet their needs for understanding they are not alone in their journey, teaches concrete tools for self-regulation, and introduces ways to look at the world they may not have previously considered. This results in benefits such as reduced stress symptoms and lower levels of mood disturbance.

As practice progresses in the drop-in group, social support deepens as relationships are further developed, and people begin to learn to be less reactive and exercise more diffuse self-regulation across a wider variety of life circumstances. Underlying this process is a theme of personal transformation, of feeling part of a larger whole. With this comes the development of positive qualities of personal growth and positive health, beyond merely the symptom reduction documented over the course of the initial program. A growing spirituality of finding meaning and purpose in one's life and feeling increasingly interconnected with others is part of this personal transformation. Even though the stance of the program was secular, participants described finding themselves feeling more connected with the larger universe and more spiritual. For example, one participant described his process of growth through meditation practice like this: "It's changed my outlook on life, my relationship to other people, and, most important, my relationship to myself." Qualities of gratitude, compassion, and equanimity may be the ultimate culmination of practice. Although this theory of the development of mindfulness practice is stated in linear terms, all of these processes likely occur simultaneously to varying degrees. Thus, the emphasis or importance of different aspects may oscillate depending on the life circumstances of each individual.

Conclusion

As this summary of research supports, mindfulness practice not only appears to decrease pathology but also can have profound effects on positive mental states and human development. With the emergence of the field of positive psychology and a host of new measures, research, and theoretical perspectives, the time is ripe to expand the focus of mindfulness from reducing symptomatology to exploring and cultivating positive mental states. The aim of positive psychology, according to Seligman and Csikszentmihalyi (2000), "is to begin to catalyze a change in the focus of psychology from preoccupation only with repairing the worst things in life to also building positive qualities" (p. 5). This aim of cultivating positive qualities, including wisdom, compassion, and virtue, is at the heart of the original intentions of mindfulness. Mindfulness offers practices that cultivate exceptional states of mental well-being and attentional control systematically developed for 2,500 years. In this way, an integrative and collaborative exploration of mindfulness may provide positive psychology with a new set of applied practices (see current research by Barbara Fredrickson, 2008, as an example) as well as help the field examine and reevaluate the current definition of "normal" and expand Western psychology's concept of mental health.

Further exploration and collaboration between the two fields are needed. This venture involves not merely building on the foundation of previous work but actually expanding this foundation and developing a new paradigm. Future work must reevaluate the lens through which mental health and well-being are viewed, and researchers must become interested in investigating the further reaches of human potential. A mindful psychology offers an opportunity to approach psychological health and well-being from a new paradigm, a new way of seeing. It is an invitation to awe.

Future Directions 10

We shall not cease from exploration
And the end of all our exploring
Will be to arrive where we started
And know the place for the first time.

—*T.S. Eliot* ("Little Gidding," 1943, p. 49)

Earlier chapters investigated the definition of mindfulness and its applications to psychotherapy and clinical training. In addition, we reviewed the body of research examining the effects of mindfulness-based interventions across diverse populations and discussed potential mechanisms of action. Finally, we explored an expanding paradigm of health, highlighting the applications of mindfulness for professional self-care as well as for cultivating positive psychological states. Within all of these areas are fruitful avenues for further exploration. In this chapter, we highlight specific suggestions under the broader topics of (a) defining and assessing mindfulness, (b) applying mindfulness to clinical research and practice, and (c) expanding the paradigm.

Defining and Assessing Mindfulness

One of the most salient issues in mindfulness research is how to operationally define it in a meaningfully quantifiable and consensual way. Several attempts have been made to develop a coherent, precise definition that could be agreed on by a large number of scholars and clinicians (Baer & Krietemeyer, 2006; Bishop et al., 2004; Brown & Ryan, 2003; S. L. Shapiro, Carlson, Astin, & Freedman, 2006). For example, Brown and Ryan (2003), in the development of the Mindful Attention Awareness Scale (MAAS), defined mindfulness as "the presence or absence of attention to and awareness of what is occurring in the present" (p. 824). They focused on the attentional component of mindfulness rather than on the attitudinal components, making present-centered awareness the foundation. Hence, this definition encompasses only one element of the IAA (intention, attention, and attitude) definition: attention.

As another example, Bishop and colleagues published the results of a consensus conference that resulted in a definition of mindfulness with two components (Bishop et al., 2004). The first component involves the self-regulation of attention to maintain focus on immediate experience, which allows for increased recognition of mental events in the present moment. The second component involves adopting an orientation toward one's experiences in the present moment that is characterized by curiosity, openness, and acceptance. Hence, in this definition, two elements of the IAA model, attention and attitude, are incorporated.

Once a consensual definition is achieved, it will be important to develop valid and reliable measures that capture the multidimensional nature of mindfulness. The most widely researched measure is the MAAS, published in 2003 by Brown and Ryan (Brown, 2003). This measure is based both on the researchers' theoretical definition of mindfulness (noted earlier) and on empirical tests of scale performance designed to enhance stability, internal consistency, and predictive and concurrent validity. It is a short 15-item scale with all items loading on one factor, which predominantly measures attentional abilities in the present moment. The scale has proven useful in some mindfulness-based stress reduction (MBSR) trials, but it has been criticized for being unidimensional and not assessing the attitudinal component of mindfulness. In response, other measures such as the Kentucky Inventory of Mindfulness Skills (KIMS) have emerged (Baer & Krietemeyer, 2006). The theoretical basis of the 39-item KIMS stems primarily from dialectical behavior therapy (DBT). It includes four subscales—observing, describing, acting with awareness, and accepting without judgment—that measure the mindfulness skills taught in DBT (outlined in chap. 4, this volume).

Baer and colleagues (Baer, Smith, Hopkins, Krietemeyer, & Toney, 2006) recently combined all the existing measures of mindfulness (five measures with a combined total of 112 items) and administered them to groups of participants in an attempt to develop an integrated and multidimensional assessment tool. The researchers also included a wide variety of other measures including mood, emotional regulation, personality, acceptance, and self-compassion. The result was a new 39-item multidimensional questionnaire called the Five Facet Mindfulness Questionnaire (FFMQ) consisting of five elements: (a) observing (e.g., I notice the smells and aromas of things); (b) describing (e.g., I am good at finding words to describe my feelings); (c) acting with awareness (e.g., I find myself doing things without paying attention); (d) nonjudging of inner experience (e.g., I think some of my emotions are bad or inappropriate and I should not feel them); and (e) nonreactivity to inner experience (e.g., I perceive my feelings and emotions without having to react to them). This questionnaire promises to be useful to researchers wanting to understand relationships between training in mindfulness and more specific changes that may occur over time in these different elements of mindfulness.

The FFMQ can also be used to assess the mechanistic relationships between mindfulness training and improvements in psychological functioning, by specifying which of the five facets is most associated with specific improvements. Indeed, preliminary research with the tool found strong correlations between the facets and a range of psychological constructs as theoretically predicted, across both meditation-naive and experienced samples (Baer et al., 2006). For example, nonjudging was strongly negatively associated with neuroticism and thought suppression (so that people who were more nonjudgmental were also less neurotic and tried less to suppress difficult thoughts). Nonreactivity was most strongly associated with self-compassion, and acting with awareness was negatively correlated with absent-mindedness and dissociation. Describing was highly correlated with emotional intelligence and negatively associated with alexithymia, the lack of awareness of one's emotional experience. In an additional study, Baer et al. (2008) found that the three facets of describing, nonjudging, and nonreactivity mediated the relationship between meditation practice and overall psychological well-being in a sample of experienced meditators. A limitation of scales such as the FFMQ is their length and associated participant burden to complete them. Depending on the needs of the researchers and the level of detail with which they want to investigate elements of mindfulness, shorter individual scales may be more useful.

All of the measures noted earlier have focused on self-report methods. However, self-report measures have significant limitations, and future research will benefit from incorporating multiple methods of assessment. Behavioral observations, proxy reports, experience sampling, and neurological data may provide more objective assessments of mindfulness. An ongoing study, the Cultivating Emotional Balance project, illustrates one example of incorporating a behavioral assessment of mindfulness. The intention of the study is to train teachers to be mindful in the classroom with students. One of the assessment measures is behavioral observation of teachers in the classroom as they interact with students. The challenge with this type of assessment is that rating scales describing which behaviors are considered to display mindfulness need to be developed and validated. A simpler method using proxy assessment would ask others in a person's environment how mindful they thought the target person was. It may be possible to adapt existing self-report scales to that purpose, although no such attempts have yet been published.

Another fruitful area for future research is to explore the measurement of mindfulness in the brain, using technology such as functional magnetic resonance imaging (fMRI) or positron emission tomography scanning. A pioneering example of this type of research was conducted by Cresswell and colleagues (Creswell, Way, Eisenberger, & Lieberman, 2007) wherein mindfulness was assessed using the MAAS scale in 27 healthy participants. Participants were then scanned by fMRI during a task in which they matched pictures of facial expressions to the corresponding affect being expressed. When affect was labeled, those who were more mindful on the MAAS showed greater prefrontal cortical and less amygdala activation, which suggests the cortex was suppressing emotional reactivity in the limbic system. The authors posited that mindfulness may act in the brain to reduce negative affect by enhancing prefrontal cortical regulation of affect. This type of study represents the tip of the iceberg in terms of understanding how mindfulness may work in neural structures to result in the types of changes documented in the growing body of clinical research discussed in chapters 5 and 6 (this volume).

Applications of Mindfulness to Clinical Research and Practice

We have considered the applications of mindfulness in psychotherapy, across three pathways: (a) the mindful therapist, (b) mindfulness-informed therapy, and (c) mindfulness-based therapy. There are numerous important future directions in the realm of each of these. Regarding the mindful therapist, further exploration is needed to explore the potential of mindfulness as a means for developing core clinical skills and to determine whether therapist mindfulness predicts patient outcome. For example, research is needed to replicate and extend preliminary evidence that mindfulness training increases attention and empathy in therapists in training, and further to document whether enhancement of these skills ultimately has an impact on patient symptomatology.

For example, multidimensional measures of mindfulness can assess therapist mindfulness, through therapist self-report, patient reports, and behavioral observation, to see whether therapist mindfulness is related to patient outcome. It will also be fruitful to build on the pioneering research by Grepmair and colleagues in Germany examining the effects of therapist mindfulness training on patient outcome across a broad range of measures, including self-report, behavioral observation, and clinician rating scales (Grepmair, Mitterlehner, Loew, Bachler, et al., 2007; Grepmair, Mitterlehner, Loew, & Nickel, 2007).

In addition to examining if therapist mindfulness affects patient outcome, second-order research examining the mechanisms through which these effects occur is needed. Through what pathways does mindfulness enhance clinical ability and patient outcome? For example, is it through augmenting the proposed common factor of the therapeutic relationship? Or is it a result of increased attentional skills or empathy on the part of the therapist? Once the process variables involved become clearer, it will be beneficial to explore questions such as How much mindfulness training does a therapist need? How can mindfulness training best be integrated into graduate curricula, professional development, and clinical health care systems? As an example, research could explore different forms of mindfulness training for clinicians to determine what is most effective in developing essential therapeutic skills. Recent interest has been sparked by Gregory Kramer's book *Insight Dialogue,* in which he describes a training process of bringing mindfulness into interpersonal dialogue (Kramer, 2007). This form of training combined with formal mindfulness practice may be more effective for training therapists than mindfulness meditation alone.

Another area of research is to examine the impact of mindfulness-informed therapy, which has received little attention, as the majority of research up to now has focused on mindfulness-based therapies. Because it is likely that mindfulness-informed therapy may ultimately represent the work of a larger number of therapists, it will be important to assess what impact the teachings, metaphors, and insights derived from Buddhism have on the therapeutic process without any introduction to formal mindfulness practice. Integrating specific mindfulness teachings without explicitly mentioning mindfulness or teaching meditation practice could be compared with therapy that includes *both* the specific teachings and the formal practice, and therapy that includes neither. An example of this type of research is currently under way in a randomized controlled trial examining the effects of MBSR versus a comparison group that includes the same workbook and didactic material but does not include any formal mindfulness practice (S. L. Shapiro, Ebert, Pisca, & Sherman, 2008).

A final direction regarding the applications of mindfulness to psychotherapy falls under the heading of mindfulness-based therapies. There are numerous avenues for future exploration, including the continued development of integrative mindfulness-based therapies, such as mindfulness-based treatment for insomnia (Ong, Shapiro, & Manber, 2008) as well as the continued movement toward empirically validating already established programs (e.g., MBSR, mindfulness-based cognitive therapy). Another direction will be to determine teacher qualifications and what level of training is important to achieve successful treatment.

Education and Parenting

There is also growing interest in the integration of mindfulness into the realms of education and parenting. For example, academia is becoming increasingly interested in the benefits meditation may provide students beyond stress reduction, and has begun to explore the possible integration of meditation into the curriculum in an attempt to enhance engagement and understanding of subject matter as well as specific skills fundamental to the learning process, such as concentration, attention, and open-mindedness (S. L. Shapiro, Brown, & Astin, 2008). At the University of Michigan School of Music, students can receive a bachelor's degree in a program called "Jazz and Contemplative Studies," which emphasizes meditation; at Brown University, a religious-studies course includes meditation "labs" as part of the curriculum (Gravois, 2005); at Santa Clara University, a counseling psychology graduate program integrates meditation into the curriculum in an effort to enhance the development of essential therapy skills such as empathy and presence (S. L. Shapiro & Izett, 2008); and Brown University has developed a Contemplative Studies Initiative spearheaded by about 20 faculty members who are in the process of establishing an undergraduate concentration in contemplative studies that will coordinate students' academic and personal studies in these areas (Roth, 2006). Preliminary research suggests the integration of mindfulness into education can be extraordinarily beneficial in terms of both student well-being and academic performance (for a review, see S. L. Shapiro, Brown, & Astin, 2008).

In addition, researchers have become interested in training teachers in mindfulness and emotional balance. The Cultivating Emotional Balance project, under way since 2002 as a direct response to encouragement from the Dalai Lama, has integrated mindfulness training and lessons in emotional intelligence for secondary school teachers in the San Francisco community. The training's purpose is to reduce emotional responses that are destructive to self and others and enhance compassion and empathy. The curriculum incorporates seven components: (a) meditation training for mindfulness of body, feelings, mental states, and mental contents; (b) empathy skills training; (c) strategies to counteract destructive thought patterns and negative emotions; (d) working with stressful situations; (e) training in visual recognition of emotions; (f) body movement practices; and (g) working with awareness in daily life. The program is in the process of being extensively evaluated, but no results have been published to date. We believe that this area of mindfulness in education will expand significantly over the next decade as evidence of its importance and efficacy in the schools continues to mount.

Mindful parenting is another clinical realm that has garnered significant interest. At the earliest stages of parenting, there has been significant interest in mindfulness training during pregnancy, as a way to reduce the damaging effects of prenatal stress to the developing infant. One review of a range of mind–body interventions during pregnancy documented outcomes such as higher birth weight, shorter length of labor, fewer instrument-assisted births, and reduced perceived stress and anxiety (Beddoe & Lee, 2008). A specific mindfulness-based intervention for pregnant parents, called mindfulness childbirth and parenting (MBCP), developed by Nancy Barnacke, teaches MBSR skills to support the greater health and well-being of expectant parents and their developing infant in pregnancy. Research into the efficacy of the MBCP program is currently under way at the University of California, San Francisco.

After birth, mindful parenting is an area ripe for clinical interventions and research. An organization called The Mindful Parent describes mindful parenting as "a contemplative practice through which our connection to our child, and awareness of our child's presence, helps us to become better grounded in the present moment" (The Mindful Parent, 2008). They offer workshops and seminars and produce a mindful parenting newsletter, drawing from Jon Kabat-Zinn and his wife Myla's book *Everyday Blessings: The Inner Work of Mindful Parenting* (M. Kabat-Zinn & Kabat-Zinn, 1998). Another recent book, *Mindful Parenting: Meditations, Verses, and Visualizations for a More Joyful Life* by Scott Rogers (S. Rogers, 2006), presents meditation techniques designed to expand present-moment awareness and bring about feelings of joyfulness through a deepening awareness of a reader's connection to his or her child.

Preliminary research examining the effects of MBSR for parents has been quite promising. For example, a recent study found that parents caring for chronically ill children benefited significantly from an MBSR intervention, decreasing levels of stress and mood disturbance (Minor, Carlson, Mackenzie, Zernicke, & Jones, 2006). Further, a mindfulness-based intervention, the Mindful Parenting Program, was developed to improve parenting after divorce by enhancing awareness and intentionality in responding to children's needs. Preliminary results from a pre–post pilot study demonstrated significant increases in parent mindfulness but no changes in parent–child interactions (Altmaier & Maloney, 2007).

Two case series by Singh and colleagues investigated the potential for mindfulness training to help parents coping with children who had autism (Singh et al., 2006) and developmental disabilities (Singh, Lancioni, Winton, Adkins, et al., 2007; Singh, Lancioni, Winton, Singh, et al., 2007). The training in each case involved 12 individual sessions covering the philosophy and practice of mindfulness plus reading the book *Everyday Blessings*. Mindfulness exercises were given for parents to apply in their interactions with their child. In the first study, three parents were trained in the program and outcomes assessed with a battery of both objective and subjective measures. Mothers' ratings of their mindful parenting were associated with decreases in their children's aggression, noncompliant behavior, and self-injury as well as increases in mothers' satisfaction with their parenting skills and interactions with their children (Singh et al., 2006). Similarly, in a different sample of four parents of children who had developmental disabilities, parents reported decreases in aggressive behavior and increases in their children's social skills (Singh, Lancioni, Winton, Adkins, et al., 2007; Singh, Lancioni, Winton, Singh, et al., 2007). They also reported increased satisfaction with their parenting, more social interactions with their children, and lower parenting stress. In addition, the children showed increased positive social interactions with their siblings.

Research into the effects of joint child–parent mindfulness courses is also beginning. Saltzman and Goldin (2008) developed a mindfulness-based intervention for fourth through sixth graders and their parents, focusing on integrating mindfulness into daily family life. Parents and children met together during the 8-week course, except for the last 15 minutes, when parents had "adult discussion" and children played outside, drew pictures, or wrote poems. The curriculum included both formal and informal mindfulness practices, as well as in-class exercises to enhance awareness, verbal communication, and artistic expression. Further, parents were asked to choose mindful activities that involve their children for home practice. Results demonstrated significant changes pre- to post-intervention; parents and children who participated in the mindfulness course showed an increase in abilities to direct attention when faced with distracters as compared with those families in the wait-list group. In addition, participants in the MBSR group reported improvements in self-compassion and self-judgment. This research suggests that mindfulness intervention for parents and children can result in increased attention, emotion, and metacognitive processes (Saltzman & Goldin, 2008).

Although research in this area is still nascent, we believe it will see much growth in the future.

Mechanisms of Change

In addition to these broader areas, there are specific lines of inquiry that merit investigation. For example, future research must continue to investigate the mechanisms underlying the mindfulness-based interventions. There are two main methodologies for exploring what happens mechanistically during mindfulness-based interventions. The first is through statistical investigation of mediators and moderators of change; the second is through the conduct of dismantling studies. For example, a researcher may want to test the hypothesis that improvements on anxiety through MBSR are the result of time spent in formal practice. To test this using mediational analysis with the Baron and Kenny model (Baron & Kenny, 1986), a relationship first has to be established between MBSR participation and improvement on the outcome of interest, in this case, anxiety. To test if home practice mediates this effect, three conditions need to be met: (a) the initial variable (MBSR program attendance) is associated with the outcome (decreased anxiety); (b) the initial variable (MBSR program attendance) is correlated with the mediator variable (home practice); and (c) the mediator variable (home practice) affects the outcome variable (anxiety). This analysis is established by entering both the initial variable and mediator in a regression equation or structural equation model and showing that the mediator is correlated with the outcomes, after controlling for effects of the initial variable. The relationships between the initial variable and the outcome may be partially or fully mediated.

In contrast to mediation, a moderated effect occurs when the moderator variable completely changes the causal relationship between the initial variable (program attendance) and the outcome (anxiety symptoms). This is usually the case with fixed moderator variables such as age, gender, or ethnicity. A classic example is that an intervention (mindfulness training) may be moderated by gender (more effective for women than men). The main distinction between moderation and mediation is that mediation is an attempt to establish mechanisms by which one variable may be affecting another, whereas moderation is looking for differences in the relationship between group assignment and outcomes based on preexisting variables.

The second method to investigate mechanisms of change is through experimental design, not statistical analyses, as some statisticians believe that dismantling studies are the only true way to establish mechanisms of action. So if the same question of whether home practice is important for improving anxiety is to be investigated, a study design would be applied that varies the level of home practice as part of the independent variable, the intervention itself. There are many ways this could be done, but most obvious would be to assign differing amounts of homework in various groups of participants while keeping everything else about the groups the same. This type of study design was used by S. L. Shapiro, Ebert, Pisca, and Sherman (2008) as described earlier.

Also important is to determine the effects of practice; frequency and duration of mindfulness practice must be recorded (e.g., in daily practice journals) to determine if greater meditation induces greater effects and, if so, whether the relationship is linear, curvilinear, or some other more intricate pattern (S. L. Shapiro & Walsh, 2003). Another important area of further study is follow-up assessment. Given that mindfulness is defined as a skill that can be developed, there is potential for longitudinal or follow-up research to test the hypothesis that even stronger results may appear than those found immediately postintervention (e.g., Oman, Shapiro, Thoresen, Plante, & Flinders, 2008).

Expanding the Paradigm

Mindful Reminder: Remember your intentions as you began reading this book. What are your intentions for continuing along this journey of mindfulness in your professional and personal life?

Finally, the continued exploration of how mindfulness can help expand the paradigm of health and healing is essential. One potential avenue is to consider the effects of mindfulness on therapist well-being. Mindfulness supports the expansion of the health care paradigm to include the well-being of the clinician as an essential part of the system. As noted in chapter 8 (this volume), preliminary evidence suggests that mindfulness training can enhance self-care for the clinician. Future research could extend these preliminary studies by including follow-up assessments as well as matched or randomized comparison groups. In addition, creative ways of integrating mindfulness practice into already packed clinical workloads and graduate training curricula could be considered.

Another important area for future research is to continue to examine dimensions of positive growth and development, and to explore the further reaches of human potential that develop with sustained meditation practice. As Elenor Rosch (1999) aptly put it, "Yes, research on the meditation traditions can provide data to crunch from the old mind-set. But they have much more to offer, a new way of looking" (p. 224). We have the opportunity to explore the unique and extraordinary capacities reported in the traditional Buddhist texts with state-of-the-art methodologies, and preliminary work has begun to verify these claims (see S. L. Shapiro & Walsh, 2007). Along these lines, future research could benefit from the inclusion of long-term meditators, such as Tibetan yogis with more than 10,000 hours of meditation practice each, to help elucidate the profound effects on development and well-being that arise with intensive and continuous meditation practice (S. L. Shapiro & Walsh, 2003). In addition, positive psychological variables such as moral development, compassion, and wisdom could be included in rigorous, controlled trials.

We believe these avenues of study will be of great benefit, helping to shift the paradigm from a patient and pathology focus to one of healing, growth, and development for all beings, patient and clinician alike.

Conclusion

The potential applications of mindfulness to Western psychological theory, research, and practice are far reaching, and the fruits of such collaborations are already visible. Three decades of research demonstrate that mindfulness-based therapies have significant beneficial effects for a wide array of clinical populations. In addition, innovative clinical applications are under way with the development of new mindfulness-based interventions for specific patient populations. Further, and specifically related to the clinician, mindfulness practice offers systematic training for key therapist skills, as well as a means of maintaining therapist health and well-being.

Finally, mindfulness practice shows promise for cultivating positive psychological qualities previously given little attention by Western researchers. Mindfulness can help enlarge the field's paradigm of health and healing, deepen the intentions we aspire toward, and expand our vision of what is possible. The field of mindfulness is quite young, and the possibilities for its integration into Western psychology and health care are vast. In fact, mindfulness has been proposed as a new model of psychotherapy, "a mindfulness-oriented model of psychotherapy," which could provide a unifying paradigm for clinicians from many diverse theoretical orientations (Germer, Siegel, & Fulton, 2005). We are hopeful the continued exploration of the art and science of mindfulness will persist in weaving together theory, research, and practice, leading to an integrated and unified model of psychotherapy, and ultimately to greater health, happiness, and freedom for all beings.

As we conclude this volume, we reflect again on our intention that it may be of benefit in your life and in all the lives you touch. We recognize that any attempt to write about mindfulness in an intellectual way will ultimately fall short, and that perhaps the essence of this rich and beautiful path of awareness is best captured through metaphor and poetry. And so we leave the final words to Jelaluddin Rumi (Barks, 1997), in his poem "The Guesthouse" (p. 77):

> This being human is a guest house.
>
> Every morning a new arrival.
> A joy, a depression, a meanness,
> some momentary awareness comes
> as an unexpected visitor.
>
> Welcome and entertain them all!
> Even if they're a crowd of sorrows,
> who violently sweep your house
> empty of its furniture,
> still, treat each guest honorably.

He may be clearing you out
for some new delight.

The dark thought, the shame, the malice,
meet them at the door laughing,
and invite them in.
Be grateful for whoever comes,
because each has been sent
as a guide from beyond.

Appendix A: The Body Scan

The body scan meditation is usually practiced in a lying-down position on your back (referred to as *rest pose* or *corpse pose* in yoga traditions), with your legs extended, feet hip-width apart, and arms by your sides with palms facing up, if this open and receptive posture is comfortable for you. The ideal environment is a warm, safe, and quiet location that has minimal distractions; for example, be sure to turn off the ringer on your phone and remove pets from the room. The technique requires focusing your awareness slowly, deliberately, and systematically throughout the body, either from toe to head or head to toe, applying moment-by-moment awareness to whatever your experience of each body part is, including awareness of sensations, emotions, and associated thoughts about the body if they arise. The body scan should ideally be practiced daily over a period of weeks to hone your abilities to closely pay attention. The entire exercise can take 30 to 45 minutes, or it can be done more quickly depending on your needs and time frame.

Begin by forming a clear intention for this practice. The intention can be whatever feels true and authentic to you in this moment: "May I be with my body in a loving way," "May I cultivate greater mindfulness," or "May this practice be of benefit to all beings." Once you have an intention, silently repeat it to yourself, and then let it go, focusing your awareness on the breath. Feel the breath move in and out of the body. Ride the waves of your own breathing from moment to moment, non-judgmentally.

When you are in touch with the flow of the breath in the body, direct your attention to the toes of your left foot. Pay close attention to any sensations (or lack of sensations) in this area of your body. If possible, feel both the tops and nails of the toes and the pads of the toes. Try to remain aware of both your breathing and sensations from your toes at the same time. Sometimes it helps to imagine that each in-breath travels all the way down to your toes and each out-breath flows back up and out from your toes. Don't worry if you get distracted or have a hard time feeling anything at all in your toes; as soon as you notice your mind wandering, gently return focus to your toes, noticing without judgment whatever your experience of that area of your body may be.

Keep this focus for a minimum of 1 minute. When you feel ready, on an out-breath, purposefully let your awareness of the toes go, allowing them to either dissolve or float away, and move your attention to the bottom of the left foot, including the sensations of pressure in the heel touching the surface you are resting on. Bring your attention and breathing to this region in the same way you just did with your toes. Just try to be in touch with your body however you can without judging yourself; there is no right or wrong way to feel. When you are ready (after a minute or 2 on the bottom of the foot), move on to the top of your left foot—the bones, skin and tendons across the top of the foot, and joint of the ankle, as well, if you choose.

In this way, move slowly and systematically through every region of your body. The order of the scan can be as follows: The left ankle, lower leg, knee, thigh, hip. The toes of the right foot, bottom of the right foot and right heel, upper foot, ankle, lower leg, knee, thigh, hip. The whole pelvis, including both hips, the genitals, buttocks, and rectum. The lower back and abdomen. The upper back, rib cage, and chest. The shoulder blades and the shoulders. For each area, check in to see what sensations are available to your awareness, dwell with the sensations, and also notice any other experience as you pay attention to different body parts, such as holding, tension, or emotions and associations that may arise. Notice any tendencies to rush ahead or dwell longer on certain areas. When moving from each area, imagine with an out-breath releasing your focus and allowing that area to dissolve from awareness as you move on to the next.

From here, move on to the fingers and hands, doing left and right together, tuning in to the fingers, thumbs, palms, back of the hands where you feel the pressure from contact with the resting surface, wrists, forearms, elbows, upper arms and shoulders. You might try expanding your awareness from one region to the next as you move up the arms until it includes the entire length of both arms, from the fingers to the shoulders. Then let go of the whole of the arms on one out-breath. They may feel hollow, warm and heavy, or weightless as you release your awareness and move on to the head and neck.

Next, move on to the neck and throat. After breathing out and letting go of awareness of muscles around the front and back of the neck, move on to the head and face. In scanning the face, start with the jaw and chin, allowing the jaw to become slack and feeling the tongue touching the back of the lower teeth in the mouth, then let the awareness gradually spread out to include sensations from the lips, teeth and gums, roof of the mouth, tongue, back of the throat, cheeks, nose (feel the air moving in and out of the nostrils), ears (and hearing), eyes, eyelids, area around the eyes, eyebrows, forehead, temples, scalp, and the entire skull beneath the skin of the scalp.

Finally, dwell for some time at the very top of your head. Imagine you have a blowhole there, like a whale or a dolphin, through which you can draw air in and out. See if you can draw the air in through the blowhole and feel it travel through your entire body to the very bottoms of your feet, then out through the top of your head again as you exhale. Perhaps feel a warmth flow through your body as your entire body breathes as a whole system, feeling complete and content. Keep up this whole-body breathing for a few minutes, and then let go of the body altogether. See if you can just stay in the present moment with a sense of the breath flowing in and out but to no particular location.

At this point, allow yourself to let go of your focus on the breath and simply be awake to whatever may arise and predominate in your field of awareness moment by moment. This may include thoughts, feelings, sensations, sounds, breath, stillness, or silence. Just pay attention and try to be with whatever comes up in the same way you paid attention to your toes and other body parts during the scan. Practice simply seeing thoughts, impulses, sensations, feeling, and emotions as they arise, and then letting go, seeing them, letting go, seeing them, letting go, moment by moment, just lying here with nothing to do other than to be present, to be awake.

When it is time to end the body scan, notice the effects of the practice on your mind and body. Notice if you feel different then you did when you began. Perhaps make an intention to bring a piece of this awareness of your body with you into your daily life. Finally, thank yourself for taking this time and giving yourself this gift of awareness.

Appendix B: Sitting Meditation

B egin by setting an intention for this sitting practice. The intention can be whatever feels most true for you in this moment: for example, "May I bring kindness and curiosity to each moment," "May I have a beginner's mind," or "May this practice be of benefit for all beings." Once you have set your intention clearly, perhaps speaking it silently to yourself, you can gently let it go as you consciously focus your attention on your body sitting. Get a sense of your feet connected to the earth, contacting both legs, your seat, your spine, and torso. Become aware of your arms, your hands resting in your lap, your shoulders, neck, face. Sense the whole body sitting. Allow the mind to be spacious and the body to relax. You don't have to make anything happen.

And notice that you are breathing. Not trying to change the breath, but simply experiencing it. Keep your attention clearly focused on the sensations of each breath as it flows in and out of the body on its own. You may notice the breath most distinctly in one part of the body—for example, the rising and falling of the abdomen, or the in and out at the nostrils. See how carefully and continuously you can feel the sensations of the entire inhalation and exhalation.

And notice the rising and falling movement of the abdomen, or the in and out of the air at the nostrils. Let the awareness be accepting and open, not trying to control the breath but simply letting it come and go in its own rhythm. Feel the sensations of each breath completely, not thinking about them but actually feeling what is here in each moment.

At times the breath will be strong and clear; sometimes it will be soft or indistinct. Simply notice what is. Is the breath long or short, rough or smooth? Be with the breath as it continually changes, feeling it, sensing it.

If while you are attending to the breath, sounds become predominant and call your attention away from the breathing, make a note of hearing. Attend to the experience of the sound, not trying to identify what's causing the sound, such as a "car" or "air conditioning" but just being with the vibration of hearing. When the hearing is no longer predominant, return to the breath.

If physical sensations in the body, emotions, or thoughts call your attention away from the breath, shift your focus to the sensation, emotion, or thought itself. Carefully and gently explore the nature of the experience. Notice what happens as you attend to it: Does it become stronger, weaker? Does it dissolve or intensify?

And once you have noted your experience, return to the breath, using the breath as an anchor, helping you return again and again to the present moment. Gently note where your mind is pulled, and then return again to the breath. The continuity of attention and of mental noting strengthens the mindfulness and concentration. When you drift and forget your focus, when the mind wanders, simply make note of "wandering" as soon as you're aware of it and gently come back to your breathing.

Keep the awareness simple, and remain grounded in the experience of breathing. Notice what calls your attention away from the breath, and then gently return, over and over again.

And when it is time for the sitting meditation to come to a close, notice how your mind, body, and heart feel. Thank yourself for taking this time to cultivate greater awareness, kindness, and insight. Perhaps make an intention to bring this mindfulness with you into your daily life. As you gently allow light to come back in through your eyes, and movement to begin in the body, see whether you can continue your mindful awareness moment by moment.

Appendix C: Walking Meditation

Meditation can be practiced in any posture, including sitting, standing, lying down, and walking. Walking meditation involves mindfully noting sensations in the body while standing and walking. It is an opportunity to intentionally train the mind to pay attention in an open, curious, and nonjudgmental way, through attending to the process of walking.

To begin a period of walking meditation, it is helpful to find a quiet place, 10 to 20 feet in length, in which to walk back and forth. It is important to remember that you are not trying to get somewhere, or to walk for exercise; you are walking to develop mindfulness. It is helpful to first make an intention for the walking period, consciously reflecting on why you are practicing in the first place. Once your intention is clear, let it fall to the background of your awareness, and focus your attention on the sensations of standing, aware of your weight, the sensations in the feet, attending to all of the subtle movements and shifting that are in play to maintain balance.

When you are ready, begin to slowly walk to the end of the path, keeping your attention on the experience of walking. You can mentally note "lifting," "stepping," "placing" as you actually experience each of these movements. Once you have reached the end of your path, pause, reestablish the body in standing, and reconnect with your breathing.

When you are ready, turn and begin to slowly walk back along the path. You can repeat this pacing back and forth a number of times for 15 to 30 minutes. If at any time during the walking meditation you notice your mind has wandered off, simply note "thinking" and then reestablish your attention on the physical sensations and movement of walking. Also continually check in with the quality of your attention; is it becoming tense and rigid, or are you able to keep it soft, fluid, and open? When you have completed the walking period, once again reflect on your intention, and thank yourself for taking this time to cultivate mindfulness.

Appendix D: Supplemental Resources

Books: Mindfulness and Psychotherapy

Aronson, H. B. (2004). *Buddhist practice on western ground: Reconciling eastern ideals and western psychology.* Boston: Shambhala.

Brantley, J. (2007). *Calming your anxious mind: How mindfulness and compassion can free you from anxiety, fear, and panic* (2nd ed.). Oakland, CA: New Harbinger.

Epstein, M. (2004). *Thoughts without a thinker: Psychotherapy from a Buddhist perspective.* New York: Perseus Publishing.

Germer, C., Siegel, R., & Fulton, P. (2005). *Mindfulness and psychotherapy.* New York: Guilford Press.

Hayes, S., Follette, V., & Linehan, M. (Eds.). (2004). *Mindfulness and acceptance: Expanding the cognitive–behavioral tradition.* New York: Guilford Press.

Kabat-Zinn, J. (1990). *Full catastrophe living: Using the wisdom of your body and mind to face stress, pain, and illness.* New York: Delacorte Press.

Kornfield, J. (2008). *The wise heart: A guide to the universal teachings of Buddhist psychology.* New York: Bantam Books.

Segal, Z., William, M., & Teasdale, J. (2001). *Mindfulness-based cognitive therapy for depression: A new approach to preventing relapse.* New York: Guilford Press.

Shapiro, D. H., & Astin, J. (1998). *Control therapy: An integrated approach to psychotherapy, health, and healing.* New York: Wiley.

Walsh, R., & Vaughan, F. (Eds.). (1993). *Paths beyond ego.* Los Angeles: Tarcher.

Books: Meditation Practice

Goldstein, J., & Kornfield, J. (2001). *Seeking the heart of wisdom: The path of insight meditation.* Boston: Shambhala.

Gunaratana, H. (2002). M*indfulness in plain English* (2nd ed.). Boston: Wisdom.

Hanh, T. N. (1999). *The miracle of mindfulness* (2nd ed.). Boston: Beacon Press.

Kabat-Zinn, J. (2005). *Wherever you go, there you are: Mindfulness meditation in everyday life* (10th ed.). New York: Hyperion.

Kornfield, J. (1994). *A path with heart: A guide through the perils and promises of spiritual life.* New York: Bantam Books.

Salzberg, S., & Kabat-Zinn, J. (2008). *Lovingkindness: The revolutionary art of happiness.* Boston: Shambhala.

Thera, N. (1973). *The heart of Buddhist meditation: Satipatthna: A handbook of mental training based on the Buddha's way of mindfulness.* New York: Weiser Books.

Web Sites: Mindfulness

Calgary MBSR Interest Group: http://www.mindfulnesscalgary.ca

Center for Contemplative Mind in Society: http://www.contemplative mind.org

Center for Mindfulness in Medicine, Health Care, and Society: http://www.umassmed.edu/cfm

Centre for Mindfulness Research and Practice: http://www.bangor.ac.uk/mindfulness

Healing and the Mind, Bill Moyers's documentary of an MBSR program: http://www.ambrosevideo.com

Institute for Meditation and Psychotherapy: http://www.meditationandpsychotherapy.org

Journal for Mindfulness Practitioners: http://www.inquiringmind.com

Mind & Life Institute: http://www.mindandlife.org

Mindful Awareness Research Center at the University of California, Los Angeles: http://www.marc.ucla.edu

Web Sites: Clinical Applications of Mindfulness

Acceptance and commitment therapy: http://www.www.contextualpsychology.org

Addictive Behaviors Research Center: http://depts.washington.edu/abrc/meditation.htm

Center for Mindful Eating: http://www.tcme.org

Dialectical behavior therapy: http://www.behavioraltech.com

Mindfulness-based cognitive therapy: http://www.mrc-cbu.cam.ac.uk/Research/cognition-emotion/researchtopics/mindfulness.shtml

Mindfulness-based symptom management: http://www.ottawamindfulnessclinic.com

Social anxiety and mindfulness: http://www.shyness.com

Web Sites: Buddhist Meditation

Dharma Seed: http://www.dharmaseed.org

Insight Meditation Community of Washington: http://www.imcw.org

Insight Meditation Society: http://www.dharma.org/ims

Spirit Rock Meditation Center: http://www.spiritrock.org

References

Abercrombie, P. D., Zamora, A., & Korn, A. P. (2007). Lessons learned: Providing a mindfulness-based stress reduction program for low-income multiethnic women with abnormal pap smears. *Holistic Nursing Practice, 21,* 26–34.

Altmaier, E., & Maloney, R. (2007). An initial evaluation of a mindful parenting program. *Journal of Clinical Psychology, 63,* 1231–1238.

Anderson, D. T. (2005). Empathy, psychotherapy integration, and meditation: A Buddhist contribution to the common factors movement. *Journal of Humanistic Psychology, 45,* 483–502.

Angutta Nikaya: Volume 1. (n.d.). P.T.S. Ed.

Arkowitz, H. (2002). Toward an integrative perspective on resistance to change. *Psychotherapy in Practice, 58,* 219–227.

Arkowitz, H., & Mannon, B. (2002). A cognitive–behavioral assimilative integration. In F. Kaslow & J. Lebow (Eds.), *Comprehensive handbook of psychotherapy* (pp. 317–337). New York: Wiley.

Arvay, M. J., & Uhlemann, M. R. (1996). Counsellor stress in the field of trauma: A preliminary study. *Canadian Journal of Counselling, 30,* 193–210.

Astin, J. A. (1997). Stress reduction through mindfulness meditation. Effects on psychological symptomatology, sense of control, and spiritual experiences. *Psychotherapy & Psychosomatics, 66,* 97–106.

Astin, J. A., Berman, B. M., Bausell, B., Lee, W. L., Hochberg, M., & Forys, K. L. (2003). The efficacy of mindfulness meditation plus qigong movement therapy in the treatment of fibromyalgia: A randomized controlled trial. *Journal of Rheumatology, 30,* 2257–2262.

Baer, R. A. (2003). Mindfulness training as clinical intervention: A conceptual and empirical review. *Clinical Psychology: Science and Practice, 10,* 125–143.

Baer, R. A., & Krietemeyer, J. (2006). Overview of mindfulness- and acceptance-based treatment approaches. In R. A. Baer (Ed.), *Mindfulness-based treatment approaches: Clinician's guide to evidence base and applications* (pp. 3–27). London: Academic Press.

Baer, R. A., Smith, G. T., Hopkins, J., Krietemeyer, J., & Toney, L. (2006). Using self-report assessment methods to explore facets of mindfulness. *Assessment, 13,* 27–45.

Baer, R. A., Smith, G. T., Lykins, E., Button, D., Krietemeyer, J., Sauer, S., et al. (2008). Construct validity of the five facet mindfulness questionnaire in meditating and nonmeditating samples. *Assessment, 15*(3), 329–342.

Barlow, D. H., & Craske, M. G. (2000). *Mastery of your anxiety and panic* (3rd ed.). San Antonio, TX: Harcourt Brace.

Baron, R. M., & Kenny, D. A. (1986). The moderator–mediator variable distinction in social psychological research: Conceptual, strategic and statistical considerations. *Journal of Personality and Social Psychology, 51,* 1173–1182.

Bateson, G., Jackson, D., Haley, J., & Weakland, J. (1956). Toward a theory of schizophrenia. *Behavioral Science, 1,* 251–264.

Bauer-Wu, S. M., & Rosenbaum, E. (2004). Facing the challenges of stem cell/bone marrow transplantation with mindfulness meditation: A pilot study. *Psycho-Oncology, 13,* S10–S11.

Beddoe, A. E., & Lee, K. A. (2008). Mind-body interventions during pregnancy. *Journal of Obstetric, Gynecologic, & Neonatal Nursing, 37,* 165–175.

Beddoe, A. E., & Murphy, S. O. (2004). Does mindfulness decrease stress and foster empathy among nursing students? *Journal of Nursing Education, 43,* 305–312.

Bien, T. (2006). *Mindful therapy: A guide for therapists and helping professionals.* Boston: Wisdom.

Baer (Ed.), *Mindfulness-based treatment approaches: Clinician's guide to evidence base and applications* (pp. 309–331). Amsterdam: Elsevier.

Carson, J. W., Keefe, F. J., Lynch, T. R., Carson, K. M., Goli, V., Fras, A. M., et al. (2005). Loving-kindness meditation for chronic low back pain: Results from a pilot trial. *Journal of Holistic Nursing, 23,* 287–304.

Cartwright-Hatton, S., & Wells, A. (1997). Beliefs about worry and intrusions: The meta-cognitions questionnaire and its correlates. *Journal of Anxiety Disorders, 11,* 279–296.

Cash, E. (2008, March 12). *Dharma talk.* Woodacre, CA: Spirit Rock Meditation Center.

Christopher, J. C., Christopher, S. E., Dunnagan, T., & Schure, M. (2006). Teaching self-care through mindfulness practices: The application of yoga, meditation, and qigong to counselor training. *Journal of Humanistic Psychology, 46,* 494–509.

Cohen-Katz, J., Wiley, S., Capuano, T., Baker, D. M., Deitrick, L., & Shapiro, S. (2005). The effects of mindfulness-based stress reduction on nurse stress and burnout: A qualitative and quantitative study, part III. *Holistic Nursing Practice, 19,* 78–86.

Cohen-Katz, J., Wiley, S. D., Capuano, T., Baker, D. M., & Shapiro, S. (2004). The effects of mindfulness-based stress reduction on nurse stress and burnout: A quantitative and qualitative study. *Holistic Nursing Practice, 18,* 302–308.

Cohen-Katz, J., Wiley, S. D., Capuano, T., Baker, D. M., & Shapiro, S. (2005). The effects of mindfulness-based stress reduction on nurse stress and burnout, part II: A quantitative and qualitative study. *Holistic Nursing Practice, 19,* 26–35.

Coppenhall, K. (1995). The stresses of working with clients who have been sexually abused. In W. Dryden (Ed.), *The stresses of counseling in action* (pp. 28–43). Thousand Oaks, CA: Sage.

Coster, J. S., & Schwebel, M. (1997). Well-functioning in professional psychologists. *Professional Psychology: Research and Practice, 28,* 5–13.

Cozolino, L. (2004). *The making of a therapist: A practical guide for the inner journey.* New York: Norton.

Creswell, J. D., Way, B. M., Eisenberger, N. I., & Lieberman, M. D. (2007). Neural correlates of dispositional mindfulness during affect labeling. *Psychosomatic Medicine, 69,* 560–565.

Cullen, M. (2006). Mindfulness: The heart of Buddhist meditation? A conversation with Jan Chozen Bays, Joseph Goldstein, Jon Kabat-

Zinn, and Alan Wallace. *Inquiring Mind: A Semiannual Journal of the Vipassana Community, 22*(2), 4–7.

Curiati, J. A., Bocchi, E., Freire, J. O., Arantes, A. C., Braga, M., Garcia, Y., et al. (2005). Meditation reduces sympathetic activation and improves the quality of life in elderly patients with optimally treated heart failure: A prospective randomized study. *Journal of Alternative and Complementary Medicine, 11,* 465–472.

Daley, D. C., & Marlatt, G. A. (1997). Relapse prevention: Cognitive and behavioral interventions. In J. Lowinson, P. Ruiz, R. B. Millman, & J. Langrod (Eds.), *Substance abuse: A comprehensive textbook* (3rd ed., pp. 458–466). Baltimore, MD: Williams & Wilkins.

Davidson, R. J., Kabat-Zinn, J., Schumacher, J., Rosenkranz, M., Muller, D., Santorelli, S. F., et al. (2003). Alterations in brain and immune function produced by mindfulness meditation [comment]. *Psychosomatic Medicine, 65,* 564–570.

Davis, L. W., Strasburger, A. M., & Brown, L. F. (2007). Mindfulness: An intervention for anxiety in schizophrenia. *Journal of Psychosocial Nursing and Mental Health Services, 45*(11), 23–29.

Deikman, A. J. (1982). *The observing self.* Boston: Beacon Press.

DeRubeis, R. J., Bortman, M. A., & Gibbons, C. J. (2005). A conceptual and methodological analysis of the nonspecifics argument. *Clinical Psychology: Science and Practice, 12,* 174–183.

di Pellegrino, G., Fadiga, L., Fogassi, L., Gallese, V., & Rizzolatti, G. (1992). Understanding motor events: A neurophysiological study. *Experimental Brain Research, 91,* 176–180.

Diebold, J. C. (2003). *Mindfulness in the machine: A mindfulness-based cognitive therapy for the reduction of driving anger.* Unpublished manuscript, Hofstra University, Hempstead, NY.

Ditto, B., Eclache, M., & Goldman, N. (2006). Short-term autonomic and cardiovascular effects of mindfulness body scan meditation. *Annals of Behavioral Medicine, 32,* 227–234.

Dobkin, P. L. (2008). Mindfulness-based stress reduction: What processes are at work? *Complementary Therapies in Clinical Practice, 14,* 8–16.

Elliot, T. S. (1943). *Four quartets.* Orlando, FL: Harcourt Inc.

Enochs, W. K., & Etzbach, C. A. (2004). Impaired student counselors: Ethical and legal considerations for the family. *The Family Journal, 12,* 396–400.

Epstein, M. (2004). *Thoughts without a thinker: Psychotherapy from a Buddhist perspective.* New York: Perseus Book Group.

Evans, S., Ferrando, S., Findler, M., Stowell, C., Smart, C., & Haglin, D. (in press). Mindfulness-based cognitive therapy for generalized anxiety disorder. *Journal of Anxiety Disorders.*

Farb, N., Segal, Z. V., Mayberg, H., Bean, J., McKeon, D., Fatima, Z., et al. (2007). Attending to the present: Mindfulness meditation reveals distinct neural modes of self-reference. *Social Cognitive and Affective Neuroscience, 2,* 313–322.

Fehr, T. G. (2006). Transcendental meditation may prevent partial epilepsy. *Medical Hypotheses, 67,* 1462–1463.

Figley, C. R. (2002). Compassion fatigue: Psychotherapists' chronic lack of self care. *Journal of Clinical Psychology, 58*(11, Suppl. 1), 1433–1441.

Finucane, A., & Mercer, S. W. (2006). An exploratory mixed methods study of the acceptability and effectiveness of mindfulness-based cognitive therapy for patients with active depression and anxiety in primary care. *BMC Psychiatry, 6*(14).

Fowler, J. (1995). *Stages of faith: The psychology of human development and the quest for meaning.* San Francisco: HarperOne.

Fredrickson, B. (2001). The role of positive emotions in positive psychology. *American Psychologist, 56*(3), 218–226.

Fredrickson, B. L., Cohn, M. A., Coffey, K. A., Pek, J., & Finkel, S. M. (2008). Open hearts build lives: Positive emotions, induced through loving-kindness meditation, build consequential personal resources. *Journal of Personal and Social Psychology, 95,* 1045–1062.

Freedman, B. (2009). *Rescuing the future.* Unpublished manuscript.

Fresco, D. M., Moore, M. T., van Dulmen, M., Segal, Z. V., Ma, H., Teasdale, J. D., et al. (2007). Initial psychometric properties of the experiences questionnaire: Validation of a self-report measure of decentering. *Behavior Therapy, 38,* 234–246.

Garland, S. N., Carlson, L. E., Cook, S., Lansdell, L., & Speca, M. (2007). A non-randomized comparison of mindfulness-based stress reduction and healing arts programs for facilitating post-traumatic growth and spirituality in cancer outpatients. *Supportive Care in Cancer, 15,* 949–961.

Germer, C. K., Siegel, R. D., & Fulton, P. R. (Eds.). (2005). *Mindfulness and psychotherapy.* New York: Guilford Press.

Gifford, E. V., Kohlenberg, B. S., Hayes, S. C., Antonuccio, D. O., Piasecki, M. M., Rasmussen-Hall, M. L., et al. (2004). Acceptance-based treatment for smoking cessation. *Behavior Therapy, 35,* 689–705.

Gilbert, P. (2005). *Compassion: Conceptualisations, research and use in psychotherapy.* London: Routledge.

Gill, J. (1980). Burnout: A growing threat in ministry. *Human Development, 1*, 21–27.

Goddard, D. (1994). *A Buddhist bible.* Boston: Beacon Press.

Goldenberg, D. L., Kaplin, K. H., Nadeau, M. G., Brodeur, C., Smith, S., & Schmid, C. H. (1994). A controlled study of a stress-reduction, cognitive–behavioral treatment program in fibromyalgia. *Journal of Musculoskeletal Pain, 2*, 53–66.

Goldstein, T. R., Axelson, D. A., Birmaher, B., & Brent, D. A. (2007). Dialectical behavior therapy for adolescents with bipolar disorder: A 1-year open trial. *Journal of the American Academy of Child and Adolescent Psychiatry, 46*, 820–830.

Goleman, D. (1971). Meditation as meta-therapy. Hypothesis toward a proposed fifth state of consciousness. *Journal of Transpersonal Psychology, 3*(1), 1–25.

Goleman, D. (1980). A map for inner space. In R. N. Walsh & F. Vaughan (Eds.), *Beyond ego* (pp. 141–150). Los Angeles: Tarcher.

Goleman, D. (2003). *Destructive emotions: A scientific dialogue with the Dalai Lama.* New York: Bantam Books.

Goleman, D. (2006). *Emotional intelligence: Why it can matter more than IQ* (10th ed.). New York: Bantam Books.

Gratz, K. L., & Gunderson, J. G. (2006). Preliminary data on an acceptance-based emotion regulation group intervention for deliberate self-harm among women with borderline personality disorder. *Behavior Therapy, 37*, 25–35.

Gravois, J. (2005). Meditate on it. *The Chronicle of Higher Education, 52*(9), A10–A12.

Gregg, J. A., Callaghan, G. M., Hayes, S. C., & Glenn-Lawson, J. (2007). Improving diabetes self-management through acceptance, mindfulness, and values: A randomized controlled trial. *Journal of Consulting and Clinical Psychology, 75*, 336–343.

Grepmair, L., Mitterlehner, F., Loew, T., Bachler, E., Rother, W., & Nickel, M. (2007). Promoting mindfulness in psychotherapists in training influences the treatment results of their patients: A randomized, double-blind, controlled study. *Psychotherapy and Psychosomatics, 76*, 332–338.

Grepmair, L., Mitterlehner, F., Loew, T., & Nickel, M. (2007). Promotion of mindfulness in psychotherapists in training: Preliminary study. *European Psychiatry, 22*, 485–489.

Gross, C. R., Kreitzer, M. J., Russas, V., Treesak, C., Frazier, P. A., & Hertz, M. I. (2004). Mindfulness meditation to reduce symptoms after organ transplant: A pilot study. *Advances in Mind-Body Medicine, 20,* 20–29.

Grossman, P., Niemann, L., Schmidt, S., & Walach, H. (2004). Mindfulness-based stress reduction and health benefits. A meta-analysis. *Journal of Psychosomatic Research, 57,* 35–43.

Grossman, P., Tiefenthaler-Gilmer, U., Raysz, A., & Kesper, U. (2007). Mindfulness training as an intervention for fibromyalgia: Evidence of postintervention and 3-year follow-up benefits in well-being. *Psychotherapy and Psychosomatics, 76,* 226–233.

Guerrero, J. M., & Reiter, R. J. (2002). Melatonin-immune system relationships. *Current Topics in Medicinal Chemistry, 2,* 167–180.

Guy, J. D., Poelstra, P. L., & Stark, M. J. (1989). Personal distress and therapeutic effectiveness: National survey of psychologists practicing psychotherapy. *Professional Psychology: Research and Practice, 20,* 48–50.

Haimerl, C. J., & Valentine, E. (2001). The effect of contemplative practice on interpersonal, and transpersonal dimensions of the self-concept. *Journal of Transpersonal Psychology, 33*(1), 37–52.

Halbesleben, J., & Rathert, C. (2008). Linking physician burnout and patient outcomes: Exploring the dyadic relationship between physicians and patients. *Health Care Management Review, 33,* 29–39.

Hanh, T. N. (2000). *Path of emancipation: Talks from a 21-day mindfulness retreat.* Berkeley, CA: Parallax Press.

Hankin, V. M. (2008). *Mindfulness-based stress reduction in couples battling multiple sclerosis.* Paper presented at the 80th Annual Midwestern Psychological Association Meeting: Stress and Coping in Clinical & Health Psychology, Chicago, IL.

Harley, R., Sprich, S., Safren, S., Jacobo, M., & Fava, M. (2008). Adaptation of dialectical behavior therapy skills training group for treatment-resistant depression. *Journal of Nervous and Mental Disease, 196,* 136–143.

Hayes, S. C. (2002). Acceptance, mindfulness, and science. *Clinical Psychology: Science and Practice, 9,* 101–106.

Hayes, S. C. (2005, July 2). *Training.* Retrieved February 10, 2009, from Association for Contextual Behavioral Science Web site: http://www.contextualpsychology.org/act_training

Hayes, S. C., Strosahl, K., & Wilson, K. G. (1999). *Acceptance and commitment therapy.* New York: Guilford Press.

Hayes, S. C., Wilson, K. G., Gifford, E. V., Bissett, R., Piasecki, M., Batten, S. V., et al. (2004). A preliminary trial of twelve-step facilitation and acceptance and commitment therapy with polysubstance-abusing methadone-maintained opiate addicts. *Behavior Therapy, 35,* 667–688.

Hebert, J., Ebbeling, C., Olendzki, D., Hurley, T., Ma, Y., Saal, N., et al. (2001). Change in women's diet and body mass following intensive intervention for early-stage breast cancer. *Journal of the American Dietetic Association, 101,* 421–431.

Heidenreich, T., Tuin, I., Pflug, B., Michal, M., & Michalak, J. (2006). Mindfulness-based cognitive therapy for persistent insomnia: A pilot study. *Psychotherapy and Psychosomatics, 75,* 188–189.

Helgeson, V. S., Reynolds, K. A., & Tomich, P. L. (2006). A meta-analytic review of benefit finding and growth. *Journal of Consulting and Clinical Psychology, 74,* 797–816.

Henry, W. P., Schacht, T. E., & Strupp, H. H. (1990). Patient and therapist introject, interpersonal process, and differential psychotherapy outcome. *Journal of Consulting and Clinical Psychology, 58,* 768–774.

Horton-Deutsch, S., O'Haver Day, P., Haight, R., & Babin-Nelson, M. (2007). Enhancing mental health services to bone marrow transplant recipients through a mindfulness-based therapeutic intervention. *Complementary Therapies in Clinical Practice, 13,* 110–115.

Jain, S., Shapiro, S. L., Swanick, S., Roesch, S. C., Mills, P. J., Bell, I., et al. (2007). A randomized controlled trial of mindfulness meditation versus relaxation training: Effects on distress, positive states of mind, rumination, and distraction. *Annals of Behavioral Medicine, 33,* 11–21.

Jaseja, H. (2006a). A brief study of a possible relation of epilepsy association with meditation. *Medical Hypotheses, 66,* 1036–1037.

Jaseja, H. (2006b). Meditation potentially capable of increasing susceptibility to epilepsy—a follow-up hypothesis. *Medical Hypotheses, 66,* 925–928.

Jaseja, H. (2007). Meditation and epilepsy: The ongoing debate. *Medical Hypotheses, 68,* 916–917.

Jayadevappa, R., Johnson, J. C., Bloom, B. S., Nidich, S., Desai, S., Chhatre, S., et al. (2007). Effectiveness of transcendental meditation on functional capacity and quality of life of African Americans with congestive heart failure: A randomized control study. *Ethnicity & Disease, 17,* 72–77.

Jha, A. P., Krompinger, J., & Baime, M. J. (2007). Mindfulness training modifies subsystems of attention. *Cognitive, Affective & Behavioral Neuroscience, 7,* 109–119.

Johanson, G. (2006). A survey of the use of mindfulness in psychotherapy. *Annals of the American Psychotherapy Association, 9*(2), 15–24.

Kabat-Zinn, J. (1982). An outpatient program in behavioral medicine for chronic pain patients based on the practice of mindfulness meditation: Theoretical considerations and preliminary results. *General Hospital Psychiatry, 4,* 33–47.

Kabat-Zinn, J. (1990). *Full catastrophe living: Using the wisdom of your body and mind to face stress, pain and illness.* New York: Delacourt.

Kabat-Zinn, J. (2003). Mindfulness-based interventions in context: Past, present, and future. *Clinical Psychology: Science and Practice, 10,* 144–156.

Kabat-Zinn, J. (2005). *Coming to our senses.* New York: Hyperion.

Kabat-Zinn, J., Lipworth, L., & Burney, R. (1985). The clinical use of mindfulness meditation for the self-regulation of chronic pain. *Journal of Behavioral Medicine, 8,* 163–190.

Kabat-Zinn, J., Lipworth, L., Burney, R., & Sellers, W. (1987). Four-year follow-up of a meditation-based program for the self-regulation of chronic pain: Treatment outcomes and compliance. *The Clinical Journal of Pain, 2,* 159–173.

Kabat-Zinn, J., Massion, A. O., Kristeller, J., Peterson, L. G., Fletcher, K. E., Pbert, L., et al. (1992). Effectiveness of a meditation-based stress reduction program in the treatment of anxiety disorders. *The American Journal of Psychiatry, 149,* 936–943.

Kabat-Zinn, J., Wheeler, E., Light, T., Skillings, A., Scharf, M. J., Cropley, T. G., et al. (1998). Influence of a mindfulness meditation-based stress reduction intervention on rates of skin clearing in patients with moderate to severe psoriasis undergoing phototherapy (UVB) and photochemotherapy (PUVA). *Psychosomatic Medicine, 60,* 625–632.

Kabat-Zinn, M., & Kabat-Zinn, J. (1998). *Everyday blessings: The inner work of mindful parenting.* New York: Hyperion.

Kaplan, K. H., Goldenberg, D. L., & Galvin-Nadeau, M. (1993). The impact of a meditation-based stress reduction program on fibromyalgia. *General Hospital Psychiatry, 15,* 284–289.

Kegan, R. (1982). *The evolving self: Problem and process in human development.* Cambridge, MA: Harvard University Press.

Kenny, M. A., & Williams, J. M. (2007). Treatment-resistant depressed patients show a good response to mindfulness-based cognitive therapy. *Behaviour Research and Therapy, 45,* 617–625.

Kingston, J., Chadwick, P., Meron, D., & Skinner, T. C. (2007). A pilot randomized control trial investigating the effect of mindfulness practice on pain tolerance, psychological well-being, and physiological activity. *Journal of Psychosomatic Research, 62,* 297–300.

Kingston, T., Dooley, B., Bates, A., Lawlor, E., & Malone, K. (2007). Mindfulness-based cognitive therapy for residual depressive symptoms. *Psychology and Psychotherapy: Theory, Research and Practice, 80*(Pt. 2), 193–203.

Kinnell, G. (1993). Saint Francis and the sow. *Three books: Body rags: Mortal acts, Mortal words: The past.* New York: Houghton Mifflin.

Klein, G. (1996). The effect of acute stressors on decision making. In J. Driskell & E. Salas (Eds.), *Stress and human performance* (pp. 49–88). Hillsdale, NJ: Erlbaum.

Koerbel, L. S., & Zucker, D. M. (2007). The suitability of mindfulness-based stress reduction for chronic hepatitis C. *Journal of Holistic Nursing, 25,* 265–274.

Kohlberg, L. (1981). *Essays on moral development: Vol 1. The philosophy of moral development: Moral stages and the idea of justice.* New York: Harper & Row.

Koons, C. R., Robins, C. J., Tweed, J. L., Lynch, T. R., Gonzalez, A. M., Morse, J. Q., et al. (2001). Efficacy of dialectical behavior therapy in women veterans with borderline personality disorder. *Behavior Therapy, 32,* 371–390.

Kornfield, J. (2003, August 4). *Monday night dharma talk.* Woodacre, CA: Spirit Rock Meditation Center.

Kornfield, J. (2008). *The wise heart: A guide to the universal teachings of Buddhist psychology.* New York: Bantam Books.

Koszycki, D., Benger, M., Shlik, J., & Bradwejn, J. (2007). Randomized trial of a meditation-based stress reduction program and cognitive behavior therapy in generalized social anxiety disorder. *Behaviour Research and Therapy, 45,* 2518–2526.

Kramer, G. (2007). *Insight dialogue: The interpersonal path to freedom.* Boston: Shambhala.

Kreitzer, M. J., Gross, C. R., Ye, X., Russas, V., & Treesak, C. (2005). Longitudinal impact of mindfulness meditation on illness burden in solid-organ transplant recipients. *Progress in Transplantation, 15,* 166–172.

Kristeller, J. L., Baer, R. A., & Quillian-Wolever, R. (2006). Mindfulness-based approaches to eating disorders. In R. A. Baer (Ed.), *Mindfulness-*

based treatment approaches: Clinician's guide to evidence base and applications (pp. 75–91). London: Academic Press.

Kristeller, J., & Hallett, C. B. (1999). An exploratory study of a mediation-based intervention for binge eating disorder. *Journal of Health Psychology, 4*, 357–363.

Kross, E., Ayduk, O., & Mischel, W. (2005). When asking "Why" does not hurt. *Psychological Science, 16*, 709–715.

Kutz, I., Leserman, J., Dorrington, C., Morrison, C. H., Borysenko, J. Z., & Benson, H. (1985). Meditation as an adjunct to psychotherapy. An outcome study. *Psychotherapy and Psychosomatics, 43*, 209–218.

Lamanque, P., & Daneault, S. (2006). Does meditation improve the quality of life for patients living with cancer? [La meditation ameliore-t-elle la qualite de vie des patients vivant avec un cancer?] *Canadian Family Physician Medecin De Famille Canadien, 52*, 474–475.

Lambert, M. J. (1992). Psychotherapy outcome research; implications for integrative and eclectic theories. In J. C. Norcross & M. R. Goldfried (Eds.), *Handbook of psychotherapy integration* (pp. 94–129). New York: Basic Books.

Lambert, M. J. (2005). Early response in psychotherapy: Further evidence for the importance of common factors rather than "placebo effects." *Journal of Clinical Psychology, 61*, 855–869.

Lansky, E. P., & St. Louis, E. K. (2006). Transcendental meditation: A double-edged sword in epilepsy? *Epilepsy & Behavior, 9*, 394–400.

Lau, M. A., Segal, Z. V., & Williams, J. M. (2004). Teasdale's differential activation hypothesis: Implications for mechanisms of depressive relapse and suicidal behaviour. *Behaviour Research and Therapy, 42*, 1001–1017.

Lazar, S. W., Kerr, C. E., Wasserman, R. H., Gray, J. R., Greve, D. N., Treadway, M. T., et al. (2005). Meditation experience is associated with increased cortical thickness. *Neuroreport, 16*, 1893–1897.

Lee, J. (2006). *Mindfulness-based cognitive therapy for children: Feasibility, acceptability, and effectiveness of a controlled clinical trial.* Unpublished doctoral dissertation, Columbia University, New York.

Lee, S. H., Ahn, S. C., Lee, Y. J., Choi, T. K., Yook, K. H., & Suh, S. Y. (2007). Effectiveness of a meditation-based stress management program as an adjunct to pharmacotherapy in patients with anxiety disorder. *Journal of Psychosomatic Research, 62*, 189–195.

Lehner, P. (1997). Cognitive biases and time stress in team decision making. *Systems, Man and Cybernetics, Part A, IEEE Transactions on, 27*, 698–703.

Lemonick, M. D. (1995, July 17). Glimpses of the mind. What is consciousness? Memory? Emotion? Science unravels the best-kept secrets of the human brain. *Time.* Retrieved February 9, 2009, from http://www.time.com/time/classroom/psych/unit3_article1.html

Lesh, T. V. (1970). Zen meditation and the development of empathy in counselors. *Journal of Humanistic Psychology, 10,* 39–74.

Linehan, M. M. (1987). Dialectical behavior therapy for borderline personality disorder. Theory and method. *Bulletin of the Menninger Clinic, 51,* 261–276.

Linehan, M. M. (1993a). *Cognitive–behavioral treatment of borderline personality disorder.* New York: Guilford Press.

Linehan, M. M. (1993b). *Skills training manual for treating borderline personality disorder.* New York: Guilford Press.

Linehan, M. M., Armstrong, H. E., Suarez, A., Allmon, D., & Heard, H. L. (1991). Cognitive–behavioral treatment of chronically parasuicidal borderline patients. *Archives of General Psychiatry, 48,* 1060–1064.

Linehan, M. M., Cochran, B. N., Mar, C. M., Levensky, E. R., & Comtois, K. A. (2000). Therapeutic burnout among borderline personality disordered clients and their therapists: Development and evaluation of two adaptations of the Maslach Burnout Inventory. *Cognitive and Behavioral Practice, 7,* 329–337.

Linehan, M. M., Comtois, K. A., Murray, A. M., Brown, M. Z., Gallop, R. J., Heard, H. L., et al. (2006). Two-year randomized trial + follow-up of dialectical behavior therapy vs. therapy by experts for suicidal behaviors and borderline personality. *Archives of General Psychiatry, 63,* 757–766.

Linehan, M. M., Dimeff, L. A., Reynolds, S. K., Comtois, K. A., Welch, S. S., Heagerty, P., et al. (2002). Dialectical behavior therapy versus comprehensive validation therapy plus 12-step for the treatment of opioid dependent women meeting criteria for borderline personality disorder. *Drug and Alcohol Dependence, 67,* 13–26.

Linehan, M. M., Schmidt, H., Dimeff, L. A., Craft, J. C., Kanter, J., & Comtois, K. A. (1999). Dialectical behavior therapy for patients with borderline personality disorder and drug dependence. *American Journal on Addictions, 8,* 279–292.

Loevinger, J. (1997). Stages of personality development. In R. Hogan, J. Johnson, & S. Briggs (Eds.), *Handbook of personality psychology* (pp. 199–208). San Diego, CA: Academic Press.

Lohr, J. M., Olatunji, B. O., Parker, L., & DeMaio, C. (2005). Experimental analysis of specific treatment factors: Efficacy and practice implications. *Journal of Clinical Psychology, 61,* 819–834.

Luborsky, L., Rosenthal, R., Diguer, L., Andrusyna, T. P., Berman, J. S., Levitt, J. T., et al. (2002). The dodo bird verdict is alive and well—mostly. *Clinical Psychology: Science and Practice, 9,* 2–12.

Luborsky, L., Singer, B., & Luborsky, L. (1975). Comparative studies of psychotherapies: Is it true that "everyone has won and all must have prizes"? *Archives of General Psychiatry, 32,* 995–1008.

Lundgren, T., Dahl, J., & Hayes, S. C. (2008). Evaluation of mediators of change in the treatment of epilepsy with acceptance and commitment therapy. *Journal of Behavioral Medicine, 31,* 225–235.

Lundgren, T., Dahl, J., Melin, L., & Kies, B. (2006). Evaluation of acceptance and commitment therapy for drug refractory epilepsy: A randomized controlled trial in South Africa—A pilot study. *Epilepsia, 47,* 2173–2179.

Lundgren, T., Dahl, J., Yardi, N., & Melin, L. (in press). Acceptance and commitment therapy and yoga for drug-refractory epilepsy: A randomized controlled trial. *Epilepsy & Behavior.*

Lushington, K., & Luscri, G. (2001). Are counseling students stressed? A cross-cultural comparison of burnout in Australian, Singaporean and Hong Kong counseling students. *Asian Journal of Counseling, 8,* 209–232.

Lutz, A., Brefczynski-Lewis, J., Johnstone, T., & Davidson, R. J. (2008). Regulation of the neural circuitry of emotion by compassion meditation: Effects of meditative expertise. *PLoS ONE, 3,* e1897.

Lutz, A., Greischar, L. L., Rawlings, N. B., Ricard, M., & Davidson, R. J. (2004). Long-term meditators self-induce high-amplitude gamma synchrony during mental practice. *Proceedings of the National Academy of Sciences of the United States of America, 101,* 16369–16373.

Lynch, T. R., Chapman, A. L., Rosenthal, M. Z., Kuo, J. R., & Linehan, M. M. (2006). Mechanisms of change in dialectical behavior therapy: Theoretical and empirical observations. *Journal of Clinical Psychology, 62,* 459–480.

Lynch, T. R., Morse, J. Q., Mendelson, T., & Robins, C. J. (2003). Dialectical behavior therapy for depressed older adults: A randomized pilot study. *American Journal of Geriatric Psychiatry, 11,* 33–45.

Lynch, T. R., Trost, W. T., Salsman, N., & Linehan, M. M. (2007). Dialectical behavior therapy for borderline personality disorder. *Annual Review of Clinical Psychology, 3,* 181–205.

Ma, S. H., & Teasdale, J. D. (2004). Mindfulness-based cognitive therapy for depression: Replication and exploration of differential relapse prevention effects. *Journal of Consulting and Clinical Psychology, 72,* 31–40.

Mackenzie, M. J., Carlson, L. E., Munoz, M., & Speca, M. (2007). A qualitative study of self-perceived effects of mindfulness-based stress reduction (MBSR) in a psychosocial oncology setting. *Stress and Health: Journal of the International Society for the Investigation of Stress, 23*(1), 59–69.

Mackenzie, M. J., Carlson, L. E., & Speca, M. (2005). Mindfulness-based stress reduction (MBSR) in oncology: Rationale and review. *Evidence-Based Integrative Medicine, 2,* 139–145.

Mackenzie, C. S., Poulin, P. A., & Seidman-Carlson, R. (2006). A brief mindfulness-based stress reduction intervention for nurses and nurse aides. *Applied Nursing Research, 19,* 105–109.

Magid, B. (2002). *Ordinary mind: Exploring the common ground of zen and psychotherapy.* Boston: Wisdom.

Majumdar, M., Grossman, P., Dietz-Waschkowski, B., Kersig, S., & Walach, H. (2002). Does mindfulness meditation contribute to health? Outcome evaluation of a German sample. *Journal of Alternative and Complementary Medicine, 8,* 719–730.

Manikonda, J. P., Stork, S., Togel, S., Lobmuller, A., Grunberg, I., Bedel, S., et al. (2008). Contemplative meditation reduces ambulatory blood pressure and stress-induced hypertension: A randomized pilot trial. *Journal of Human Hypertension, 22,* 138–140.

Mann, S. (2004). 'People-work': Emotion management, stress and coping. *British Journal of Guidance & Counselling, 32,* 205–221.

Marlatt, G. A., & Chawla, N. (2007). Meditation and alcohol use. *Southern Medical Journal, 100,* 451–453.

Marlatt, G. A., & Gordon, J. R. (Eds.). (1985). *Relapse prevention: Maintenance strategies in the treatment of addictive behaviors.* New York: Guilford Press.

Marlatt, G. A., & Witkiewitz, K. (2005). Relapse prevention for alcohol and drug problems. In G. A. Marlatt & D. M. Donovan (Eds.), *Relapse prevention* (pp. 1–44). New York: Guilford Press.

Martin, J. R. (1997). Mindfulness: A proposed common factor. *Journal of Psychotherapy Integration, 7,* 291–312.

Maslow, A. (1971). *The farther reaches of human nature.* New York: Viking Press.

Massion, A. O., Teas, J., Hebert, J. R., Wertheimer, M. D., & Kabat-Zinn, J. (1995). Meditation, melatonin and breast/prostate cancer: Hypothesis and preliminary data. *Medical Hypotheses, 44,* 39–46.

Matchim, Y., & Armer, J. M. (2007). Measuring the psychological impact of mindfulness meditation on health among patients with cancer: A literature review. *Oncology Nursing Forum, 34,* 1059–1066.

McCartney, L. (2004). *Counsellors' perspectives on how mindfulness meditation influences counsellor presence within the therapeutic relationship.* Unpublished master's thesis, University of Victoria, British Columbia, Canada.

McCracken, L. M., & Vowles, K. E. (2007). Psychological flexibility and traditional pain management strategies in relation to patient functioning with chronic pain: An examination of a revised instrument. *The Journal of Pain, 8,* 700–707.

McCracken, L. M., Vowles, K. E., & Eccleston, C. (2005). Acceptance-based treatment for persons with complex, long standing chronic pain: A preliminary analysis of treatment outcome in comparison to a waiting phase. *Behaviour Research and Therapy, 43,* 1335–1346.

Mehling, W. E., Hamel, K. A., Acree, M., Byl, N., & Hecht, F. M. (2005). Randomized, controlled trial of breath therapy for patients with chronic low-back pain. *Alternative Therapies in Health and Medicine, 11*(4), 44–52.

Melden, A. I. (Ed.). (1950). *Ethical theories: A book of readings.* New York: Prentice Hall.

Miller, J. J., Fletcher, K., & Kabat-Zinn, J. (1995). Three-year follow-up and clinical implications of a mindfulness meditation-based stress reduction intervention in the treatment of anxiety disorders. *General Hospital Psychiatry, 17,* 192–200.

The mindful parent. (2008). Retrieved September 10, 2008, from http://themindfulparent.org/

Minor, H. G., Carlson, L. E., Mackenzie, M. J., Zernicke, K., & Jones, L. (2006). Evaluation of a mindfulness-based stress reduction (MBSR) program for caregivers of children with chronic conditions. *Social Work in Health Care, 43*(1), 91–109.

Moffitt, P. (2008). *Dancing with life: Buddhist insights for finding meaning and joy in the face of suffering.* New York: Rodale Books.

Monti, D. A., Peterson, C., Kunkel, E. J., Hauck, W. W., Pequignot, E., Rhodes, L., et al. (2005). A randomized, controlled trial of mindfulness-based art therapy (MBAT) for women with cancer. *Psycho-Oncology, 15,* 363–373.

Morone, N. E., Greco, C. M., & Weiner, D. K. (2008). Mindfulness meditation for the treatment of chronic low back pain in older adults: A randomized controlled pilot study. *Pain, 134,* 310–319.

Myers, M. F. (1994). *Doctors' marriages: A look at the problems and their solutions* (2nd ed.). New York: Plenum Press.

Myers, S. G., & Wells, A. (2005). Obsessive–compulsive symptoms: The contribution of metacognitions and responsibility. *Journal of Anxiety Disorders, 19,* 806–817.

Mytko, J. J., & Knight, S. J. (1999). Body, mind and spirit: Towards the integration of religiosity and spirituality in cancer quality of life research. *Psycho-Oncology, 8,* 439–450.

Neff, K. D., Kirkpatrick, K. L., & Rude, S. (2007). Self-compassion and adaptive psychological functioning. *Journal of Research in Personality, 41,* 139–154.

Newsome, S., Christopher, J. C., Dahlen, P., & Christopher, S. (2006). Teaching counselors self-care through mindfulness practices. *Teachers College Record, 108,* 1881–1900.

Nielsen, L., & Kaszniak, A. W. (2006). Awareness of subtle emotional feelings: A comparison of long-term meditators and nonmeditators. *Emotion, 6,* 392–405.

Nolen-Hoeksema, S., Morrow, J., & Fredrickson, B. L. (1993). Response styles and the duration of episodes of depressed mood. *Journal of Abnormal Psychology, 102,* 20–28.

Oman, D., Shapiro, S. L., Thoresen, C. E., Plante, T. G., & Flinders, T. (2008). Meditation lowers stress and supports forgiveness among college students: A randomized controlled trial. *Journal of American College Health, 56,* 569–578.

Ong, J. C., Shapiro, S. L., & Manber, R. (2008). Combining mindfulness meditation with cognitive–behavior therapy for insomnia: A treatment-development study. *Behavior Therapy, 39,* 171–182.

Orme-Johnson, D. (2006). Evidence that the transcendental meditation program prevents or decreases diseases of the nervous system and is specifically beneficial for epilepsy. *Medical Hypotheses, 67,* 240–246.

Orzech, K., Shapiro, S., Brown, K., & Mumbar, M. (in press). Intensive mindfulness training-related changes in cognitive and emotional experience. *Journal of Positive Psychology.*

Ospina, M. B., Bond, T. K., Karkhaneh, M., Tjosvold, L., Vandermeer, B., Liang, Y., et al. (2007). *Meditation practices for health: State of the research* (Evidence Report/Technology Assessment No. 155). Rockville, MD: Agency for Healthcare Research and Quality.

Ost, L. G. (2008). Efficacy of the third wave of behavioral therapies: A systematic review and meta-analysis. *Behaviour Research and Therapy, 46,* 296–321.

Ott, M. J., Norris, R. L., & Bauer-Wu, S. M. (2006). Mindfulness meditation for oncology patients. *Integrative Cancer Therapies, 5,* 98–108.

Pagnoni, G., & Cekic, M. (2007). Age effects on gray matter volume and attentional performance in zen meditation. *Neurobiology of Aging, 28,* 1623–1627.

Penzer, W. N. (1984). The psychopathology of the psychotherapist. *Psychotherapy in Private Practice, 2*(2), 51–59.

Phongsuphap, S., Pongsupap, Y., Chandanamattha, P., & Lursinsap, C. (in press). Changes in heart rate variability during concentration meditation. *International Journal of Cardiology.*

Plews-Ogan, M., Owens, J. E., Goodman, M., Wolfe, P., & Schorling, J. (2005). A pilot study evaluating mindfulness-based stress reduction and massage for the management of chronic pain. *Journal of General Internal Medicine, 20,* 1136–1138.

Pradhan, E. K., Baumgarten, M., Langenberg, P., Handwerger, B., Gilpin, A. K., Magyari, T., et al. (2007). Effect of mindfulness-based stress reduction in rheumatoid arthritis patients. *Arthritis & Rheumatism, 57,* 1134–1142.

Radeke, J. T., & Mahoney, M. J. (2000). Comparing the personal lives of psychotherapists and research psychologists. *Professional Psychology: Research and Practice, 31,* 82–84.

Rajesh, B., Jayachandran, D., Mohandas, G., & Radhakrishnan, K. (2006). A pilot study of a yoga meditation protocol for patients with medically refractory epilepsy. *Journal of Alternative and Complementary Medicine, 12,* 367–371.

Randolph, P. D., Caldera, Y. M., Tacone, A. M., & Greak, M. L. (1999). The long-term combined effects of medical treatment and a mindfulness-based behavioral program for the multidisciplinary management of chronic pain in West Texas. *Pain Digest, 9,* 103–112.

Reibel, D. K., Greeson, J. M., Brainard, G. C., & Rosenzweig, S. (2001). Mindfulness-based stress reduction and health-related quality of life in a heterogeneous patient population. *General Hospital Psychiatry, 23,* 183–192.

Renjilian, D. A., Baum, R. E., & Landry, S. L. (1998). Psychotherapist burnout: Can college students see the signs? *Journal of College Student Psychotherapy, 13*(1), 39–48.

Robert McComb, J. J., Tacon, A., Randolph, P., & Caldera, Y. (2004). A pilot study to examine the effects of a mindfulness-based stress-reduction and relaxation program on levels of stress hormones, physical functioning, and submaximal exercise responses. *Journal of Alternative and Complementary Medicine, 10,* 819–827.

Robinson, F. P., Mathews, H. L., & Witek-Janusek, L. (2003). Psycho-endocrine-immune response to mindfulness-based stress reduction in individuals infected with the human immunodeficiency virus: A quasiexperimental study. *Journal of Alternative and Complementary Medicine, 9,* 683–694.

Rogers, C. R. (1957). The necessary and sufficient conditions of therapeutic personality change. *Journal of Consulting Psychology, 21,* 95–103.

Rogers, C. R. (1961). *On becoming a person.* Oxford, England: Houghton Mifflin.

Rogers, S. (2006). *Mindful parenting: Meditations, verses, and visualizations for a more joyful life.* Miami Beach, FL: Mindful Living Press.

Rosch, E. (1999). Is wisdom in the brain? *Psychological Science, 10,* 222–224.

Rosenberg, T., & Pace, M. (2006). Burnout among mental health professionals: Special considerations for the marriage and family therapist. *Journal of Marital and Family Therapy, 32,* 87–99.

Rosenzweig, S. (1936). Some implicit common factors in diverse methods of psychotherapy. *American Journal of Orthopsychiatry, 6,* 412–415.

Rosenzweig, S., Reibel, D. K., Greeson, J. M., Brainard, G. C., & Hojat, M. (2003). Mindfulness-based stress reduction lowers psychological distress in medical students. *Teaching and Learning in Medicine, 15,* 88–92.

Rosenzweig, S., Reibel, D. K., Greeson, J. M., Edman, J. S., Jasser, S. A., McMearty, K. D., et al. (2007). Mindfulness-based stress reduction is associated with improved glycemic control in type 2 diabetes mellitus: A pilot study. *Alternative Therapies in Health and Medicine, 13*(5), 36–38.

Roth, B., & Robbins, D. (2004). Mindfulness-based stress reduction and health-related quality of life: Findings from a bilingual inner-city patient population. *Psychosomatic Medicine, 66,* 113–123.

Roth, H. (2006). Contemplative studies: Prospects for a new field. *The Teachers College Record, 108,* 1787–1815.

Rumi, J. (1995). Childhood friends. In *The essential Rumi* (C. Barks, Trans., p. 139). San Francisco: HarperCollins.

Rumi, J. (1997). The guesthouse. In *The illuminated Rumi* (C. Barks, Trans., p. 77). New York: Broadway Books.

Ryan, R. M., & Deci, E. L. (2000). Self-determination theory and the facilitation of intrinsic motivation, social development, and well-being. *American Psychologist, 55,* 68–78.

Ryan, R. M., Kuhl, J., & Deci, E. L. (1997). Nature and autonomy: An organizational view of social and neurobiological aspects of self-regulation in behavior and development. *Development and Psychopathology, 9,* 701–728.

Sadlier, M., Stephens, S. D., & Kennedy, V. (2008). Tinnitus rehabilitation: A mindfulness meditation cognitive behavioural therapy approach. *Journal of Laryngology & Otology, 122,* 31–37.

Safer, D. L., Telch, C. F., & Agras, W. S. (2001). Dialectical behavior therapy for bulimia nervosa. *American Journal of Psychiatry, 158,* 632–634.

Safran, J. (2003). *Psychoanalysis and Buddhism: An unfolding dialogue.* Boston: Wisdom Publications.

Safran, J. D., & Segal, Z. V. (1990). *Interpersonal process in cognitive therapy.* New York: Basic Books.

Saltzman, A., & Goldin, P. (2008). A mindfulness meditation training program for school-age children. In S. Hayes & L. Greco (Eds.), *Acceptance and mindfulness interventions for children, adolescents, and families.* Oakland, CA: New Harbinger.

Santorelli, S. (1999). *Heal thy self: Lessons on mindfulness in medicine.* New York: Random House.

Saxe, G. A., Hebert, J. R., Carmody, J. F., Kabat-Zinn, J., Rosenzweig, P. H., Jarzobski, D., et al. (2001). Can diet in conjunction with stress reduction affect the rate of increase in prostate specific antigen after biochemical recurrence of prostate cancer? *Journal of Urology, 166,* 2202–2207.

Schneider, R. H., Alexander, C. N., Staggers, F., Orme-Johnson, D. W., Rainforth, M., Salerno, J. W., et al. (2005). A randomized controlled trial of stress reduction in African Americans treated for hypertension for over one year. *American Journal of Hypertension: Journal of the American Society of Hypertension, 18,* 88–98.

Schneider, R. H., Alexander, C. N., Staggers, F., Rainforth, M., Salerno, J. W., Hartz, A., et al. (2005). Long-term effects of stress reduction on mortality in persons ≥ 55 years of age with systemic hypertension. *The American Journal of Cardiology, 95,* 1060–1064.

Schure, M. B., Christopher, J., & Christopher, S. (2008). Mind-body medicine and the art of self-care: Teaching mindfulness to counseling students through yoga, meditation, and qigong. *Journal of Counseling & Development, 86*(1), 47–56.

Segal, Z. V., Williams, M. G., & Teasdale, J. D. (2002). *Mindfulness-based cognitive therapy for depression: A new approach to preventing relapse.* New York: Guilford Press.

Seligman, M. E. P. (1995). The effectiveness of psychotherapy: The Consumer Reports study. *American Psychologist, 50,* 965–974.

Seligman, M., & Csikszentmihalyi, M. (2000). Positive psychology: An introduction. *American Psychologist, 55,* 5–14.

Semple, R. J., Lee, J., & Miller, L. F. (2006). Mindfulness-based cognitive therapy for children. In R. A. Baer (Ed.), *Mindfulness-based treatment approaches* (pp. 143–166). New York: Academic Press.

Sephton, S. E., Salmon, P., Weissbecker, I., Ulmer, C., Floyd, A., Hoover, K., et al. (2007). Mindfulness meditation alleviates depressive symptoms in women with fibromyalgia: Results of a randomized clinical trial. *Arthritis & Rheumatism, 57*(1), 77–85.

Sephton, S. E., Sapolsky, R. M., Kraemer, H. C., & Spiegel, D. (2000). Diurnal cortisol rhythm as a predictor of breast cancer survival. *Journal of the National Cancer Institute, 92,* 994–1000.

Shanafelt, T. D., Bradley, K. A., Wipt, J. E., & Back, A. L. (2002). Burnout and self-reported patient care in an internal medicine residency program. *Annals of Internal Medicine, 136,* 358.

Shapiro, D. H. (1992). Adverse effects of meditation: A preliminary investigation of long-term meditators. *International Journal of Psychosomatics, 39*(1), 62–67.

Shapiro, S. L., Astin, J. A., Bishop, S. R., & Cordova, M. (2005). Mindfulness-based stress reduction for health care professionals: Results from a randomized trial. *International Journal of Stress Management, 12,* 164–176.

Shapiro, S. L., Bootzin, R. R., Figueredo, A. J., Lopez, A. M., & Schwartz, G. E. (2003). The efficacy of mindfulness-based stress reduction in the treatment of sleep disturbance in women with breast cancer: An exploratory study. *Journal of Psychosomatic Research, 54,* 85–91.

Shapiro, S. L., Brown, K. W., & Astin, J. (in press). Toward the integration of mediation into high education: A review of research evidence. *Teachers College Record.*

Shapiro, S. L., Brown, K. W., & Biegel, G. M. (2007). Teaching self-care to caregivers: Effects of mindfulness-based stress reduction on the mental health of therapists in training. *Training and Education in Professional Psychology, 1,* 105–115.

Shapiro, S. L., Carlson, L. E., Astin, J. A., & Freedman, B. (2006). Mechanisms of mindfulness. *Journal of Clinical Psychology, 62,* 373–386.

Shapiro, S. L., Ebert, S., Pisca, N., & Sherman, J. (2008). *Exploring the value added of meditation practice in MBSR.* Unpublished manuscript.

Shapiro, S. L., & Izett, C. (2008). Meditation: A universal tool for cultivating empathy. In D. Hick, & T. Bien (Eds.), *Mindfulness and the therapeutic relationship* (pp. 161–175). New York: Guilford Press.

Shapiro, S. L., & Schwartz, G. E. (2000a). Intentional systemic mindfulness: An integrative model for self-regulation and health. *Advances in Mind-Body Medicine, 16,* 128–134.

Shapiro, S. L., & Schwartz, G. E. (2000b). The role of intention in self-regulation: Toward intentional systemic mindfulness. In M. Boekaerts, P. R. Pintrich, & M. Zeidner (Eds.), *Handbook of self-regulation* (pp. 253–273). New York: Academic Press.

Shapiro, S. L., Schwartz, G. E., & Bonner, G. (1998). Effects of mindfulness-based stress reduction on medical and premedical students. *Journal of Behavioral Medicine, 21,* 581–599.

Shapiro, S. L., Shapiro, D. E., & Schwartz, G. E. (2000). Stress management in medical education: A review of the literature. *Academic Medicine, 75,* 748–759.

Shapiro, S. L., & Walsh, R. (2003). An analysis of recent meditation research and suggestions for future directions. *Humanistic Psychologist, 31,* 86–114.

Shapiro, S. L., & Walsh, R. (2007). Meditation: The farther reaches. In T. Plante & C. E. Thoresen (Eds.), *Spirit, science and health: How the spiritual mind fuels physical wellness* (pp. 57–71). Westport, CT: Praeger/Greenwood.

Shapiro, S. L., Walsh, R., & Britton, W. B. (2003). An analysis of recent meditation research and suggestions for future directions. *Journal for Meditation and Meditation Research, 3,* 69–90.

Sheppard, L. C., & Teasdale, J. D. (1996). Depressive thinking: Changes in schematic mental models of self and world. *Psychological Medicine, 26,* 1043–1051.

Sibinga, E. M., Stewart, M., Magyari, T., Welsh, C. K., Hutton, N., & Ellen, J. M. (2008). Mindfulness-based stress reduction for HIV-infected youth: A pilot study. *Explore: The Journal of Science & Healing, 4,* 36–37.

Siegel, D. (2007a). *The mindful brain: Reflection and attunement in the cultivation of well-being.* New York: Norton.

Siegel, D. (2007b). Mindfulness training and neural integration: Differentiation of distinct streams of awareness and the cultivation of well-being. *Social Cognitive and Affective Neuroscience, 2,* 259–263.

Silva, J. M. (2007). Mindfulness-based cognitive therapy for the reduction of anger in married men. *Dissertation Abstracts International: Section B: The Sciences and Engineering, 68*(3-B), 1945.

Simons, D. J., & Chabris, C. F. (1999). Gorillas in our midst: Sustained inattentional blindness for dynamic events. *Perception, 28,* 1059–1074.

Simpson, E. B., Yen, S., Costello, E., Rosen, K., Begin, A., Pistorello, J., et al. (2004). Combined dialectical behavior therapy and fluoxetine in the treatment of borderline personality disorder. *Journal of Clinical Psychiatry, 65,* 379–385.

Singh, N. N., Lancioni, G. E., Singh, A. N., Winton, A. S., Singh, J., McAleavey, K. M., et al. (2008). A mindfulness-based health wellness program for an adolescent with Prader-Willi syndrome. *Behavior Modification, 32,* 167–181.

Singh, N. N., Lancioni, G. E., Winton, A. S., Adkins, A. D., Singh, J., & Singh, A. N. (2007). Mindfulness training assists individuals with moderate mental retardation to maintain their community placements. *Behavior Modification, 31,* 800–814.

Singh, N. N., Lancioni, G. E., Winton, A. S. W., Fisher, B. C., Wahler, R. G., McAleavey, K., et al. (2006). Mindful parenting decreases aggression, noncompliance, and self-injury in children with autism. *Journal of Emotional and Behavioral Disorders, 14,* 169–177.

Singh, N. N., Lancioni, G. E., Winton, A. S. W., Singh, J., Curtis, W. J., Wahler, R. G., et al. (2007). Mindful parenting decreases aggression and increases social behavior in children with developmental disabilities. *Behavior Modification, 31,* 749–771.

Skosnik, P. D., Chatterton, R. T., Swisher, T., & Park, S. (2000). Modulation of attentional inhibition by norepinephrine and cortisol after psychological stress. *International Journal of Psychophysiology, 36,* 59–68.

Slagter, H. A., Lutz, A., Greischar, L. L., Francis, A. D., Nieuwenhuis, S., Davis, J. M., et al. (2007). Mental training affects distribution of limited brain resources. *PLoS Biology, 5*(6), e138.

Smith, J. E., Richardson, J., Hoffman, C., & Pilkington, K. (2005). Mindfulness-based stress reduction as supportive therapy in cancer care: Systematic review. *Journal of Advanced Nursing, 52*, 315–327.

Snyder, C., & Lopez, S. (Eds.). (2005). *Handbook of positive psychology.* New York: Oxford University Press.

Soler, J., Pascual, J. C., Campins, J., Barrachina, J., Puigdemont, D., Alvarez, E., et al. (2005). Double-blind, placebo-controlled study of dialectical behavior therapy plus olanzapine for borderline personality disorder. *American Journal of Psychiatry, 162*, 1221–1224.

Speca, M., Carlson, L. E., Goodey, E., & Angen, M. (2000). A randomized, wait-list controlled clinical trial: The effect of a mindfulness meditation-based stress reduction program on mood and symptoms of stress in cancer outpatients. *Psychosomatic Medicine, 62*, 613–622.

St. Louis, E. K., & Lansky, E. P. (2006). Meditation and epilepsy: A still hung jury. *Medical Hypotheses, 67*, 247–250.

Swinehart, R. (2008). Two cases support the benefits of transcendental meditation in epilepsy. *Medical Hypotheses, 70*, 1070.

Tacon, A. M., Caldera, Y. M., & Ronaghan, C. (2004). Mindfulness-based stress reduction in women with breast cancer. *Families, Systems, & Health, 22*, 193–203.

Tacon, A. M., McComb, J., Caldera, Y., & Randolph, P. (2003). Mindfulness meditation, anxiety reduction, and heart disease: A pilot study. *Family and Community Health, 26*, 25–33.

Teasdale, J. D., Segal, Z. V., Williams, J. M., Ridgeway, V. A., Soulsby, J. M., & Lau, M. A. (2000). Prevention of relapse/recurrence in major depression by mindfulness-based cognitive therapy. *Journal of Consulting and Clinical Psychology, 68*, 615–623.

Telch, C. F., Agras, W. S., & Linehan, M. M. (2001). Dialectical behavior therapy for binge eating disorder. *Journal of Consulting and Clinical Psychology, 69*, 1061–1065.

Thompson, B. L., & Waltz, J. (2007). Everyday mindfulness and mindfulness meditation: Overlapping constructs or not? [references]. *Personality and Individual Differences, 43*, 1875–1885.

Trungpa, C. (1975). *The Tibetan book of the dead* (F. Fremantle & C. Trungpa, Trans.). Boston: Shambhala.

Turner, R. M. (2000). Naturalistic evaluation of dialectical behavioral therapy–oriented treatment for borderline personality disorder. *Cognitive and Behavioral Practice, 7,* 413–419.

Tyssen, R., Vaglum, P., Grønvold, N. T., & Ekeberg, O. (2001). Factors in medical school that predict postgraduate mental health problems in need of treatment. A nationwide and longitudinal study. *Medical Education, 35,* 110–120.

van den Bosch, L. M., Koeter, M. W., Stijnen, T., Verheul, R., & van den Brink, B. W. (2005). Sustained efficacy of dialectical behaviour therapy for borderline personality disorder. *Behaviour Research and Therapy, 43,* 1231–1241.

van den Bosch, L. M. C., Verheul, R., Schippers, G. M., & van den Brink, W. (2002). Dialectical behavior therapy of borderline patients with and without substance use problems: Implementation and long-term effects. *Addictive Behaviors, 27,* 911–923.

Vaughan, F., & Walsh, R. (Eds.). (1992). *Accept this gift. Selections from A Course in Miracles.* Los Angeles: Tarcher.

Verheul, R., Van Den Bosch, L. M., Koeter, M. W., De Ridder, M. A., Stijnen, T., & van den Brink, W. (2003). Dialectical behavior therapy for women with borderline personality disorder: 12-month, randomised clinical trial in The Netherlands. *British Journal of Psychiatry, 182,* 135–140.

Vijayalaxmi, T. C. R., Jr., Reiter, R. J., & Herman, T. S. (2002). Melatonin: From basic research to cancer treatment clinics. *Journal of Clinical Oncology, 20,* 2575–2601.

Vowles, K. E., & McCracken, L. M. (2008). Acceptance and values-based action in chronic pain: A study of treatment effectiveness and process. *Journal of Consulting and Clinical Psychology, 76,* 397–407.

Vowles, K. E., McCracken, L. M., & Eccleston, C. (2007). Processes of behavior change in interdisciplinary treatment of chronic pain: Contributions of pain intensity, catastrophizing, and acceptance. *European Journal of Pain, 11,* 779–787.

Vredenburgh, L. D., Carlozzi, A. F., & Stein, L. B. (1999). Burnout in counseling psychologists: Type of practice setting and pertinent demographics. *Counseling Psychology Quarterly, 12,* 293–302.

Wachs, K., & Cordova, J. V. (2007). Mindful relating: Exploring mindfulness and emotion repertoires in intimate relationships. *Journal of Marital and Family Therapy, 33,* 464–481.

Wallace, A. B., & Bodhi, B. (2006). The nature of mindfulness and its role in Buddhist meditation: A correspondence between B. Alan Wallace and the venerable Bhikkhu Bodhi. Unpublished manuscript, Santa Barbara Institute for Consciousness Studies, Santa Barbara, CA.

Wallace, A. B., & Shapiro, S. L. (2009). *Ethics as inquiry.* Manuscript in preparation.

Walsh, R. (1983). Meditation practice and research. *Journal of Humanistic Psychology, 23,* 18–50.

Walsh, R. (2000). *Essential spirituality: The 7 central practices to awaken heart and mind.* New York: Wiley.

Walsh, R., & Vaughan, F. (1993). *Paths beyond ego: The transpersonal vision.* New York: Tarcher.

Walton, K. G., Schneider, R. H., & Nidich, S. (2004). Review of controlled research on the transcendental meditation program and cardiovascular disease. Risk factors, morbidity, and mortality. *Cardiology in Review, 12,* 262–266.

Watzlawick, P. (1990). *Münchhausen's pigtail: Or psychotherapy and "reality"—essays and lectures.* New York: Norton.

Weinberger, J. (2002). Short paper, large impact: Rosenweig's influence on the common factors movement. *Journal of Psychotherapy Integration, 12,* 67–76.

Weiss, L. (2004). *Therapist's guide to self-care* . New York: Routledge.

Weiss, M., Nordlie, J., & Siegel, E. P. (2005). Mindfulness-based stress reduction as an adjunct to outpatient psychotherapy. *Psychotherapy and Psychosomatics, 74,* 108–112.

Weissbecker, I., Salmon, P., Studts, J. L., Floyd, A. R., Dedert, E. A., & Sephton, S. E. (2002). Mindfulness-based stress reduction and sense of coherence among women with fibromyalgia. *Journal of Clinical Psychology in Medical Settings, 9,* 297–307.

Wells, A. (1990). Panic disorder in association with relaxation-induced anxiety: An attentional training approach to treatment. *Behavior Therapy, 21,* 273–280.

Wells, A. (1999). A cognitive model of generalized anxiety disorder. *Behavior Modification, 23,* 526–555.

Wells, A., & Cartwright-Hatton, S. (2004). A short form of the metacognitions questionnaire: Properties of the MCQ-30. *Behaviour Research and Therapy, 42,* 385–396.

Wetter, D. W. (2008). *Smoking relapse prevention among postpartum women* [abstract]. Retrieved March 17, 2008, from http://crisp.cit.nih.gov/ crisp/CRISP_LIB.getdoc?textkey=7169647&p_grant_num=5R01CA0 89350-06&p_query=&ticket=57814319&p_audit_session_id= 293544573&p_keywords=

Wicks, R. (2007). *The resilient clinician: Secondary stress, mindfulness, positive psychology, and enhancing the self-care protocol of the psychotherapist, counselor, and social worker.* New York: Oxford University Press.

Wilber, K. (1999). *The collected works of Ken Wilber series: Vol. 3. A sociable god/Eye to eye.* Boston: Shambhala.

Wilber, K. (2000). *Integral psychology: Consciousness, spirit, psychology, therapy.* Boston: Shambhala.

Williams, A. L., Selwyn, P. A., Liberti, L., Molde, S., Njike, V. Y., McCorkle, R., et al. (2005). A randomized controlled trial of meditation and massage effects on quality of life in people with late-stage disease: A pilot study. *Journal of Palliative Medicine, 8,* 939–952.

Williams, J. M., Alatiq, Y., Crane, C., Barnhofer, T., Fennell, M. J., Duggan, D. S., et al. (2008). Mindfulness-based cognitive therapy (MBCT) in bipolar disorder: Preliminary evaluation of immediate effects on between-episode functioning. *Journal of Affective Disorders, 107*(1–3), 275–279.

Williams, J. M., Duggan, D. S., Crane, C., & Fennell, M. J. (2006). Mindfulness-based cognitive therapy for prevention of recurrence of suicidal behavior. *Journal of Clinical Psychology, 62,* 201–210.

Williams, J. M., & Swales, M. (2004). The use of mindfulness-based approaches for suicidal patients. *Archives of Suicide Research, 8,* 315–329.

Williams, J. M., Teasdale, J., Segal, Z., & Kabat-Zinn, J. (2000). *The mindful way through depression: Freeing yourself from chronic unhappiness.* New York: Guilford Press.

Williams, J. M., Teasdale, J. D., Segal, Z. V., & Soulsby, J. (2000). Mindfulness-based cognitive therapy reduces overgeneral autobiographical memory in formerly depressed patients. *Journal of Abnormal Psychology, 109,* 150–155.

Williams, K. A., Kolar, M. M., Reger, B. E., & Pearson, J. C. (2001). Evaluation of a wellness-based mindfulness stress reduction intervention: A controlled trial. *American Journal of Health Promotion, 15,* 422–432.

Winnicott, D. W. (1965). *Maturational processes and the facilitating environment.* New York: International Universities Press.

Woods, D. W., Wetterneck, C. T., & Flessner, C. A. (2006). A controlled evaluation of acceptance and commitment therapy plus habit reversal for trichotillomania. *Behaviour Research and Therapy, 44,* 639–656.

Young-Eisendrath, P., & Muramoto, S. (Eds.). (2002). *Awakening and insight: Zen Buddhism and psychotherapy.* New York: Routledge.

Zautra, A. J., Davis, M. C., Reich, J. W., Nicassario, P., Tennen, H., Finan, P., et al. (2008). Comparison of cognitive behavioral and mindfulness meditation interventions on adaptation to rheumatoid arthritis for patients with and without history of recurrent depression. *Journal of Consulting and Clinical Psychology, 76,* 408–421.

Zettle, R. D. (2003). Acceptance and commitment therapy (ACT) vs. systematic desensitization in treatment of mathematics anxiety. *The Psychological Record, 53*(2), 197–215.

Zylowska, L., Ackerman, D. L., Yang, M. H., Futrell, J. L., Horton, N. I., Hale, S., et al. (2007). Mindfulness meditation training in adults and adolescents with ADHD: A feasibility study. *Journal of Attention Disorders, 11,* 737–746.

Index

About the Authors

Shauna L. Shapiro, PhD, is a professor of counseling psychology at Santa Clara University and previously served as adjunct faculty for Andrew Weil's Center for Integrative Medicine at the University of Arizona. Dr. Shapiro's research focuses on mindfulness meditation and its applications to psychotherapy and health care. She began her study of psychology and meditation at Duke University, graduating summa cum laude, and received her doctorate in clinical psychology from the University of Arizona. Dr. Shapiro pursued her study of meditation in Thailand and Nepal, as well as in the West, training in mindfulness-based stress reduction and mindfulness-based cognitive therapy. She has conducted extensive clinical research investigating the effects of mindfulness-based therapies across a wide range of populations, and she has published over 50 book chapters and peer-reviewed journal articles. She is the recipient of the American Council of Learned Societies teaching award, acknowledging her outstanding contributions to graduate education in the area of mindfulness and psychotherapy. Dr. Shapiro lectures and leads mindfulness training programs nationally and internationally for health professionals on the growing applications of mindfulness in psychology and health care.

Linda E. Carlson, PhD, holds the Enbridge Endowed Research Chair in Psychosocial Oncology and is an Alberta Heritage Foundation for Medical Research Health Scholar, associate professor in psychosocial oncology in the Department of Oncology, Faculty of Medicine, and adjunct associate professor in the Department of Psychology at the University of Calgary. She is director of research and works as a clinical psychologist in the Department of Psychosocial Resources at the Tom Baker Cancer Centre, where her program has offered mindfulness-based stress reduction (MBSR) to cancer patients and their families since 1997. Dr. Carlson trained as a clinical health psychologist at McGill University in Montreal, researching the area of psychoneuroendocrinology. She received the Kawano New Investigator Award from the International Psycho-Oncology Society in 2006 and the William E. Rawls Prize in cancer control from the National Cancer Institute of Canada/Canadian Cancer Society in 2007. She has practiced meditation with the Insight Meditation Society in Burma and Canada, and trained in MBSR with Jon Kabat-Zinn and Saki Santorelli. She presented her work at Mind and Life XVI: Investigating the Mind–Body Connection: The Science and Clinical Applications of Meditation at the Mayo Clinic with His Holiness the Dalai Lama in 2008. Dr. Carlson has published over 90 book chapters and research articles in peer-reviewed journals, holds more than $6 million in grant funding, and presents her work at national and international conferences.